Richer Lives
why rich people give

Beth Breeze

Theresa Lloyd

DIRECTORY OF SOCIAL CHANGE

Published by the Directory of Social Change (Registered Charity no 800517 in England and Wales)

Head office: 24 Stephenson Way, London NW1 2DP

Northern office: Federation House, Hope Street, Liverpool L1 9BW

Tel: 08450 77 77 07

Visit www.dsc.org.uk to find out more about our books, subscription funding websites and training events. You can also sign up for e-newsletters so that you're always the first to hear about what's new.

The publisher welcomes suggestions and comments that will help to inform and improve future versions of this and all of our titles. Please give us your feedback by emailing publications@dsc.org.uk

It should be understood that this publication is intended for guidance only and is not a substitute for professional or legal advice. No responsibility for loss occasioned as a result of any person acting or refraining from acting can be accepted by the authors or publisher.

First published 2013

ISBN 978 1 906294 79 3

British Library Cataloguing in Publication Data

A catalogue record for this book is available from the British Library

This book has been produced by Alliance Publishing Trust www.alliancepublishing.org

Edited and designed by Laura McCaffrey, London, UK

Printed and bound by Hobbs the Printers, Totton, Hampshire, UK

This book is printed on FSC approved paper

For Michael and Tim

Contents

About the funders

Pears Foundation is a British family foundation rooted in Jewish values. Its work is concerned with identity and citizenship. The Foundation's support for *Richer Lives* is part of its programme on Exploring Philanthropy - one of five strategic programme areas. The Foundation's work in this area also includes the Pears Business Schools Partnership with three of the UK's leading business schools and a long-standing research partnership with the Centre for Charitable Giving and Philanthropy at Cass Business School to produce the annual *Family Foundation Giving Trends* report. www.pearsfoundation.org.uk

The **University of Kent** was established at Canterbury in 1965. Known as the UK's European university, it has almost 20,000 students studying at its campuses or centres in Canterbury, Medway, Brussels and Paris. It is a major educational, economic and cultural force in Kent and the Southeast, supporting innovation and enterprise across the region. The university runs a matched funding scheme to encourage philanthropic donations, and was pleased to offer a 1:3 match of the funds provided by the Pears Foundation and the anonymous donor. www.kent.ac.uk

Foreword

I am delighted to have been asked to write the Foreword to *Richer Lives*, which makes an important contribution to the enduring issue of philanthropy and its role in building a better society.

The National Council for Voluntary Organisations (NCVO) champions volunteering and civil society, both of which are inextricably linked with philanthropy. Developing a better understanding of philanthropy remains critical to strengthening volunteering and civil society: while much has been written about the role of statutory funding in recent years, it is the donations of individuals, rich and poor alike, that are still a defining characteristic of civil society. And long may that continue.

Despite the upheavals of the 20th century, I believe that there remains a strong culture and practice of philanthropy and voluntary action in the UK in the 21st century. Building upon that culture and practice continues to be a particular policy challenge in relation to the wealthy. This is not a criticism of either those who ask or those who give: but a healthy starting point for this publication is that we still have much to learn.

When *Why Rich People Give* was published in 2004 there was very little understanding of the motivations and practice of the wealthy; indeed, the review presented here of how the philanthropy landscape has since been transformed is illuminating. Over that period, our understanding of the role and practice of philanthropy has advanced greatly. Moreover, as the relative positions of the state, businesses and households have ebbed and flowed, so philanthropy too has changed. We are at an inflection point today, when important questions are being asked, and addressed by this book with reference to the richer members of society: How much should people give and to whom? For what purpose should people give? How can we give effectively? It also asks more fundamental ethical and moral questions, such as whether it is good for society that we give at all.

This book provides us with a number of insights. We learn of philanthropists' response to matched funding and tax incentives; of how the attitudes of the wealthy are changing and what they look for in the organisations they fund, what they regard as a major donation, and what kind of engagement they seek. And we also hear more about philanthropists' experience of being asked and thanked, which makes for sobering reading for all with an interest in increasing major philanthropy. Running throughout the analysis are some enduring questions: How do we make it a social norm for the wealthy to give? What can be done about the sometimes ambivalent attitudes of the media? And just how important is public recognition to donors?

These and other questions are addressed in what is both a substantial and accessible text, relevant to donors, recipients and those working to advise or better understand both parties. Not everybody will agree with the messages of this book – few issues drive as much disagreement as a discussion of philanthropy and its role, motivations and characteristics. This is particularly the case at a time when a relatively small number of people in our society share an increasingly disproportionate share of our nation's wealth. But I hope most will agree with the purpose of the book: to stimulate our understanding of philanthropy and build upon what is best about voluntary action in the UK.

Sir Stuart Etherington, Chief Executive, NCVO

Acknowledgements

This project would not have been possible without generous funding from the Pears Foundation. We are particularly grateful to Trevor Pears who has given far more than financial support. Without his wholehearted encouragement and genuine interest in this project, it would not have got off the ground or been completed. We also thank our other financial backer who wishes to remain anonymous.

The matched funding scheme run by the University of Kent enabled our funding to grow by a third – we are grateful to Professor Keith Mander for initiating this scheme and to the university's Director of Development, Alison Coles, for her attentive assistance. Paul Glover and Mandy Twyman in the finance office of the School for Social Policy, Sociology and Social Research were patient and supportive in administering the funds.

We are also very grateful to Charles Keidan, former Director of the Pears Foundation, and to his successor Amy Braier and Programme Director Bridget McGing for their professional input and personal support.

Sir Stuart Etherington is often described as 'the voice of the UK charity sector' and we are deeply grateful that he has written such a supportive foreword.

We would like to acknowledge our debt, and that of the sector as a whole, to the original funders of the project that resulted in the initial publication *Why Rich People Give*, being revisited here 10 years on: the Esmée Fairbairn Foundation, the Gatsby Charitable Foundation and the Lloyds-TSB Foundation for England and Wales. We hope they are pleased to see their investment grow in this way.

We are particularly grateful to those who were helpful in identifying and recruiting new donor interviewees for the research; among them were some of the 12 professional advisers who contributed significantly to the research in their own right, and others with links into different sectors. Detailed surveys were also completed by 16 expert observers of the world of philanthropy, whom we also thank, while respecting their confidentiality.

We are also very grateful to those organisations that contributed information to support our description of the current philanthropy landscape, including Philanthropy Impact, the Charities Aid Foundation, the Esmée Fairbairn Foundation, the Impetus Trust, Pilotlight and Coutts. Andrew Milner provided a very helpful summary of the findings from *Why Rich People Give*, which we were able to draw on for our analysis. We thank Caroline Underwood of The Philanthropy Company for the illuminating case study in Chapter 7.

We also thank Jennie Bristow for editing and structuring our initial texts and helping to unify our different writing styles, and Laura McCaffrey who managed the editorial, design and production process for Alliance Publishing to a tight timetable with charming efficiency.

We are also appreciative of the help and guidance of Caroline Hartnell, Editor, *Alliance* Magazine and John Martin, Publisher, Directory of Social Change.

Finally, it is no exaggeration to say that there is a group of people without whom this research and report could not have taken place: the 82 donors (including couples) from a range of ages, backgrounds, sources of wealth and approaches to philanthropy who agreed to complete an extensive survey, and the 20 donors (including couples) who were willing to speak at length about some of their most private concerns, motivations and attitudes. That they did so was itself a further generous contribution to society, and our understanding of those of substantial means. Their willing introspection made the months spent gathering the information among the most rewarding of our professional lives. We hope we have done justice to their faith in our ability to explain and reflect upon their hopes, concerns and aspirations. While giving reduces their monetary wealth, the paradox is that philanthropy has enriched their lives, and our society would be a much poorer place without their generous contribution.

If, in spite of this wealth of advice and interest, there are mistakes or misinterpretations, they are entirely our own responsibility.

Key findings

Here we highlight the main messages from our research, outline the analysis and findings from each chapter, and conclude with a summary of the recommendations.

Main messages

Philanthropy matters to donors and society

Philanthropy is of growing importance in donors' lives; they feel an obligation to use their wealth for the good of society, and to do so in an increasingly thoughtful and strategic way. While donors often feel unappreciated and unfairly criticised, overall, they sense that the political and cultural climate for giving has improved over the past decade.

Being philanthropic enriches the lives of donors

Philanthropic acts are motivated by a complex array of factors, including different drivers for the same donor giving to different causes at different times. But the one shared motivation is that it is a means of enriching donors' lives in many ways. These include feelings of satisfaction at using their private wealth to support the causes they care about; the enjoyment of having unusual experiences and developing relationships with interesting people working in charities, as well as fellow donors and beneficiaries; the opportunity to integrate giving into their social life and retirement activities; and the beneficial impact on their family, as a way of sharing values across the generations and leaving a meaningful legacy beyond a simple sum of money.

Philanthropy is not a simple, static activity and philanthropists are open to change

Despite a widespread view of philanthropy as a straightforward, unchanging activity and the tendency to pigeonhole donors into 'types' (such as 'driven by religious belief' or 'focused on local causes'), these simplifications sit uncomfortably with the reality of a complex, ever-changing sphere of activity populated by donors who are open to new ideas about how to best use their private wealth for the public good. This book charts the emergence of new ideas, including a concern to be more strategic, a desire to focus on underlying problems rather than symptoms, and a willingness to be more open about giving. These trends are aligned with new approaches and mechanisms, including social investment, venture philanthropy and taking up professional advice. At the same time, we see renewed interest in old ideas such as tithing, giving anonymously and collaborative giving.

The end of the armchair philanthropist

Almost all those who give substantial amounts of money also give substantial amounts of time. Donors want to be involved with the cause they are supporting, though the level of engagement varies from donor to donor and from cause to cause, and changes over time, depending on their other commitments. The desire for involvement may create new pressures for time-stretched charities, but project visits ('seeing is believing') can lead to more donations.

Fundraising is improving but needs the input of donors as askers

Donors feel that fundraising has become more professional over the past decade, especially in terms of the right research being conducted before approaches are made, and a better understanding of how different donors might want to engage with causes. However, donors want to have relationships with the charity chief executive and the trustees, not just the fundraisers, and believe that sizable donations ought to create access to the charity leadership. Fundraisers also need more support from major donors. While many major donors do get involved in asking, a sizable proportion (especially of newly emerging philanthropists) have never asked others to give. This needs to change, given the importance attached to being asked by someone known and trusted by the potential donor, and the role of peer pressure in securing a positive response.

Feelings of financial security matter more than actual financial resources

Many very wealthy people do not feel financially secure, despite objectively having 'enough to spare'. This is a genuine barrier both to giving and to giving more. The size of donations is largely unrelated to donors' income and net worth, which shows that actual capacity to give is less important than confidence on the part of donors that they can afford to give money away, as well as factors such as the strength of connection to the cause and receiving an appropriate request for support.

Reciprocity matters but should not be misinterpreted

Philanthropists give primarily to the causes they are personally passionate about, but they sometimes also give to charities and projects proposed by family members and respected peers, even in some cases when it is not one of their priority areas. Donations made in these circumstances tend to be one-off and smaller than gifts to a preferred organisation, though a 'nominal' or 'token' gift from a rich person may still be worth £5,000 or more. Many fundraisers misinterpret gifts at this level as indicative of serious interest and potential. Rich people themselves define a gift as major from £10,000 upwards.

Recognition and role models are important

Appropriate and dignified recognition, such as through the honours system, naming opportunities and positive media coverage, are all useful and appreciated by many donors. The desire to be recognised as a good person who uses their wealth well is not an improper motive and can help inspire others to give, and to give more. However, this strategy can backfire if it leads to a re-definition of philanthropy as something that only a tiny number of the super-wealthy can do. It is unhelpful for philanthropy to be viewed as an unattainable option by the mass of the population, or for rich people to have the opt-out of thinking: 'We'll leave saving the world to you'.

Donors are offended by slurs but willing to engage in thoughtful debates

Many philanthropists were shocked by the unexpected proposal in the 2012 Budget to cap charity tax relief and offended by the language used during that period, and need reassurance that government does not view them as 'tax dodgers', nor their causes as 'dodgy'. Despite this, donors largely agree there is an important debate to be had about the trade-off between paying tax and making donations, they understand concerns about the redirection of tax revenues to favoured causes, and they are willing to engage with the argument about how private giving fits into a modern democratic society.

There is a culture gap between donors and charity staff

Many donors perceive people working in charities as good-hearted but often inefficient. Rich people need more proof that charities can and will make best use of donations, otherwise they will bypass the traditional charity sector and set up their own delivery mechanisms. Well-run charities should be efficient and collect evidence on impact for their own management purposes, not just to please donors. However, donors should be aware of the inherent inconsistency in complaining about high administration costs while simultaneously demanding super-efficiency and outstanding management.

The paradox of philanthropy is that you don't 'get it' until you do it

Philanthropy is an experience that can only be understood as a result of actually having that experience. One reason that many rich people don't give, and don't believe it when others tell them that giving will be enriching, is because these arguments only make sense to those who have actually done it. Ensuring that young people get involved in giving from an early age, and helping potential donors to 'dip their toe in' with smaller gifts before making bigger commitments, can help them to 'get it'.

Summary of analysis, findings and recommendations

Who participated in the study? (Chapter 3)

We surveyed and interviewed 110 people:

- 40 established philanthropists, comprising half of the original sample of wealthy donors who participated in the 2002 research.
- 42 emerging philanthropists, who were not part of the original study, although in some cases they were actively giving in 2002.
- 16 people who work in the philanthropy sector, with responsibilities ranging from roles in infrastructure and support bodies to major donor fundraisers, as well as policy-makers and media commentators.
- 12 people who work as providers of philanthropy advice to wealthy clients.

The typical profile of the philanthropists we spoke to is that of a self-made man, aged 55 or older, with two or more children. They have had a religious upbringing, are well educated and now enjoy an annual income of at least £250,000 and a net worth of £10m or more. They give away on average £300,000 per year.[1] For those with a net worth below £100m, the size of donation is not, on the whole, related to the size of their wealth.

However, there was much variety within our sample, not least between the established and emerging groups of donors.

Why do rich people give? (Chapter 4)

Every donor in our study rates philanthropy as important in their life today. On a scale of 1-10, over a quarter (27%) rate it 10/10. Furthermore, philanthropy has grown in importance over the past decade for the vast majority (80%) of the people we spoke to – rising to 90% for the emerging donors. This is related to a belief that wealth-holding brings extremely strong responsibilities and obligations to society.

An overwhelming majority feel that the profile of philanthropy in the UK has improved over the past 10 years. Two-thirds (67%) of all donors feel that public opinion in 2012 was more positive than in 2002, with emerging donors slightly more concerned about hostile public opinion. Over half (55%) feel the political climate for philanthropy in the UK has improved; this perception is also shared by most of the experts we surveyed.

Only a third (32%) of all the donors we spoke to cite tax reliefs on charitable donations as an incentive behind their giving decisions, with matched funding schemes seen as a better incentive for individual donations.

Two-thirds (67%) of the rich donors we surveyed are concerned about leaving an over-large inheritance to their children, and of these half see philanthropy as a solution to that problem. Philanthropy also plays a role in parenting by enabling the demonstration of values in action, by bringing the family unit together to discuss good works, and by creating a family legacy that is about more than money.

We find 10 key answers to our core question 'why do rich people give?':

- Because they believe in the cause.
- Because they want to be a catalyst for change.
- Because philanthropy helps them achieve self-actualisation.
- Because they feel a duty and responsibility to share their wealth.
- Because they enjoy the relationships that develop with the charity leadership, with fellow donors and with the beneficiaries.
- Because they believe philanthropy is the right use of surplus money.
- Because they are clear about the complementary roles of government and philanthropy.
- Because they believe philanthropy is a good parenting tool.
- Because they appreciate the recognition that comes with being philanthropic.
- Because philanthropy enriches their life.

What do rich people give to? (Chapter 5)

All types of cause receive some degree of support from rich UK donors. The three most popular cause areas are:

- Arts and culture (supported by 59% of the sample with average annual gift size of £225,000).
- Human services and welfare (supported by 50% of the sample, with average gift size of £195,000).
- Higher education (supported by 40% of the sample, with average gift size of £260,000).

There are many similarities in the causes supported by both established and emerging donors, with two key exceptions. Firstly, 'religious organisations and causes' is the fifth most popular cause (by incidence) for established donors, but by far the least popular area for emerging donors. Secondly, 'higher education' attracts almost double the incidence of donations among established donors; however, those emerging donors who do support this area make gifts that are on average twice as large. 'Charitable foundations' are slightly more popular for emerging donors, but we believe this is because the more established donors had already settled their foundations.

The four factors that prompt rich people to consider a request for support are:

- The nature of the cause – such that the donor has some prior interest or experience.
- A personalised approach, ideally being asked by someone known and respected.
- A 'fit' with pre-determined giving objectives, indicating a rise in strategic approaches to giving.
- A belief that their donation will 'really make a difference'.

While there is some inertia in giving, such that people stick with the same causes over a long period of time, many donors do switch to support new causes, and this is more likely to happen when:

- They have personal experience of the cause (47%).
- They are inspired by the work of a charitable organisation (31%).
- They are approached by a fundraiser (17%).

How do rich people give? (Chapter 6)

Donors are becoming more strategic in their giving. This is evidenced through a rise in giving through a personal foundation (which enables planned, long-term, tax-efficient giving), from around half of the sample in 2002 to nearly three-quarters in 2012.

Foundations are often established as permanent grant-making bodies that distribute the interest and retain the principal to exist in perpetuity. However, an alternative 'spend out' model, which involves distributing both the capital and interest within a set period, is becoming increasingly popular. Over a quarter (28%) of the donors we spoke to who have a foundation have decided to spend out, and a further quarter (25%) are actively considering this option.

Despite giving often being viewed as a solo activity, almost half (44%) the people we surveyed are part of a regular or occasional group of donors and less than a third (30%) have no intention of giving this way. Giving collaboratively may be one of the 'best kept secrets' of the rich donor community.

Attitudes towards allocating a proportion of income for donations vary. Just over a quarter (27%) are already allocating a set proportion (reported as being between 5-50%) of income; 29% do not intend to go down this path; and many others (41%) feel that having a charitable foundation makes this question redundant. Only 3% feel this question remains open.

Giving while living, as opposed to in a charitable legacy, is the dominant plan. 75% are primarily giving their money away during their lifetime, only 6% are giving mostly through their Will and the rest are undecided.

Only 14% give anonymously on a regular basis but almost three-quarters (72%) have made an anonymous gift at some point in their lives. The most common position (35%) is to do so on a case-by-case basis.

The vast majority of our respondents (82%) volunteer as well as make donations, and tend to concentrate their gifts of time on charitable organisations that they also support with financial gifts. The amount of time committed by rich donors is substantial. Almost three-quarters commit 20 hours per month or more to volunteering, which is more than the general population.

Rich people's experience of being asked and asking (Chapter 7)

The majority (83%) of the experts we consulted believe that a more professional approach by those seeking funding has been one of the significant developments in UK philanthropy over the past decade. This improvement will be pleasing to a fundraising sector that has invested heavily in professionalisation, for example, by writing new codes of practice, renewing policies, and enhancing the suite of accredited qualifications.

A third (31%) of donors cite liking the approach of the fundraiser as a factor in their decision to consider a request, compared with the importance of being asked by somebody they know, which mattered to two-thirds (69%) of donors. The combination of the right asker and excellent research is very powerful.

'Major donor fundraising' is the fastest growing element of UK charity fundraising activity, but rich people and fundraisers differ in their definition of what constitutes a 'major donation'. The industry standard definition of £5,000 is inconsistent with 90% of our respondents who cite a higher figure as indicative of their serious interest. Almost all (90%) define a major donation as £10,000 or above, and 65% believe the bar should be set at £50,000 or more.

A third of our respondents do not expect access to the charity leadership until they have given a donation worth £50,000 or more. However, a quarter expect access with smaller gifts, and a third feel that such access should not be dependent on the size of gift.

Most (85%) of the donors we surveyed have also been involved in asking for money for the charities that they support. This question generated one of the sharpest distinctions between the established and emerging donors. Almost every established donor (97%) has at some point asked others to make a donation to a cause, but a quarter (26%) of the emerging group have never done so.

We identify 10 guidelines for donors when asking:

- Credibility in asking comes from giving.
- Donors who become askers must be passionate and knowledgeable champions of the cause.
- Just as with professional fundraisers, donors who ask must invest time in developing a relationship with those they wish to ask.
- Askers must be prepared for rejection and not take it personally, or make it a personal issue.
- Askers may take advantage of norms of reciprocity.
- Askers must realise that their efforts may produce gifts of increasing value over time.
- Some people prefer to ask one-to-one, others prefer asking in small groups, and others prefer to facilitate situations in which the charity can make the ask. There will be an approach that is right for the person being asked, and right for the asker.
- Some people find asking much easier than others.
- Asking gets easier with practice and success.
- Donors who ask can emphasise the life-enriching aspects of giving, because they have first-hand experience of it.

Why rich people don't give (Chapter 8)

We find there is no simple answer to the question 'why don't rich people give, or give more?' but we identify one dominant reason and five further factors that contribute to non-giving and under-giving.

The main reason is that, despite their objective levels of wealth, some rich people still feel financially insecure and that they have 'nothing to spare' to give away. Despite most (67%) of our sample who shared this information having a net worth of over £10m, many of them express feelings of some degree of financial insecurity.

We propose using the system devised by the founder of the New Tithing Group, Claude Rosenberg, (reproduced in Appendix 4) that helps people to calculate how much they can afford to donate.

Further reasons why rich people do not give are:

- Because they lack empathy for potential beneficiaries.
- Because they don't feel it is their responsibility to help.
- Because they were not brought up or socialised with philanthropic values.
- Because they have fears about the consequences of starting to give.
- Because they lack faith in the capacity of philanthropically-funded organisations (i.e. charities) to spend their money wisely.

This chapter also explores how to encourage those who do give, but who could give more. The idea of a benchmark (e.g. donating a percentage of income, or a proportion of wealth) is one solution to help giving become more proportionate to capacity to give, but many respondents are resistant to this idea, either because it feels too prescriptive – and therefore against the spirit of voluntary giving – or because such figures tend to be set too low. The Giving Pledge, initiated by Bill Gates and Warren Buffet in 2010, has a benchmark of giving away 50% of wealth either during lifetime or in a Will. A number of British donors have now signed this pledge, indicating that a higher bar may be more attractive.

The precise role that tax breaks could play in encouraging non-donors and under-givers is not clear, and more research is needed in this area. But we advocate the introduction of a new tax relief, commonly known as 'lifetime legacies'.

We note the important role of early education and socialisation in giving, and advocate greater investment by both government and existing philanthropists in teaching children about philanthropy, and providing them with role models so that they have an understanding of how giving helps to improve society and how it can be personally enriching.

Who advises the rich on giving? (Chapter 9)

We note that the past decade has seen a rapid expansion in the provision of philanthropy advice, and we explore the ways in which this activity has become more professionalised over the same period.

Over a quarter (28%) of the people we surveyed have sought philanthropy advice, and in most cases this has influenced their giving plans. The newer or emerging donors are more than twice as likely to seek such advice.

The two overarching concerns of clients seeking philanthropy advice are:

• The maintenance of their wealth and confidence in the future value of their assets.
• The right amount to leave to children.

Philanthropy advisers are more likely to get involved with giving to some cause areas where the donor has less personal knowledge – notably international development, human services and welfare and schools. Donors are less likely to seek input on giving to areas such as higher education or religion where they may be more recently, or more intimately, involved with the recipient organisation.

Despite widespread assumptions by many charities, who see advisers as a source of potential donors, only a quarter of the advisers we surveyed made suggestions as to which charities their clients might support.

Donors who do not seek professional advice are not necessarily making giving decisions without any other input. Most consult a range of others including: their fellow trustees, in the case of those who give through a personal trust or foundation; two-thirds (67%) who consult their partner; and a third (31%) who consult family members, most often their children. We find that emerging donors are not only more likely to consult experts, they are also twice as likely to involve their children in giving decisions.

Conclusions and recommendations

We conclude with a series of recommendations addressed to different audiences, summarised here:

Recommendations to government

- Seek cross-part consensus to clarify a long-term strategy on philanthropy with regards to specific issues, notably tax reliefs, as well as broader issues, such as how philanthropy interacts with public sector provision.

- Implement the charity tax relief known as 'lifetime legacies', as recommended by numerous previous reports.

- Extend the concept of matched funding to cause areas that have not yet benefitted from this successful incentive.

- Invest in schools training to ensure philanthropy is embedded in future generations.

- Fund the Charity Commission adequately so it can fulfil its regulatory role and raise donors' confidence.

- Instruct HMRC to co-operate with those researching philanthropy, to improve both the quality and the quantity of relevant data.

- Ensure that the honours system respects and recognises significant and sustained philanthropic contributions, rather than just those who give the largest amounts.

- Consider the simplification of the tax system surrounding charitable giving, both to make the process easier to understand and to assuage public concerns that donors can benefit financially from giving.

Recommendations to charities

- Invest in fundraising to improve efforts in asking, and the donors' experience of being asked, in ways that involve trustees and senior staff as well as fundraisers.

- Ensure that experiences of serious donors are positive and reinforcing by improving the after-care and stewardship of those who make substantial gifts.

- Integrate legacy promotion with other forms of relationship development to take advantage of new incentives and expanded opportunities in this area.

- Consider matched funding schemes and challenge grants instigated by current donors to incentivise new donors.

- Address donors' lack of confidence in the competence and efficiency of charitable organisations by funding and implementing more rigorous management processes.

Recommendations to philanthropists

- Talk more openly in the media about giving, to encourage peers and to assist charities in their promotional activities.

- Be willing to act as role models for the next generation by visiting schools and universities to talk about giving.

- Invest in fundraising training and support for charity trustees and senior management.

- Encourage other donors by being willing to ask for their support, as well as getting involved in donor care.

- Contribute to public debates about philanthropy in local and national media, as well as other forums such as events and online discussions.

Recommendations to advisers

- Develop a standardised code of practice for those offering philanthropy advice.

- Be more confident in raising the issue of how much people can afford to give, in order to address the important barrier of financial insecurity.

- Incorporate philanthropy advice and services in routine dealings with clients.

- Make more efforts to promote social investment products.

- Track and share with colleagues the nature of the advice that donors are seeking, to help improve provision in this field.

- Test and share knowledge of donors' attitudes towards paying for advice, to help improve the structure of this field.

Recommendations to the media

- Normalise' philanthropy by presenting it as a regular part of a rounded life for the rich and not-so rich.

- Be accurate in discussions of charity tax reliefs and other donor benefits.

- Highlight philanthropy in a regular and routine way, in all types of media: broadcast, print and online.

- Be more responsible and proactive in educating and convening opinion on philanthropic matters.

Further research

The final chapter ends with suggestions for research in this field to develop further our collective knowledge and understanding of philanthropy, and notes that we intend to repeat the 'why rich people give' study in 2022, and every 10 years thereafter. All profits from the sale of this book will be used to fund this longitudinal study of major giving in the UK.

Notes

[1] This is the median figure, considered the best measure of a 'typical' sum. For information, the mean annual donation is £1.4m and the mode is £1m.

1

Introduction

'We believe, we really sincerely believe, that we get more fulfilment and joy out of giving than the recipients do.'

In researching this book, almost every rich donor we interviewed expressed the view that giving enriches their life. In taking this observation as the title for our work, we intend that the research and analysis presented here will both advance understanding of philanthropy in the UK today, and also challenge some of the misconceptions about the rich, the reasons behind their giving, and their general outlook on money and society.

This work is based on, and is a development from, the research undertaken in 2002 by Theresa Lloyd and published as *Why Rich People Give in 2004*,[1] from now on referred to as *WRPG*. In the decade since, there has been an explosion of activity in the philanthropy sector. This is covered in detail in Chapter 2. However, despite the plethora of books, reports and reviews, it is apparent that many of the implications and recommendations remain to be implemented. Key messages are still not getting through to key constituencies.

In revisiting *WRPG* ten years on, we share the belief that the value of this kind of research lies in the potential to build evidence-based practice that will influence and strengthen a culture of giving and engagement among the wealthy in the UK, and in this book we combine the rigour of data analysis with the passion and direct voices of the philanthropists themselves.

The purpose of this introductory chapter is, first, to put into context the philanthropy and motivations of the wealthy in the 21st century, by providing a short history and a few examples of the past contribution of rich people to British philanthropy. We conclude this introduction with a brief discussion of our research methodology, and an outline of the contents of the succeeding chapters.

Why did rich people give? The historical context

Philanthropy is sometimes discussed as though it is a new phenomenon in the UK. But talk of 'new philanthropy' in the final years of the 20th century referred to the novelty of the context, of increasing wealth, notably from entrepreneurial activity, information technology, the financial sector and real estate and, concurrently, changes in the role of the state, rather than the novelty of the act. This gave rise to new approaches and mechanisms, which we discuss later on.

Philanthropy has been practised in the UK for many centuries. For as long as there have been rich people, some of them have been giving away some of their wealth. As others have noted, philanthropy is 'as old as humanity itself; we can safely consider it universal'.[2]

There are several claimants for the title of oldest registered charity in the UK. The King's School Canterbury, founded in 597 and re-founded in about 1541, is certainly among the leaders. The Hospital of St Cross in Winchester was founded by Bishop Henry de Blois, a grandson of William the Conqueror, in 1136; today, it still provides care for the elderly and bread and ale to passing travellers who ask. Schools, hospitals, help for the old and poor have been the major focus for philanthropy in the UK for well over 1,000 years.

The 14th century poet William Langland, in his work *Visions of Piers Plowman*, provides a useful glimpse into medieval notions of what constituted charitable activity:

> And therewith repair hospitals,
> Help sick people,
> Mend bad roads,
> Build up bridges that had been broken down,
> Help maidens to marry or to make them nuns,
> Find food for prisoners and poor people,
> Put scholars to school or to some other craft,
> Help religious orders and
> Ameliorate rents or taxes.[3]

The combination of causes that are still widely supported (such as schools, hospitals, the poor) with entirely outdated causes (helping maidens to marry or become nuns!), is striking. As the range of charitable activity grew, an attempt was made to classify or provide guidelines for the identification of charitable purposes, published in the Preamble to the Charitable Uses Act 1601.[4] The Preamble set out the following charitable purposes:

> The relief of the aged, impotent and poor people; the maintenance of sick and maimed soldiers and mariners, schools of learning, free schools and scholars in universities; the repair of bridges, ports... sea-banks and highways; the education and preferment of orphans; the... maintenance of houses of correction; the marriages of poor maids, the... aid... of young tradesmen; ... the relief or redemption of prisoners; ... and the aid or ease of any poor inhabitants concerning payment of fifteens [a tax of one fifteenth, formerly imposed on personal property], setting out of soldiers and other taxes.

The Preamble was not, even in 1601, an exhaustive list of charitable purposes. Despite the dominance of religious activity as a charitable objective during the medieval and early modern period, trusts for the advancement of religion were omitted (perhaps because this was self-evidently a charitable activity), as were some other trusts – for example, some educational institutions – that were considered to be adequately administered and so not requiring the protection of the Act. Purposes much broader than relief of poverty, sickness or distress were also included in the Preamble.

Over the subsequent centuries charitable giving developed with the wealth of the country, and the basic methods of fundraising and providing recognition for donors were established. For example, hospitals in London were founded on City wealth, as two notable cases illustrate. Thomas Guy, born in 1644, was a bookseller whose gains from timely investing in the South Sea Company (responsible for the notorious 'South Sea Bubble'[5]), funded the endowment that still bears his name and sustains the well-known hospital in south London. The 18th century Great Hall of St Bartholomew's Hospital is covered inside with large wallboards listing individual donors, including members of the royal family, and the amount they contributed.

Even 'strategic' philanthropic investment is not new. Banker Henry Hoare, who also invested in the South Sea Bubble, provided not only funding but also initiated a new approach: in January 1716 he met with three others to 'consult upon the most effectual methods for relieving the Sick and Needy': a forerunner of the concepts of collaboration and a desire for impact that we see today. Hoare's initiative was not only about the 'deserving poor': the first practical measures taken as a result of the work of his committee were organised visits to ill inmates of London's prisons.[6]

As we move into the 19th century, what is striking is the innovative and indeed to us familiar nature of the investment by wealthy private individuals in the Victorian age. As with so much philanthropy in this period, it is hard to disentangle the motivations of a humanitarian commitment to social justice and a less polarised society, the paternalism of good works, and the desire to keep the lid on potential social unrest.

This period witnessed a complex approach to philanthropy and the development of new models. An example is Octavia Hill (1838-1912) who identified the lack of housing for unskilled labourers as a key problem and collaborated with John Ruskin (a relatively wealthy man) to develop a model in which investors were provided with a guaranteed return of 5%, with any additional profits ploughed back into property acquisition and development for the benefit of new residents. A team of female rent collectors ensured weekly personal contact with tenants and minimal bad debts. Within 10 years of the first house purchase in 1865, Octavia Hill had some 3,000 tenants in 15 housing schemes.

Another outstanding Victorian philanthropist was the American entrepreneur and banker George Peabody, whose Model Dwellings Company was established in 1859. Three years later he established the Peabody Donation Fund, which continues to this day as the Peabody Trust,[7] to provide housing of a decent quality for the 'artisans and labouring poor of London'. It now has over 19,000 properties housing about 50,000 people.

What we see in this idea, and the model developed by Octavia Hill, is an investment that provides both a financial and a social return. Another example of so-called 'five per-cent philanthropy', or philanthropy that made a return on its investment, is The East End Dwellings Company, incorporated in 1884. Its aim was to 'house the very poor while realising some profit.'[8] Along the principles of Octavia Hill's schemes, the company used female rent collectors, including Beatrice Potter (later Webb), one of the founders of the London School of Economics.

A different approach is that exemplified by Lord Leverhulme. William Lever set up Port Sunlight, his model village, in 1887, with the idea that good housing would ensure a contented and productive workforce. This was closely followed in 1893 when George Cadbury funded the development of 120 acres of land close to the Cadbury factory at Bourneville. By 1900 there were some 330 acres allocated to housing on the estate. The designs became a blueprint for many other model village estates around Britain.

Most of these philanthropists – mainly entrepreneurs and bankers – and many others at that time were driven by a profound religious conviction, as well as what might be called enlightened self-interest. Two of today's significant grant-making trusts were created by Lord Leverhulme and George Cadbury, although neither now has a focus on housing. The Leverhulme Trust (set up in 1925) supports 'scholarships for the purposes of research and education'. The Barrow Cadbury Trust, founded in 1920 'promotes social justice through grant-making, research, influencing public opinion and policy and supporting local communities'.

But these very well intentioned initiatives were characterised by what we would now regard as paternalistic supervision. The lives of Hill's tenants were closely monitored by the weekly rent collectors; a similar approach operated at the Peabody Trust, where there were rules such as a night-time curfew.

The model villages were essentially tied to employment, generally for life, unless a worker was dismissed, when they might be evicted. Lever (who became Viscount Leverhulme in 1917) stated: 'A good workman may have a wife of objectionable habits, or may have objectionable habits himself, which make it undesirable for us to have him in the village.'[9] As a review of a biography of Lever notes, 'Tenants of the ideal villas could find themselves evicted for slothfulness, gambling, reluctance to participate in community activities or even failing to grow the species of flowers approved by the boss.'[10] And in a move that would be regarded as draconian nowadays, no public houses have ever been built in Bourneville because George Cadbury was a temperance Quaker.[11]

Nevertheless, throughout this period, while the state in the form of Parliament and various reviews was attempting to come to terms with the challenges of providing decent affordable housing for the poor, private philanthropists were also developing practical financial solutions and models to address the problem. These concerns were echoed in other sectors, leading to the development of nursing care, better working conditions for labourers and the provision of education for children in poorer families.

As well as what might be regarded as prototype social investment structures, many more traditional or donation-based organisations were established in the 19th century, including some that are now household names such as the RNLI (Royal National Lifeboat Institution) in 1824, the Salvation Army in 1865, Barnardo's in 1866, and the NSPCC (National Society for the Prevention of Cruelty to Children) in 1884. These developments happened in a society in which growing wealth based on industrial, imperial and trade expansion was accompanied by desperate poverty. There were also disputes – still relevant today – about the merits of addressing symptoms or underlying causes, and the risks of creating dependency.

Another aspect of what is often viewed as a central plank of a 'new philanthropy' in the 21st century was already evident in the 19th century: a focus on impact and the effectiveness of charitable giving. 1869 saw the founding (by Octavia Hill among others) of the Society for Organising Charitable Relief and the Repression of Mendicity, also known as the Charity Organisation Society.[12] The intention was to use 'scientific principles to root out scroungers and target relief where it was most needed'.[13] Its reputation remains disputed; while it and similar organisations may have started with the best of intentions, with a focus on collecting data and evidence for the effectiveness of different interventions, the concentration on minimising dependency and categorising the poor as deserving or undeserving had inevitable, if unintended, consequences.

Another aspect of Victorian philanthropy, unfortunately still held by a minority today, involved overlooking the economic and structural reasons for poverty and laying the blame on causes such as improvidence and alcoholism among the poor. By 1914 it had largely been agreed that the state should play a greater role in providing the basic necessities of life for all the population, whether by clearing slums to build better housing or by paying a pension to old people. Despite the ever-growing role of the state, and regardless of an opinion poll in 1948 which found that an astonishing 98% of the population felt that the new institutions of the welfare state would make philanthropy superfluous,[14] voluntary work, funded by voluntary donations, continued and remains as important today as it was in the past. The number of new charities continued to grow throughout the 20th century, which witnessed the founding of some of today's most popular causes, including Save the Children (1919), Oxfam (1942), the Samaritans (1953), Shelter (1966) and Comic Relief (1985). The entrepreneurialism of philanthropists willing to complement state action has continued to the present day, due to the combination of energetic founders and a cause that captures the imagination of generous donors. This has resulted in new major charities such as Kids Company (1996), the Teenage Cancer Trust (1997), Teach First (2002) and Help for Heroes (2007), which were either very new or not in existence when the original study of *WRPG* was published.

The definition of charity: the debate continues

The context within which charity and philanthropy operates has, of course, changed over the centuries. Since the 1601 Preamble, the definition of charity has been restated a number times, notably in 1891 when Lord Macnaghten set out what became known as the Pemsel classification or 'the four heads of charity': the relief of poverty, the advancement of education, the advancement of religion, and other purposes beneficial to the community.[15]

The following century brought immense social change in terms of public attitudes and outlooks, but the definition of charity did not legally alter again until 2006, when the Charities Act listed 13 categories of activity (including a catch-all class) that the state recognises as charitable:

- The prevention or relief of poverty.
- The advancement of education.
- The advancement of religion.
- The advancement of health or the saving of lives.
- The advancement of citizenship or community development.
- The advancement of the arts, culture, heritage or science.
- The advancement of amateur sport.
- The advancement of human rights.
- The advancement of environmental protection.
- The relief of those in need, by reason of youth, age, ill-health, disability, financial hardship or other disadvantages.
- The advancement of animal welfare.
- The promotion of the efficiency of the armed forces, police, fire and rescue or ambulance services.
- Any other purposes currently recognised as charitable and any new charitable purposes which are similar to another charitable purpose.

Debates about what is – and what should count as – charitable continue today.

Philanthropy, the welfare state, public benefit and taxation

Registered charities are now legally required to demonstrate that they provide 'public benefit', and it is noticeable that it is in those very areas that were the cradle of philanthropy in the UK – private schools and hospitals – where the tensions are now greatest. Some, including a number of our interviewees, question why institutions that are mainly or only open to those able to afford to pay the high fees expected from schoolchildren and patients in the private sector should benefit from the tax reliefs and other privileges that are available to registered charities.

It is not only in education and healthcare where times have changed. The focus of philanthropy in previous centuries included many tasks that would now be regarded as the role of the public sector, such as the repair of bridges and the maintenance of highways. Yet quirks remain, including the philanthropically-funded Rochester Bridge Trust which still maintains two heavily-used bridges carrying the A2 road and a rail track across the Medway river.

The centuries of charitable giving described here took place in a specific environment: one dominated by Christianity, in which the philanthropy of piety (paying for priests, prayers, shrines, care of the sick and needy and anything else that sprung from religious conviction or was deemed helpful in purchasing a ticket to paradise) was the main driver of much giving. Organised religion continues to commend the duty of charitable giving: indeed, every major faith commands its adherents to undertake philanthropic acts.[16]

The establishment of the welfare state in the middle of the 20th century raised questions about the respective role of private individuals versus the state, and the responsibility for the provision of public goods, especially those relating to meeting basic needs, such as healthcare, housing and education. The idea that philanthropy is no longer needed because 'it is the job of the state' still lingers as an excuse for non-givers, as we explore in Chapter 8. However, as noted above, philanthropists have always demonstrated an entrepreneurial ability to spot and fill gaps in private sector and public sector provision. Meanwhile today, in the UK at least, the influence of organised Christianity is significantly diminished and the role of the state in funding most of the activities undertaken in hospitals, schools, and to a significant extent the arts and higher education, is being rolled back. As one person interviewed in 2002 said: 'It is the role of the state to provide the basics; it's the role of the philanthropist to make the basic the best'.

Many of our interviewees, both donors and expert commentators, have commented thoughtfully on this complex issue. We explore the changing attitudes to the role of the state and whose responsibility it is to pay for (some) public goods in Chapter 4.

A 'new philanthropy'?

This book charts developments in UK philanthropy from roughly 2002 to 2012. But how new are the ideas and approaches that are often referred to as 'new philanthropy'? While there is some new terminology, such as 'venture philanthropy' or 'social investment', arguably philanthropy is not distinctively 'newer' at the start of the 21st century than in any previous era. The role of philanthropy and philanthropists has continually been re-invented to reflect contemporary needs, dominant values, available wealth, technological developments, new financing and tax structures and the broader socio-political context. In other words: philanthropy cannot be divided into 'old' and 'new' but is always evolving as a product of its time.

We suggest that there is much that is the same as it ever was – motivation, passion and the desire to make a difference to individual lives. Education and health (including medical research) are still priority causes for wealthy donors, along with social welfare and the arts (if not nowadays for religious purposes). The biggest historic change is the shift from helping people and causes that are personally known to the donor, to helping unknown recipients and contributing to causes far from where the donor lives. While people have helped each other for as long as human societies have existed, donating money to help total strangers away from one's own community is a relatively new development, brought about by the same forces that have shaped globalisation: fast, affordable international travel and immediate global communications, especially via the internet. But there have also been significant developments in the focus and scope of giving – particularly in international development, and for causes linked to the environment and climate change.

We also see, as with the example of Henry Hoare described above, that collaboration for leverage and shared learning is not a new phenomenon. Contemporary UK philanthropy differs from the past because we are drawing ideas from beyond our shores – both geographic and sectoral borders. For example, there is much exchange between those working in, and studying, philanthropy in the US and the UK, and there is a blurring of boundaries between philanthropy and social investment. We are observing openness to learning how to be more effective donors with the encouragement of organisations such as NPC (New Philanthropy Capital), and, as we describe in Chapter 9, we are witnessing the rise of a new professional on this scene: the philanthropy adviser. We are also seeing governmental developments, as described in the next chapter, notably government-funded matched funding schemes, investment in research and a focus on philanthropy in the honours system. Surrounding all of these developments is an increasing awareness of and debate about the role of philanthropy in 21st century Britain, with a philanthropist-funded campaign to Give More, the involvement in the discourse of opinion-formers and politicians, and more wealthy people willing to talk openly about their money and their giving, which makes the present study possible.

Why do rich people give? How we have approached this research

How did we go about capturing the evidence for our research in 2012? We have used what we believe is a unique methodology: a cohort analysis over time. Half of the donors we survey for this book were drawn from the original interviewees for *WRPG* ('established donors'), and the other half are new to this analysis ('emerging donors').[17] It is the intention that this approach will be repeated in another decade, and in subsequent 10-year intervals, in order that a unique and informed portrait of the changing face of the philanthropy of the rich in the UK can be developed over time.

Unless otherwise attributed, all the quotes in this book come from our interviewees. Anonymity and confidentiality were conditions for the research, and this allowed us to gather the candid opinions on which we base our findings.

We have supplemented our surveys and interviews with donors by drawing on the views of a dozen philanthropy advisers and 16 experts, including policy-makers and politicians, journalists and other opinion-formers, and those with expertise in developing strategies for organisations seeking funding from the wealthy. The views and experiences of the advisers are discussed in detail in Chapter 9. Those of the experts are not covered as a separate chapter, but are referenced throughout the book, implicitly or explicitly, to support or elaborate points made.

In Chapter 3 we describe in detail the social, economic and demographic characteristics of the donors we surveyed and interviewed. (A full description of the methodology, along with information on the survey questions, is given in Appendix 1).

In Chapter 4 we discuss why some rich citizens choose to give away some of their private wealth for public good. We look at the reasons given in our recent research, and compare them to those identified 10 years ago in *WRPG*. The focus of their giving, the basis for supporting different causes and the satisfaction (or otherwise) of their experiences is discussed in Chapter 5. In Chapter 6 we review the approaches and methods used by wealthy donors to organise their philanthropic activity.

A crucial issue for those who wish to understand how to encourage more rich people to give more, is to understand how people get started; how donors decide whether to consider a request for funding, and what is likely to influence their response. What do they look for in the relationships with the organisations they fund? What are the characteristics of good and bad experiences and what can be learned from them? These elements are covered in Chapter 7, which explores experiences of asking and being asked.

But what about those people who are not givers, or who give very little? Like other researchers in this field, we have had to come at this question somewhat indirectly, since we have not, despite some attempts, managed to persuade non-givers to be interviewed in depth about their attitudes. We base our analysis in Chapter 8 on the views, experiences and informed speculation of our interviewees, including donors who also ask for support from their peers, and advisers, as well as existing research on this topic. We include suggestions from our expert observers, and some of the reasons given for not responding to requests. And we explore ideas as to what can be done to change this situation.

We then consider whether the rich ask for advice, and if so, from whom and on what topics. The question of the scale and nature of the advisory sector, the provision of advice and its influence on donors, is discussed in Chapter 9. Finally, Chapter 10 sets out the recommendations that emerge from this work.

Some of these recommendations have been made before, by ourselves and by others. Indeed, the consistent nature of the recommendations emanating from various studies over the years is itself noteworthy. It is regrettable that they need to be re-stated, but they bear repetition until they are acted upon. Our work is partly prompted and inspired by the fact that these messages are still not getting through to, or are being ignored by, some of the key constituencies that need to hear them. This is despite the significant developments in the philanthropy sector in the UK over the past decade, and the many papers, reviews and recommendations, from the proposals in *WRPG* onwards, including notable reports such as the Philanthropy Review.[18]

Our hope is that the combination of research and analysis, combined with the verbatim and unvarnished voices of donors themselves, will provide convincing proof of the need and opportunity for those seeking funding, government, advisers, the press and the wealthy themselves, together to build on this work and body of evidence, and have the courage and vision to make a step change in the culture, practice and extent of giving by the wealthy in the UK.

Notes

[1] Theresa Lloyd (2004) *Why Rich People Give*. London: Association of Charitable Foundations.

[2] Robert Payton and Michael Moody (2008). *Understanding Philanthropy*. Indiana University Press p.14.

[3] Cited in W.K. Jordan (1959). *Philanthropy in England 1480-1660: A study of the changing pattern of English social aspirations*. London: George Allen & Unwin p.112.

[4] The Charitable Uses Act of 1601 (known as the Statute of Elizabeth) is an Act (43 Eliz I, c.4) of the Parliament of England. It was repealed by section 13(1) of the Mortmain and Charitable Uses Act 1888 (c.42) (but see section 13(2) of that Act).

[5] In 1720 the South Sea Company collapsed after engaging in practices such as bribery and insider trading. The collapse caused the ruin of investors who, unlike Thomas Guy, did not sell their stock in time.

[6] A detailed description of the many charitable activities and investments of Henry Hoare and other family members can be found in Victoria Hutchings (2005) *Messrs Hoare Bankers A history of the Hoare Banking Dynasty*. London: Constable.

[7] www.peabody.org.uk/about-us/history.aspx

[8] www.british-history.ac.uk/report.aspx?compid=22752

[9] The life of Lord Leverhulme is told in Adam Macqueen (2011) *The King Of Sunlight: How William Lever Cleaned Up The World*. London: Corgi.

[10] www.spectator.co.uk/books/20957/a-bully-with-a-heart-of-gold

[11] However, since the late 1940s, there has been a licensed members' bar at the sports centre built on the estate.

[12] M.J.D. Roberts (2003) 'Charity disestablished? The origins of the Charity Organisation Society revisited, 1868-1871'. *Journal of Ecclesiastical History*, vol 54, pp. 40-61.

[13] Rosemary Rees (2001) *Poverty and Public Health 1815-1949*. London: Heinemann.

[14] This survey is reported by Chesterman (1979), as cited in J Kendall and M Knapp (1996). *The Voluntary Sector in the UK*. Manchester: Manchester University Press.

[15] For an example of this classification being cited, see p2 of the Charity Commission 2001 report 'Recognising New Charitable Purposes'.

[16] W.F. Ilchman, S.N. Katz et al., Eds. (1998). *Philanthropy in the World's Traditions*. Bloomington, Indianapolis: Indiana University Press.

[17] As we discuss in Chapter 3, not all of the emerging donors are new to philanthropy, but new to this analysis. We have used the terms established and emerging for simplicity.

[18] www.philanthropyreview.co.uk

21st century developments

2

In this chapter we review the developments over the past decade, with a focus on six main themes:

- Wealth, inequality and philanthropy.
- Growing government interest in encouraging philanthropy.
- Development of the UK philanthropy infrastructure.
- New forms of philanthropic engagement.
- Transformations triggered by technology.
- The rise of 'enrichment' as a key driver of philanthropic activity.

Wealth, inequality and philanthropy

This section discusses the context for philanthropy today in terms of changing patterns of wealth and heightened inequality.

The rich are getting richer

Despite the economic crisis of 2008/09, and the large financial losses experienced by many wealthy people, there has been a sharp increase in wealth among the richest members of society over the past decade. The number of UK-based billionaires has risen four-fold – from 21 in 2003 to 88 in 2013 – and the combined wealth of Britain's 1,000 richest people rose almost three-fold from £156bn to £450bn over the same decade.[1]

This trend is not confined to one society. Across the world 210 new billionaires emerged in 2013, who joined the largest number of dollar billionaires yet recorded (1,426), with an all-time high collective net worth of $5.4 trillion.[2]

The Barclays Wealth *2011 UK Wealth Map*[3] reports on wealth distribution in the UK. It identifies 619,000 millionaires in 2010 – a number that has grown by almost 100,000 since 2008 when 528,000 millionaires resided in the UK. This number is predicted to keep growing and reach 826,000 by 2020. The same report also finds a 19% growth in the number of people with a net worth of £5m or more, which leapt from 70,000 in 2008 to 86,000 in 2010.

In June 2013 *The Guardian*[4] cited figures from HM Revenue & Customs showing that 18,000 people in the UK now earn at least £1m, which is the highest number of income millionaires ever recorded. This figure has risen steeply from 1999-2000 when there were only 4,000 people earning a seven-figure salary, and represents a huge year-on-year increase from 2010-11, when 10,000 earned more than £1m. The same report also noted huge growth in the numbers earning six-figure salaries, for example, 5,000 more people earned between £500,000 and £1m in 2012-13, compared with 2012-11.

In May 2013 a report from Boston Consulting Group[5] also told a similar story, identifying over 1,000 ultra-high net worth UK households, defined as those with more than $100m (£65m) in private financial wealth, not including property.

Growing inequality

Much of the 20th century saw a closing of the gap between rich and poor in Western consumer societies, as mass affluence spread and inequality narrowed. But from the 1980s on this pattern reversed. This recent increase in wealth among the richest strata of society has been described by noted sociologists[6] as:

> 'The most rapid and dramatic shift of income, assets and resources in favour of the very rich that has ever taken place in human history...
> We can see the rise of the 'super rich' in the 'old' capitalist nations, especially those such as the UK and USA, which have enthusiastically embraced neo-liberalism from the early 1980s. In both countries the top one or five per cent of income earners have more or less doubled their share of total income since the early 1980s and we have now almost returned to pre-1914 levels of income inequality.'

As the top 1% get richer, the poorest get relatively poorer. Alongside massive increases in wealth and wealth disparity, we note the parallel phenomenon of growing polarisation in incomes. A 2011 report[7] published by the Organisation for Economic Co-operation and Development (OECD) finds growing income inequalities across most

OECD countries, such that the average income of the richest 10% of the population is now nine times that of the poorest 10%. The report notes that in the UK the ratio is slightly higher at 10 to 1. According to the 2013 annual report of the Resolution Foundation[8] (a philanthropically-funded think tank focused on low pay), the share of post-tax income of the bottom half of the UK population fell year on year, while the post-tax income of the top 1% increased. The Resolution Foundation concludes: 'The very richest in Britain thus moved ever further away from the vast majority in society over the past two decades.'

Widening inequality is most pronounced in the US. According to a 2012 special report in *The Economist*,[9] since 1980 the richest 1% of American households have doubled their share of national income, from 10% to 20%. Within that statistic is an even more remarkable figure: the richest 0.01% (which constitutes just 16,000 individuals and families) now enjoy 5% of national income – up from 1% in 1980.

Giving in relation to wealth

Analysis of giving in relation to wealth, like so many other questions related to giving and philanthropy, is bedevilled by lack of consistent and current data – a point we cover in our recommendations. Nevertheless, the pattern is broadly that of the rich (as a group) giving more than they did in previous decades, but still less than their share. Research published by the UK's Centre for Giving and Philanthropy (CGAP)[10] finds that the 10% of households with the highest expenditure accounted for 22% of the total value of donations made in the period 1978-1982, while that same decile accounted for 31% of the total value of donations made between 2004-08 (the latest financial year for which such data is available). Despite this welcome increase, it is still less than the contribution that might be expected, given the Office for National Statistics report[11] in 2012 which found the wealthiest 10% in the UK own 40% of the national wealth and were over 850 times wealthier than the poorest 10% of households (the inclusion of wealth as well as income makes these figures more extreme than the OECD ratios discussed above). Despite its relative poverty, the bottom decile in terms of expenditure still collectively donated 2% of all donations in 2004-08, according to the CGAP report – very much punching above its weight.

However, research also indicates that the propensity to donate is higher among those with greater resources. The *UK Giving 2008* report[12] finds the likelihood of giving increases with income: whereas 52% of the lower quartile (the 25% of households having the least income) gave to charity in 2007/08, this figure rises to 68% of the upper quartile. The same report shows that the size of typical monthly donations is also related to household income, with donors in the upper quartile giving a median gift of £20 against £8 given by lower quartile donors – though again this differential does not reflect the vastly larger differential in potential to give. Indeed, the CGAP paper discussed above reinforces the point that givers within poorer households are much more generous in terms of the proportion of their total budgets given to charity. Giving comprises 3.6% of total spending among the poorest 10 % of givers, compared to 1.1% for the richest 10%.

One of the most startling findings from the *UK Giving* annual surveys is how few people give an amount that might be described as significant. The 2012 edition[13] of this study reported that just 6% of donors gave £100 or more per month in 2011/12, but the collective donations of this group known as 'high level donors' accounted for 40% of the value of donations made in that year. The disproportionately large contribution of fewer than 10% of the population has been a recurrent picture in UK giving statistics for many years.

Beyond these headline figures on wealth inequalities and giving by the wealthy, what do we know about the rich, and giving by the rich in general? The annual *Coutts Million Pound Donors Report*[14] and the data presented in this book, make clear that there are some very generous wealthy givers. Further, this generosity is on the increase – observe the increased philanthropic donations of the *Sunday Times Giving List*,[15] from £299m in 2004 to the £1.7bn in 2013, as shown in Table 2.1. Some of this six-fold increase may be due to better data collection and greater willingness on the part of donors to declare their giving (in other words, a 'reveal effect'), but clearly there has been a significant growth in elite philanthropy, alongside the growth in wealth.

The role of The Giving Pledge, and the high profile examples it makes of leading philanthropists, is considered later in this chapter.

Table 2.1 shows the progression in both the collective value of donations made by those included in the *Sunday Times Giving List*, and the percentage of wealth given away by the donor ranked 30th most generous as an indicator of how giving as a proportion of wealth has changed over time.

Table 2.1: Philanthropic donations 2004-2013

Year	Total donations	% of wealth given by donor ranked 30th most generous
2004	£299m	0.59
2005	£333m	0.68
2006	£453m	0.89
2007	£1.2bn	1.36
2008	£2.4bn	3.00
2009	£2.8bn	4.50
2010	£2.5bn	3.20
2011	£1.6bn	3.42
2012	£1.3bn	4.01
2013	£1.7bn	2.62

Source: adapted from the Sunday Times Rich List 2004-2013

The underlying trend shows a significant increase, and although we see a peak in 2009, and subsequent volatility, the amounts being donated at the start of the second decade of the 21st century appear to be much higher than a decade before.

Such is the extent of some individuals' giving that a rich person can 'donate themselves' off the Sunday Times Rich List. One example is Dame Stephanie ('Steve') Shirley, Britain's first Ambassador for Philanthropy and an extraordinary entrepreneur and philanthropist.[16] Dame Stephanie used to appear in the Rich List, but as she explained to the BBC in December 2011:

> 'I was worth £150m, but I have given away enough, together with the dot.com collapse, to take me out of the Rich List. I am terribly proud of that, because money to me that is not working has a sort of obscenity about it.'[17]

But there is clearly capacity to give more, particularly among the very wealthy. While recognising the generosity of many, it is worth considering why so many people are not giving, or not giving at levels that might be thought appropriate for their wealth. We explore the question of why some rich people don't give in Chapter 8.

The global context

Our research is focused on the UK, but we are aware that some of those we surveyed and interviewed enjoy international networks and are giving outside the UK, sometimes in collaboration with others.

Looking briefly at the international context, we see, despite the blip of the recession, a very significant rise in the numbers of the super-rich. *The Wealth Report 2012*, produced by Knight Frank and Citibank, finds that the number of people with $100m or more has increased by 29% since 2006, and that the number of these 'centa-millionaires' in South-East Asia, China and Japan is greater (18,000) than in North America (17,000).[18] These trends are underpinned by rapid growth in GDP, which in turn provides the framework for wealth creation.

The same report highlights concerns about growing income inequality, evidenced in demonstrations such as the Occupy movement and the high profile of this issue at the 2012 World Economic Forum.[19] As Wilkinson and Pickett (2009) argue in *The Spirit Level*, income inequality has negative impacts on all in a society, not just on those who are economically marginalised.

It is possible that increasing wealth and recognition of the dangers of increasing inequality in emerging markets will act to encourage philanthropy among those with money who are concerned to try to alleviate its worst effects (The Giving Pledge, discussed later in this chapter along with other philanthropist-led initiatives, could be seen in this light). However, this inequality has also led to a growing debate about how much the rich ought to be able to distribute at their own discretion in the form of philanthropy, and how much governments should appropriate and distribute for the public benefit. As one of our respondents suggested:

> 'Philanthropy alone cannot end poverty, nor end environmental destruction, nor, alone, build a cultural sector. In all of these areas it needs a state partner either to tax wealth and support the poor, or to legislate against polluters, or to take the arts to the public. Philanthropists and their non-profit partners can innovate, and pressurise, and demonstrate how to do these things better; philanthropists can identify and focus on minorities or neglected causes in a way that the state (or rather, the politicians) cannot or will not. And philanthropy provides for the donor a satisfaction that paying taxes never can.'

As we have noted, this is a familiar question, which has merely been sharpened by rising inequality of wealth. The other side of this is increasing distrust of governments to distribute money wisely, or even honestly.

Some of the wealthiest people are themselves deeply uncomfortable with this situation of massive wealth-holding by a few in the face of increasing need, and have responded accordingly:

> 'We have to change the situation when you have "haves" and "have nots"; it's a fundamental problem and touches on all the key issues of our life: moral, ethical, behavioural. Will we ever stop? Our entire basis for living is based on consumption.'

Growing government interest in encouraging philanthropy

While tax reliefs on charitable donations are the most widely known aspect of government support for giving, a number of other government-funded initiatives to promote philanthropy have occurred over the past decade or so.

The Giving Campaign

An early government initiative, embarked on concurrently with the development of pioneering organisations such as Philanthropy UK, NPC (New Philanthropy Capital) and the Institute for Philanthropy, was the Giving Campaign, which ran from 2001 to 2004. Chaired by Lord Joffe, it was a three-year project funded by the then-named Office of the Third Sector, CAF (Charities Aid Foundation) and a number of the top 100 fundraising charities. The main aims of the campaign were to promote more tax-effective giving, primarily through Gift Aid, payroll giving and share giving, as well as to create a stronger culture of giving in the UK. Among its achievements were building media interest, developing a brand for Gift Aid, payroll giving training courses and a Giving Nation project for schoolchildren. After its closure in 2004, some of the projects it had created spun off into independent programmes, such as Giving Nation, while its programmes around tax-effective giving were passed on to CAF. Its greatest legacy is probably the 'Gift Aid It' brand, which is now almost ubiquitous in fundraising and recognised and trusted by the public.

Subsequent government investments include the strategic funding of Philanthropy UK and now Philanthropy Impact.

Matched funding and capacity building schemes

A crucial development, strongly influenced by the 2004 Thomas Report on increasing voluntary giving to higher education,[20] was the launch of a matched funding scheme for the higher education sector. This scheme, and its impact, are described in the report by the More Partnership of September 2012.[21] The Government made available up to £200m for a matched funding initiative for England, intended to incentivise giving to universities and to encourage professionalism within institutions. It allowed universities to apply to take part in one of three tiers, related to their historic success in fundraising. In Wales a separate matched funding scheme drew on £10m from the Higher Education Council for Wales (HEFCW) and was structured in two capped tiers, matching 1:1 for lower-level fundraising operations, and 1:2 for universities with more developed fundraising capabilities. Funds were also made available for capacity building.

The scheme was a success. Funds raised by universities in the UK increased from £513m in 2006/07 to £693m in 2010/11. This represents an overall rise of 35% in funds raised, and 54% more donors. The More Report assessment suggests that if universities continue to invest in the same way, they have the potential to receive £2bn per annum from some 630,000 donors by 2022.

An example of matched funding in a different sector was Grassroots Grants. This was a £130m government-funded programme that ran from September 2008 to March 2011. It supported the voluntary sector in building stronger, more active communities. Grassroots Grants included an £80m small grants programme and a £50m endowment match challenge. Both elements were delivered by funders who had local knowledge and experience in grant-making and managing endowment funds. Local groups meeting all the criteria could apply for a Grassroots Grant of £250 to £5,000. This programme succeeded in reaching grassroots activity, and eventually supported around 19,000 groups. According to the evaluation report:[22]

> 'Thirty-nine per cent of those funded were under-the-radar groups; their Grassroots Grant was the first publicly-funded grant they had received. The majority of groups funded (59%) had an annual turnover of less than £5,000.'

In September 2011 the Department for Culture, Media and Sport (DCMS), the Arts Council England (ACE) and the Heritage Lottery Fund (HLF) announced details of a £100m Catalyst scheme to boost private giving to culture. The scheme is designed to enable arts and heritage organisations to diversify the way they generate income, increase their fundraising potential and develop new ways to secure private giving. It includes a £55m endowment scheme with a matched funding incentive jointly funded by DCMS, ACE and HLF, and multi-million-pound capacity building schemes funded by ACE and HLF. These provide investment in training organisations in the cultural sector to help them become more effective at governance, clarify their business model, make their case for support, identify and look after major donors, and develop a legacy income stream.[23] That such training is necessary is evidenced in Chapters 7 and 8, which discuss experiences of asking and being asked, and why rich people don't give.

Another government department making use of matched funding schemes to incentivise donations is the Department for International Development (DfID), which launched UK Aid Match[24] in 2012, offering charities working on poverty reduction projects in developing countries the opportunity to apply for 'pound for pound' matching, up to a cap of £5m. A further DfID matched funding scheme was announced in June 2013 when £280m of matched funding was made available to tackle global malnutrition.[25]

It is too early to report on the impact of these initiatives, but as well as the success of the scheme in the Higher Education sector we note (in Chapter 4) the positive responses by some of those interviewed to the concept of matched funding, because of the attractive idea of a 'deal'.

The Big Society

The Big Society[26] was the flagship policy idea of the 2010 UK Conservative Party general election manifesto. It now forms part of the legislative programme of the Conservative-Liberal Democrat Coalition Agreement. The stated aim is to create a climate that empowers local people and communities, building a 'Big Society' that will take power away from politicians and give it to people. While some have responded to the policy favourably, its aims have been queried and disputed by other commentators, from all sides of the political spectrum.

An early legislative realisation of the Big Society concept came in 2011 with the publication of a Giving White Paper,[27] which introduced a raft of measures designed to stimulate charitable giving. Among these is the move to promote legacy giving, encouraging people to leave 10% of their money to charity in exchange for an equal reduction in inheritance tax.[28] (The impact of this measure on our interviewees is discussed in Chapter 4). It has also simplified the rules surrounding Gift Aid, enabling charities to claim Gift Aid on up to £5,000 of small donations a year without the need for declarations.[29]

Another pertinent development for this study is the formation of Big Society Capital as a UK Social Investment Bank in 2011, and the launch of the £600m investment fund in April 2012.[30] The Bank's mission will be 'to catalyse the growth of a sustainable social investment market, making it easier for social ventures to access the finance and advice they need at all stages of their development'.[31] It is independent from government and will act as a wholesaler, not investing directly in projects but 'will invest in products developed by intermediaries and encourage others to do likewise'. We discuss this further in the context of social investment later in this chapter.

A key element in the relationship between government and charitable giving is the nature and extent of the ways in which the tax system encourages philanthropy. This is both about its simplification (as many have advocated, particularly in respect of Gift Aid) and its effectiveness as an incentive. We explore the Government's 2012 proposals to cap tax relief for charitable giving in Chapter 4. Despite these proposals being rescinded, rich donors acknowledge that many important issues remain to be addressed.

Recognition and awards

Along with investment in the encouragement of philanthropy has come the realisation that those who respond should be recognised and celebrated. This complex area, and the extent to which such recognition is an incentive for individuals, is discussed in Chapter 4. In addition, the growing number of awards for philanthropists, family businesses and, indeed, professional advisers, represents another strand that is increasing awareness of philanthropy. Such awards are promoted by government (through the honours system discussed further below), as well as by the private sector and by charitable entities (discussed in the next section).

Government honours

The stated intention of recognising those who contribute to society has been underpinned with the formation of the Philanthropy Honours Committee. The Chair of this committee, Dame Mary Marsh, described its terms of reference to the House of Commons' Public Administration Select Committee in May 2012. She stated that philanthropists would be considered if they had given 'time, commitment and sustained engagement with their particular cause... and have made a significant difference through their philanthropy'.

Obviously, the process of selecting recipients is a complex area and the terms of reference are designed to address the cynicism that has surrounded some aspects of this system in the past. It is difficult to be precise on the resulting number of wealthy people who have been recognised for their philanthropy in recent years, not least because the wording varies from one recipient to another, and in many cases philanthropy is only one of the reasons for their recognition.

Along with public honours, we have seen an increase in the number of other ways in which individual philanthropists are celebrated. These include the Beacon Awards, The Prince of Wales medals for Arts Philanthropy[32] and the Spears Wealth Management Awards.[33] We look at the Beacon Awards in detail in the next section as the most established example.

Development of the UK philanthropy infrastructure

Growth in the voluntary sector

The past two decades have seen an unprecedented growth in the scale and scope of the 'voluntary sector'. According to the UK Charity Commission (which publishes data relating to charities in England and Wales), the annual gross income of registered charities (including grant-making trusts, and including public sector funding and contracts) grew from just under £24bn in 1999 to over £58bn in 2012.[34] Over the same period the total number of charities fluctuated at around 163,000, reaching over 169,000 in 2007 and falling to under 163,000 in 2012.[35] This same source of information shows that income for larger charities (those whose annual income exceeds £10m) has grown from just over £10bn (43% of the total) to £33.5bn (57% of the total). This represents a growing concentration of resources in these largest organisations, which constitute less than 1% of all charities. This may be because (as suggested in the Charity Commission report from which this data is drawn) they are better placed to bid for the public funding and contracts that form a substantial element in their funding portfolio.

As well as income generation, volunteering is vitally important for charities. Many people give both money and time. More than half (58%) of the 2,705 people interviewed in England for *Helping Out:*

A National Survey of Volunteering and Charitable Giving[36] had both volunteered and donated to charity in the last 12 months, and 81% had given to a charity within the last four weeks. All three mainstream political parties (the Conservatives, the Liberal Democrats and Labour) are at pains to stress the importance of the 'voluntary sector' to ensure a healthy public sphere, a thriving civil society, and the effective delivery of welfare services. Much of the increase in the income of the sector has come from the state contracting with the charitable sector to deliver a wide range of services, from nursery places to working with offenders, and from delivering training to youth work.

Over the same period there has been a step change in the relationship between the public and private sector. A report in 2010 by the Third Sector Research Centre[37] indicated that around 36% of the charities surveyed received some income from statutory sources, while 14% (23,000 organisations) regarded statutory funding as their most important source of income. In the same year the Charity Commission reported that a quarter of large charities said that funding from the public sector was their main source of income.[38] There has been some criticism of the perceived risk to the independence of charities because of their reliance on state funding.

Developments in researching and encouraging philanthropy

As wealth creation exploded at the end of the 20th century, many people started asking whether the newly rich entrepreneurs, and those from the banking and IT sectors, would become the philanthropists of tomorrow, how this might be encouraged, and what could be learned from the US.

At the same time, donors were becoming more strategic in their giving and wanting to see the impact of their support beyond evidence of outputs, such as the number of people served, to a desire for evidence on the longer-term outcomes and impacts on beneficiaries, such as improved health or self-esteem. New tools for measuring social returns as well as financial returns needed to be developed, and donors demanded increased accountability and transparency from charities.

A number of organisations and initiatives emerged to research and address these questions and information needs, some of which are described below in this section and all of which are also listed in Appendix 5, which provides details on how to access further information about them online. The fact that there is now a plethora of such organisations is a testimony to the vibrancy and diversity of the sector.

Concurrently with the development of these types of organisations, which are themselves charities, there has also been also a growth in the number of wealth managers and advisers in banks and law firms becoming engaged with the potential and actual philanthropic interests of their clients. Partly stimulated by Philanthropy UK research showing that some wealthy people were looking for expert values-based advice, partly looking at US experience, and partly in direct response to client interest, a growing number of commercial firms have invested in establishing specialist departments over the last decade. Indeed, more and more firms are realising that, to quote Philanthropy Impact:

> 'Too few financial advisers take the initiative when it comes to engaging clients on the question of philanthropy. Yet, having a meaningful conversation about charitable giving is an effective way of deepening client relationships and differentiating one's firm. What is important, however, is that advisers frame the discussion around the client's values, interests, and goals – not simply around the technical aspects of taxes and philanthropic vehicles.'[39]

An example is Coutts Bank, which in 2005 became one of the first private banks in the UK to set up a philanthropy advisory service, now called the Coutts Institute:[40] an initiative soon replicated by many of its competitors. Its advisers act as facilitators assisting individuals and families to focus on the 'governance of wealth' and making decisions on matters such as preparing children for inheritance, making a difference to the causes and communities they care about and planning for the future of their family business.

In addition to helping clients create personal giving strategies, the Coutts Institute publishes research, such as the *Coutts Million Pound Donors Report* (in association with the University of Kent),[41] and runs education programmes, such as Coutts Philanthropy and Family Business Forums.

We consider the development of the provision of philanthropy advice, and the importance of training 'frontline' staff to be confident in raising the topic of philanthropy, below and in Chapter 9.

Despite the apparent blooming of philanthropy organisations, we should view the field with some caution, since, as we discuss in Chapter 9, many donors continue to say they have chosen not to take advantage of advice. Ninety per cent of respondents to a 2007 survey of ultra high net worth Europeans thought that traditional wealth advisers do not meet their philanthropic needs,[42] while according to a 2010 edition of *Alliance* magazine,[43] 'few [philanthropy advice] organisations have managed to grow beyond a dozen staff. Small boutiques and solo practitioners are the norm'. Size may not matter if standards are high, but not all donors expect to be charged or are willing to pay for a service – the same article warns of plenty of free, but not necessarily informed, advice. We are now a few years on from that 2010 report and the market is expanding all the time, but the provision of philanthropy advice is still nowhere near being a mature profession.

In the UK, although a Philanthropy Advisers Forum was established in 2010 (now incorporated with Philanthropy Impact), there is no standard code of practice within the advice industry and, indeed, anyone can put themselves forward as a 'philanthropy adviser'. Reputable organisations ensure that they offer a combination of experience and expertise, provide staff training and adhere to ethical business practice. The Society of Trust and Estate Practitioners[44] (STEP) has also developed a training partnership with Philanthropy Impact.[45] This includes a step-by-step guide with a framework for advising clients on philanthropy, case studies and key questions and answers, with signposts to more detailed information and other helpful resources. However, the sector still needs to develop an agreed code of practice and set of professional standards.

Another aspect to the provision of advice, as we report in Chapter 7, is that only a minority of interviewees (28% overall and just 15% of the emerging donors) think that fundraisers have become better at explaining tax breaks and helping with planned giving. Any perceived lack of understanding and expertise in beneficiary organisations is a matter of concern, and improvement in this area is a necessary component of the general raising of standards in the management of relationships with wealthy donors.

We also note three other significant developments that have emerged from within the philanthropy sector: the Philanthropy Review, the Give More campaign and the Beacon Awards.

The Philanthropy Review

One of the most influential recent non-governmental initiatives is the Philanthropy Review. In December 2010, leaders from the worlds of philanthropy, business and the charitable sector came together to identify new and already existing opportunities to catalyse a step change in the level of giving of money in the UK. The aim, similar to other initiatives in the past decade, was to identify, gather evidence and advocate for practical actions that can build a stronger culture of philanthropy in the UK. The detailed final report[46] describes the work in depth, and sets out a series of recommendations. These are encapsulated in three goals:

- It must be easier for people to give.
  - Every bank or building society account holder should have the option to hold a charity account.
  - Every chief executive must champion payroll giving in the workplace and lead by example, giving through their own payroll.
- Giving must be encouraged.
  - Current tax incentives must be simplified and applied equally to all assets including cash.
  - Living legacies must be introduced to allow families to make significant gifts and enjoy large-scale giving in their lifetime, not solely through their Wills.
- Giving should become a social norm.
  - 'Giving' education must be provided in every school.
  - Planned giving must be championed by professional advisers.

Not surprisingly, many of the suggestions in these recommendations were put forward by our interviewees, and we explore some of these in Chapter 10.

Give More

Another key non-governmental initiative is the Give More campaign,[47] funded by the Pears Foundation. (Trevor Pears was a member of the Philanthropy Review team and is Executive Chairman of the Pears Foundation, a significant funder of the present research.) This is a short-term campaign to encourage everyone across the UK to make a public pledge to give a little more of their time, money or energy to a cause or charity they care about, as a response to current economic difficulties. By July 2013 the campaign had secured over 24,000 pledges and signed up 120 charity and business partners.

Beacon Awards

The Beacon Fellowship Charitable Trust[48] was set up in 2003 with the aim of promoting effective philanthropic giving through the creation of a nationally-recognised awards scheme with winners forming a fellowship body of philanthropists to promote best practice and innovation in philanthropy. Since 2010 the Beacon Awards have been managed by UK Community Foundations (formerly known as Community Foundation Network).

The Awards celebrate outstanding philanthropic achievement by individuals, families and small groups of individuals working collaboratively across seven categories. They highlight key trends in philanthropic giving, along with pioneering developments including the growing focus on donations not only of money, but also of time, talents and social capital, to support future generations and local initiatives in the UK.

Since the first Beacon Awards ceremony in 2003, more than 100 individuals have been honoured as Beacon Fellows in recognition of their exceptional contribution to charitable and social causes.

Public awareness of wealth and philanthropy

Such awards, along with the honours system and the *Sunday Times Giving List*, highlight exemplary philanthropy and best practice. Awards events are complemented by reports in local papers, and celebration and recognition of major donations by recipient charities, universities and cultural organisations.

There is also an increasing number of role models who are very public about their giving and focus. These have both increased the visibility of the issues and set an example for current and emerging donors. In some cases – The Giving Pledge (discussed below) is an obvious example here – they are actively encouraging others to become more involved in addressing global issues. Conversely, role models can provoke resentment as well as admiration. The quiet culture of giving in the UK militates against such public demonstrations of giving (in many religions giving is supposed to be 'unheralded'). We explore the extent to which people give anonymously in Chapter 6.

Global networks

There is evidently a developing infrastructure of philanthropy both in the UK and globally. This includes philanthropic networks such as the Global Philanthropy Forum[49] and Worldwide Initiatives for Grant-maker Support (WINGS).[50] Cross-border giving in Europe has been facilitated by the Transnational Giving Europe initiative[51] and by legislation in EU member states, and in May 2013 the legal affairs (JURI) committee of the European Parliament voted in favour of the report on the European Foundation Statute, indicating that the European Foundation Centre's pressure for a European foundation statute is about to bear fruit.[52] Global developments in philanthropy and social investment (see below) are extensively covered in *Alliance* magazine[53] and through regular news bulletins, for example from Philanthropy Impact.[54] Appendix 5 contains further details of these sources of information.

Development of philanthropy as an academic study

The need to understand the attitudes and motivations of the wealthy, with particular reference to charitable giving, was the impetus for the original *Why Rich People Give* study. The intention was not research for its own sake, but to underpin the provision of advice for would-be donors, for those seeking funding, and for policy-makers and others with an interest in strengthening a culture of giving in the UK.

At that time there was a very limited body of reliable research about the wealthy, and although the *Sunday Times Rich List* was already being published, the *Sunday Times Giving List*, which describes the giving of the most generous members of the main rich list, did not appear until 2003. This is valuable data that now shows trends over a decade, but it has limitations, notably the historic inclusion of pledges rather than gifts that have actually been made. It also excludes donors who are not counted among the nation's 1,000 richest people. Furthermore, the reported donations include one-off large gifts to, for example, charitable foundations established by the donor. Not only is it possible that subsequent gifts from those charitable trusts are counted again, but the analysis behind the *Giving List* may miss people who give regularly but at lower levels. Someone very wealthy who gives, say, £2m a year for 10 years may not feature on the radar, whereas someone making a one-off commitment of £20m might.

While charitable organisations such as Philanthropy UK, NPC and the Institute for Philanthropy began and continue to provide a range of research, advisory and training services, there is now a growing body of research produced by academic institutions, independent think tanks and research organisations, funded by government, charitable foundations, private sponsors and those who advise the wealthy such as banks.

The establishment of the Centre for Giving and Philanthropy (CGAP) in 2008 was a step change in investment in academic research, receiving £2.2m in funding from the Economic and Social Research Council, Cabinet Office, the Scottish Government and Carnegie UK Trust. CGAP involved a consortium of five universities (City University London, Strathclyde University, University of Southampton, University of Kent and the University of Edinburgh) and ran from 2008 to 2013.

A number of academic centres undertaking research and teaching courses related to philanthropy have also emerged in the past 10 years, some as a result of the CGAP funding. These include the Centre for Philanthropy at the University of Kent, the Centre for Voluntary Sector Research at Sheffield Hallam University and the Centre for Charity Effectiveness at Cass Business School.

New forms of philanthropic engagement[55]

There is a growing number of more engaged donors who plan their giving, and become involved through 'venture philanthropy', providing expertise and business skills. This approach of strategic engagement is sometimes referred to as 'philanthrocapitalism' (a term coined by Matthew Bishop of *The Economist*).[56]

Venture philanthropy

The terms 'venture philanthropy' and 'high-engagement' are often used interchangeably. Essentially, the approach involves long-term support for an organisation that is not simply financial but can also include using the expertise of the donor or his or her networks to build the capacity of the recipient organisation, the direct involvement of the donor in the organisation's management (for example, through taking a seat on the board), and identifying clear measures of performance to judge the impact of investment. Venture philanthropy uses the language of finance, comparing the relationship the donor has with the beneficiary organisation to that of an investor in a company.

We invited the Impetus Trust to explain the concept and how it has developed (Box 2.1).

Box 2.1: The development of venture philanthropy

Venture philanthropy is an active approach to philanthropy that involves giving skills as well as money. The principles of venture capital are at the core of this form of engaged giving, with the investee organisation receiving management support, expertise and financial resources over a period of time in order to scale up its capacity to make a greater social impact.

In the 1990s, the concept of venture philanthropy made its debut in the US. In an article published by the *Harvard Business Review*, it suggested that traditional grant-making foundations could borrow practices from the venture capital sector.[57] By mixing methods such

---

as due diligence and performance management with a well-honed growth strategy and grant funding, stronger organisations could be built to produce greater impact. In the case of venture philanthropy, the emphasis would be on social, rather than financial, return.

In the UK there was interest from individuals with financial and entrepreneurial backgrounds to find organisations that would link business skills with the social sector through high level, high impact engagement. Impetus Trust was founded in 2002 and Private Equity Foundation in 2006, both pioneering venture philanthropy in the UK and focusing expertise and resources on supporting some of the most deprived people in society.

As interest spread across Europe, the European Venture Philanthropy Association (EVPA) was established to provide a forum for this form of philanthropy. In 2011, EVPA research estimated that €1bn had been invested by European venture philanthropy funds.[58] According to the same research, venture philanthropy organisations in Europe had achieved a diverse funding base: 40% coming from foundations or endowments; 23% from private equity, venture capital and hedge funds; 17% from high net worth individuals and the remaining from other sources, including corporations, government, and income recycled from earnings.[59]

In 2013, Impetus Trust and Private Equity Foundation announced they would merge to achieve greater scale to support more investee organisations to reach more people. In the previous year, both venture philanthropy organisations helped over half a million people through their combined portfolio of investments.[60]

In a little over a decade, the nascent industry had come into its own. Today, it continues to play a crucial role in reducing the risk in early-stage social innovations, enabling additional forms of social investment to scale further and have a greater impact on social problems.

There is further information and a number of resources on the EVPA website.[61]

Another approach to the provision of the business skills that many charities, particularly but not only small ones, are perceived to lack is that developed by Pilotlight,[62] which matches philanthropists with charities in need of their expertise. A similar course is taken by the Engaging Experience Philanthropy Network,[63] a project of The Bulldog Trust.

Social investment

Venture philanthropy is one element of a trend that has seen some blurring of the distinction between philanthropy and investment. While with venture philanthropy, the 'return' on an 'investment' is a social rather than a financial one, other forms of investment where some degree of financial return is also sought have come increasingly into vogue. 'Impact investment', 'social investment', 'mission-related investment' – these terms are not always precisely defined or differentiated one from the other, but all of them seek to use capital in ways that differ from traditional donations or grants.

Social investors utilise risk-based capital and quasi-equity to finance charities and social enterprises, filling a gap in the funding market. By seeking a financial return, in addition to a social return, investors are able to attract significant private investment. Examples of new models in the UK to stimulate this trend include Community Development Finance Institutions (CDFIs) and Community Development Venture Capital (CDVC). Community Investment Tax Relief (with a draw-down of £65m), introduced by the UK Government in 2002, has given a big boost to CDFIs (whose combined loan portfolio stood at £394m in 2009).

Charities are increasingly looking to social investment as an element of their funding. UK advisory organisation CAF Venturesome reported late in 2012 that it had received 224 enquiries for a loan since June 2011, which has led to 15 investments, while in 2011 the disability charity Scope launched a £20m bond scheme to expand its fundraising programme and charity shops. Another example is the over-subscribed Mencap Bond, launched in association with Triodos Bank[64] early in 2013. The Government has committed to supporting this emerging market with the launch of Big Society Capital, a wholesale bank that began investing in 2012. In addition, the Charity Commission moved to clarify its guidance on social investment by charities, publishing new guidelines in October 2011.

In the US, the number of foundations using mission investment (either mission- or programme-related investment) is increasing, according to a report produced by the Foundation Center in 2011.[65] Some 14% (168) of the foundations surveyed were making some kind of programme- or mission-related investment. More than half of those began doing so within the past five years, and a quarter (28%) within the past two years.

In terms of impact investment, a report in January 2013[66] by JP Morgan and the Global Impact Investing Network (GIIN) indicates a growing market, with respondents planning to commit $9bn to impact investing in 2013, up from a total commitment of $8bn in 2012. Additionally, the vast majority of investors surveyed reported that their impact investment portfolio performance is meeting or exceeding social, environmental and financial expectations, with two-thirds of respondents principally pursuing market-rate financial returns.

The growth in social investment has been reflected (if not matched exactly stride for stride) by the growth of an industry to advise this new breed of investor, with the launch of organisations such as NPC in the UK and PHINEO in Germany.[67] The US, meanwhile, has a Social Investment Forum, which serves as an umbrella body for organisations and individuals concerned to advance the practice of socially responsible investment.[68]

In addition, a handful of social stock exchanges[69] have appeared. A UK version is the Social Stock Exchange (SSE)[70], which announced the first batch of companies to be admitted to its platform in June 2013.

It is hoped that the SSE will address some of the key constraints for advisers – the lack of evidence and measurement, and the cost of due diligence (as we discuss in Chapter 9) – by providing a single reference point for investors as well as standardised and comparable social impact disclosure.

Donors too, are defining new roles for private donations and investment within public services. These include testing and promoting new, innovative approaches serving people who do not receive sufficient government funding and subsidising a higher level of care than government provides. These can be combined using instruments such as Social Impact Bonds (SIBs).

The concept of the SIB developed from the realisation that while investing in effective preventative approaches to social problems saves public money in the long term, making the case for and finding the public funding for upfront investment is increasingly difficult. Essentially, the idea is that of a partnership with an operational charity. Private investors put money into non-profit organisations with a track record in addressing the identified problem. The investment is made on the basis of proposed social targets, and if these are reached the investors make a profit.

The first such SIB in the UK addressed prisoner rehabilitation and re-offending.[71] This pilot scheme was launched in March 2010, in a partnership between the Ministry of Justice, Social Finance[72] and the St Giles Trust, a charity that works with ex-offenders. Investors collectively funded a £5m intensive programme for short-term prisoners leaving Peterborough prison in Cambridgeshire. The idea is that a total of 3,000 offenders will be supported over six years; if reoffending rates fall by 7.5% or more, investors will make a profit. The more government saves on not having to prosecute and jail recidivists, the higher the profits, to a ceiling of 13%.

Also with help from Social Finance, in 2012 the Greater London Authority (GLA) awarded SIB contracts to two providers to pay for interventions to tackle rough sleeping in London,[73] to be funded by the Department of Communities and Local Government (DCLG). The SIBs are being used to develop new services designed to address the individual needs of a number of rough sleepers. This is a three-year programme, and payment for these services of up to £5m will depend on the extent to which agreed outcomes are achieved.

Another sector experimenting with this funding model is children's services. In November 2012 Essex County Council became the first local authority in the UK to commission a SIB with a focus on children aged 11 to 16 who are at risk of going into care.

Nick Hurd, Minister for Civil Society at the time, commented: 'Social impact bonds are opening up serious resources to tackle social problems in new and innovative ways. This is about communities, businesses and charities all working together to change people's lives, while at the same time making savings for the taxpayer.'

The end of April 2013 saw the launch by Bridges Ventures and Big Society Capital of the £14m Bridges Social Impact Bond Fund. The first of its kind, the fund will invest in charities and social enterprises to deliver programmes designed to improve social outcomes in areas such as education, employment, housing, and care for vulnerable young people.

The extent of interest in, and awareness of, these products is as yet unclear, as the Future for Children Bond announced by charitable social investment organisation Allia in February 2013 was withdrawn because of inadequate interest.[74]

However, it is widely thought that the development of social investment is potentially very significant. Yet the lack of widespread understanding of the concept, track record, critical mass of opportunities, and recognised standards for due diligence have made it difficult up to 2013 for new products of this nature to be promoted by advisers such as banks. As we suggest above, it is hoped that the launch of Social Stock Exchanges will address these constraints. We discuss this point further in Chapter 9.

We note that data on giving do not include this investment strand. As this form of engagement with the non-profit sector becomes more common, further thought will have to be given to how to capture and report on this market.

Transformations triggered by technology

Over the past decade the revolution in the world of digital media has had a major impact in three areas relevant to the development of charitable giving: opportunities to donate; opportunities to communicate; and opportunities to view and be involved with the work of the beneficiary organisations. In some instances existing charities have developed their own capacity to take advantage of the new technology; in others new organisations have been created that depend on and exploit the mechanisms underpinned by the internet and social media. There is increasing interest in this area[75] and the 2013 Technology4Good Awards[76] offered a digital giving category for the first time.

Giving

A milestone in online giving was passed in 2013 when the UK Disasters Emergency Committee appeal for Syria became the first fundraising appeal to process more than half of its donations online.[77] A year earlier, the Institute of Fundraising (IoF) and Give as you Live launched the *Digital Giving Review 2012*.[78] It found that across the UK charity sector only a minority of donations are received through online channels. Respondents to the survey reported that 90% of their online donations in 2012 came through online donation platforms, while the other 10% came via email (7%) and Facebook (3%). No charities in the review claim to have received donations through Twitter, indicating that some social media may be less about processing donations and more about disseminating timely information and enthusing potential donors, who then make their donation using other channels.

The growing significance of donation by text message was already evident during the Haiti earthquake of 2009, where within two weeks, $30m had been raised by text messaging, mostly in the US.[79] More recently, in the UK Comic Relief 2011 raised more than £7m from text message donations.[80]

As the popularity of this form of giving grows, mobile phone operators have come under increasing pressure to waive their fees and, in Spring 2011, the mobile phone provider Vodafone and the donation website JustGiving launched JustTextGiving, a service to allow UK-registered charities to raise money through text donations without charge.

March 2013 saw the launch of a pilot scheme called DONATE[81] from the National Funding Scheme, designed to enable mobile giving to cultural causes and campaigns through a wide number of routes (text message, debit or credit card and Paypal). As with other charitable causes experimenting with these new methods of giving, the arts sector hopes that some of the people who today give £10 through the DONATE phone app – say, to conserve a painting or in response to a wonderful performance – will be the major donors to the arts of tomorrow.

Research[82] from the US has highlighted inter-generational differences in engaging with online fundraising: a fifth (19%) of Generation X (born 1965-1980) and a quarter (27%) of Generation Y (born 1981-1991) were found to begin their engagement with a charity by visiting its website, whereas older donors were more likely to initiate contact with a donation, often in response to a piece of direct mail. However, donors of all ages were found to 'channel hop', switching between different sources of online and offline information and making donations through various channels at different times. For example, a donor may go online to make a donation as a result of receiving a piece of direct mail in the post, while another donor may put a cheque in the post after reading material in a blog or on Twitter.

Communicating with donors

The *Digital Giving Review* discussed above notes that although the majority of donations continue to be received through offline channels, a charity's online audience is now likely to be slightly larger than its offline audience, and the frequency of communication with that audience is greater. Nearly half (47.5%) of the charities surveyed communicate daily through social media channels, and over a third (34%) of charities communicate via email on a monthly basis. Offline communication clearly happens far less frequently given the costs involved in printing and posting materials to supporters. The most common frequency reported for such traditional communications was quarterly or less often. The low cost of transmitting online messages is appealing to charities and donors alike, as giving decisions are known to be affected by perceptions of cost control and efficiency in communications.[83] Many donors, especially from younger generations, expect to interact with charities in a multimedia way, just as they communicate with their friends in multiple ways: in person, by phone, text, email and on social networking sites. While this gives charities a plethora of new methods to interact with their supporters, it also involves new costs in maintaining these multiple channels.

Seeing and being involved with the work

As well as the significant growth of digital giving, technology has created the means for donors to see the work of, and have some involvement with, the organisations they support. Online giving portals, such as the various CAF affiliates, GiveIndia, JustGive, GlobalGiving, Give2Asia, CharityNavigator and a host of others, allow donors to select the organisations they wish to support, pre-screened by those who host or run the site on the basis of their effectiveness and the causes they address. The relationship between even fairly modest donors and the organisations they support, wherever they are in the world, has thus become more direct. The increasing appeal of this approach is shown by a report produced by Network for Good,[84] which charted growth in giving through its portal rising from $50m in 2003 to $381m by 2009.

At the same time as allowing donors to give globally, the internet and social media have also helped to heighten awareness of global problems, which may explain recent increases in support for international causes. For example, a report on 'The rise of international giving'[85] found that US giving to international causes grew by 6.2% in 2009, despite a general decline in giving to all causes in the same time period.

There are also web-based opportunities for investment and lending. A leading and striking example is Kiva,[86] based in San Francisco. Set up in 2005 it allows people to lend money via the internet to people in developing countries through its 191 field partners, which include microfinance institutions, social businesses, schools and non-profit organisations. Kiva includes personal stories of each person who needs a loan to enable lenders to connect on a human level with the entrepreneurs they support. Kiva itself does not collect any interest on the loans it facilitates, but rather is funded by grants, loans, and donations from its users, corporations, and national institutions.

As of June 2013, Kiva has distributed over $442m in loans from over 900,000 lenders to over one million borrowers. The average loan size is $407 and the scheme enjoys a repayment rate of 99%.

Digital giving is not just restricted to money. The potential that technology offers for other kinds of giving has only just begun to be tapped. According to a report[87] on how digital media is transforming philanthropy:

> 'Open-source collaborative projects have facilitated new ways for people to donate by offering their expertise and time rather than financial aid. Innovations such as crowd-sourcing crisis information transformed the landscape for a targeted disaster response when Hurricane Sandy hit in 2010. As a result, the International Network of Crisis Mappers[88] has become a hugely influential humanitarian technology forum, bringing together experts from diverse fields to collaborate in complex emergency situations.'

Although perhaps not directly relevant to all of the current generation of wealthy donors, especially some of the older philanthropists we surveyed, the use of the web as a source of information and the development of models and networks of the type discussed earlier are already integral parts of the practice of some major donors, who may use the internet to monitor the impact of their donations or, in one case noted by an interviewee, to watch a live webcast of a feeding programme they had funded to see where their money was going. Tracking developments in this digital sector, particularly for larger donations and wealthier donors, should be a key element in future research.

The rise of 'enrichment' as a key driver of philanthropic activity

> 'Seeing these projects develop and bring major benefits to people has been a life-enhancing experience.'

The concept that it is more blessed to give than to receive has been known since biblical times. But as we discuss in Chapter 4, a noticeable feature of our research findings is the openness, joy and passion with which our interviewees talk about the personal fulfilment that comes with their giving, and the fact that the more one engages in philanthropy the more enjoyable and rewarding it becomes.

This feeling of personal enrichment is captured in the letters from philanthropists committing support to The Giving Pledge, initiated in 2010 by Bill and Melinda Gates and Warren Buffett. In their letter, Bill and Melinda Gates write:

> 'The idea of the pledge came out of discussions we had with other givers about what they were doing, about what had worked in philanthropy and what had not worked. Everyone shared how giving had made their lives richer.'

The Giving Pledge involves a public commitment (moral rather than legally enforceable) from billionaires who pledge to give away at least half their wealth either during their life or upon death. The public nature of making such a pledge is arguably as striking as the commitment itself. The transcripts of the letters from philanthropists (all named) making this pledge are in the public domain,[89] and make moving and inspiring reading. We recommend examining them for the range of motivations and focus they reveal. Here is a typical example:

> 'We are deeply indebted to our community and our country for the many opportunities granted to us, and for a social and economic environment in which we could make the most of those opportunities. We consider it our responsibility to ensure the same opportunities for others. We view our wealth in this light – not as an end in itself, but as an instrument to effect positive and transformative change. To this end, we have contributed a significant portion of our wealth to the Laura and John Arnold Foundation and will continue to do so during our lifetime. Upon our death, the vast majority of our assets will be left to the Foundation.'

The effort is not limited to donors in the US. In February 2013, 12 families from Australia, Britain, Germany, India, Malaysia, Russia, and South Africa signed the pledge.

Charles Feeney, who established what became Atlantic Philanthropies[90] in 1985 – a foundation that has now distributed well over $5.5bn – says:

> 'I cannot think of a more personally rewarding and appropriate use of wealth than to give while one is living – to personally devote oneself to meaningful efforts to improve the human condition. More importantly, today's needs are so great and varied that intelligent philanthropic support and positive interventions can have greater value and impact today than if they are delayed when the needs are greater. I urge those who are taking up the Giving Pledge example to invest substantially in philanthropic causes soon and not postpone their giving or personal engagement.'

This quote illustrates the combination of personal fulfilment and recognition of great need that characterises the philanthropy of nearly all those we surveyed and interviewed. We return to the theme of giving while living in Chapter 6.

By May 2013 the Pledge had 114 signatories and was worth a minimum (i.e. if people give away no more than 50%) of £500bn. Among the UK signatories are David and Susie Sainsbury. In his letter David Sainsbury says:

> 'The approach of my wife, Susie, and I to philanthropy is very simple. We do not believe that spending any more money on ourselves or our family would add anything to our happiness. However, using it to support social progress we have found deeply fulfilling. We focus on a few areas which require investment and which we care about deeply, and seeing these projects develop and bring major benefits to people has been a life-enhancing experience.'

While this initiative has attracted many positive headlines, some have made the point that, if there are 1,223 billionaires in the world (according to *Forbes 2012*), the headlines could also read: 'Over 1,100 billionaires refuse to give away surplus wealth'. Yet others make the more positive reflection that:

> 'If this initiative succeeds in galvanising other wealthy potential philanthropists into action, even if their motivation is the positive publicity and the opportunity to avoid looking like shame-faced jerks, many would consider that a very good thing.'[91]

This quote takes us back to the purpose of the present study: to examine the motivation of rich donors. In the remainder of this book we build on the openness and generosity of spirit demonstrated by those we surveyed and interviewed, and explore in some detail why and how rich people give, their experiences, concerns and fears, why some people do not give and what can be done about it, and the immeasurably richer lives that result from passionate, committed, informed and effective philanthropy by the wealthy.

Notes

1 Figures based on data published in the 2003 and 2013 editions of the *Sunday Times Rich List*.
2 All data from www.forbes.com/billionaires
3 www.barclayswealth.com/insights/uk-wealth-map-2011.htm#
4 www.guardian.co.uk/politics/2013/jun/01/top-earners-millionaires-inequality-city-finance
5 http://tinyurl.com/o3pxa5d
6 Mike Savage and Karel Williams in an article entitled 'Elites: remembered in capitalism and forgotten by social sciences', published in a 2008 edition of *Sociological Review* 56(4), pp.1-24.
7 www.oecd.org/els/soc/49499779.pdf
8 http://squeezedbritain.resolutionfoundation.org
9 www.economist.com/node/21564414
10 http://tinyurl.com/42eermv
11 http://tinyurl.com/cgzccbc
12 www.cafonline.org/pdf/UKGiving2008.pdf
13 www.cafonline.org/PDF/UKGiving2012Full.pdf
14 Full copies of all editions of the *Coutts Million Pound Donors Report* are available online www.kent.ac.uk/sspssr/cphsj/research/couttsmilliondonor.html
15 The *Sunday Times Giving List* (formerly known as the Giving Index) is published within the annual *Sunday Times Rich List*. It is a measure of relative generosity because it identifies the members of the *Rich List* who gave most in that year relative to their wealth, rather than those who made the largest donations in absolute terms.
16 As told in her autobiography *Let It Go: The Entrepreneur Turned Ardent Philanthropist* by Dame Stephanie Shirley and Richard Askwith (2012). UK: Andrews.
17 www.bbc.co.uk/news/business-15949480
18 www.thewealthreport.net/economic-trends/rise-of-the-new-rich.aspx
19 www.weforum.org/content/inequality-occupying-minds-davos
20 http://tinyurl.com/pdu5dec
21 www.hefce.ac.uk/pubs/rereports/year/2012/philanthropyreview
22 www.cdf.org.uk/wp-content/uploads/2012/02/CDF-Grassroots-Grants-Executive-summary-.pdf
23 www.artscouncil.org.uk/funding/our-investment/funding-programmes/catalyst-arts
24 www.gov.uk/uk-aid-match
25 www.telegraph.co.uk/news/10108151/Britain-commits-to-375m-extra-in-aid.html
26 www.gov.uk/government/publications/big-society-faqs-and-useful-links
27 www.official-documents.gov.uk/document/cm80/8084/8084.pdf
28 This received a boost when, in January 2012, the three major party leaders jointly undertook to leave 10% of their estate to charity. See http://tinyurl.com/lw3odf4
29 See www.guardian.co.uk/uk/2011/mar/23/budget-2011-charities-gift-aid-boost
30 http://tinyurl.com/nlsf86b
31 http://tinyurl.com/mxudurm
32 http://tinyurl.com/pllqzyx
33 www.spearswms.com/wm-awards/46752/spearand39s-wealth-management-awards-2013.thtml
34 http://tinyurl.com/p2w87w6 The table showing data on the 'recent history' – 1999 to 2012 is near the end of this web page.
35 This fluctuation is partly related to intermittent attempts to 'clean up' the Register of Charities and remove inactive organisations.
36 Commissioned by the Office for Civil Society within the Cabinet Office, and conducted by the National Centre for Social Research and the Institute for Voluntary Action Research (IVAR).
37 Dr David Clifford, Frida Geyne Rajme, and Professor John Mohan (2010). *How dependent is the third sector on public funding? Evidence from the National Survey of Third Sector Organisations*. TSRC Working Paper 45 www.tsrc.ac.uk/LinkClick.aspx?fileticket=TiDxGXmS2Ko%3D&tabid=741
38 www.charitycommission.gov.uk/media/89574/downturn4.pdf
39 http://tinyurl.com/q42ryrp
40 www.coutts.com/private-banking/coutts-institute
41 This is researched and written by Beth Breeze, all editions of the report are freely available online www.kent.ac.uk/sspssr/cphsj/research/couttsmilliondonor.html
42 Research commissioned by NPC, Wise and Bertelsmann Stiftung.
43 Vol 15, No 3, September 2010.
44 www.step.org
45 www.philanthropy-impact.org/giving-advice

46 http://tinyurl.com/3v7ck55
47 www.givemore.org.uk
48 http://beaconfellowship.org.uk/about-us
49 http://philanthropyforum.org
50 www.wingsweb.org
51 www.givingineurope.org
52 See http://tinyurl.com/p8trryr
53 www.alliancemagazine.org
54 http://www.philanthropy-impact.org
55 Some of this section is drawn from the chapter on *Motivational factors in International Philanthropy*, by Theresa Lloyd, published by the Open University Press in 2012.
56 http://philanthrocapitalism.net
57 Harvard Business Review (March 1997) *Virtuous Capital: What Foundations Can Learn from Venture Capitalists*.
58 The European Venture Philanthropy Industry 2010/2011.
59 ibid
60 Impetus Trust 2011/12 and Private Equity Foundation 2012.
61 http://tinyurl.com/p3lfbar
62 www.pilotlight.org.uk
63 www.bulldogtrust.org/philanthropy_network.htm
64 http://tinyurl.com/naxuk8l
65 The Foundation Center (2011). *Key Facts on Mission Investing*.
66 http://tinyurl.com/apkj6bo
67 www.phineo.org/english
68 www.ussif.org
69 While there is no agreed definition of the term, the aim of an SSE 'can be broadly understood as an environment where donors can make informed decisions about which non-profit organisations' social and environmental projects to fund in a transparent and reliable manner'. www.gexsi.org/en/building-the-sector
70 http://tinyurl.com/qjhz8wo
71 House of Commons Home Affairs Section (2010). *Social Impact Bonds: the Pilot at Peterborough Prison*. http://tinyurl.com/qfhk5aj
72 Social Finance is an independent organisation whose aim is to support charities and social enterprises with investment and models for revenue generation. www.socialfinance.org.uk/sib
73 www.socialfinance.org.uk/homelessness
74 http://allia.org.uk
75 See for example http://tinyurl.com/p5kdruo
76 www.technology4goodawards.org.uk
77 http://tinyurl.com/nrgl2z5
78 www.digitalgivingreview.com
79 http://tinyurl.com/peuptwl
80 'Mobile phone charges drain text donations to charities', http://tinyurl.com/qf5lhaz
81 www.nationalfundingscheme.org/about
82 Convio/Edge Research (2010) *The Next Generation of American Giving: A study on the contrasting charitable habits of Generation Y, Generation X, Baby Boomers and Matures*.
83 See, for example, the discussion in Beth Breeze (2010) *How Donors Choose Charities*, p.34-36.
84 Network for Good (2010). T*he Online Giving Study: A Call to Reinvent Donor Relationships* http://tinyurl.com/qczt7wk
85 Global Impact (2011) *Moving Beyond Boundaries*.
86 www.kiva.org
87 http://tinyurl.com/p5kdruo
88 http://crisismappers.net
89 http://givingpledge.org
90 www.atlanticphilanthropies.org
91 http://tinyurl.com/qdpdsqd

3

Which rich people?
About our research

Philanthropists are not an easy population to study. Although charitable giving is generally viewed as admirable behaviour, donors often shy away from the researcher's gaze, and are reluctant to discuss their generous acts. Some of the unwillingness stems from a concern about seeming boastful or appearing to lay claim to the moral high ground; others are deterred by more practical reasons – if they are still engaged in creating their wealth then they may be too busy; if they are well known they may have privacy or security concerns for themselves and their families. Whatever the reason, the lack of enthusiastic participants in research creates a very real barrier to advancing our common knowledge of philanthropy. It may even contribute to the slower development of a philanthropic culture in the UK than in comparable countries where donors are less reticent, notably the US.

Nonetheless, our study reached a significant sample of wealthy donors and experts. It took us almost eight months to achieve our goal of surveying at least 80 rich donors (we obtained completed questionnaires from 82, despite counting couples who give together as one donor), and conducting in-depth interviews with 20 of them. We also ran a different survey of a further 28 people who work in and around the philanthropy sector in the UK, making a total of 110 people who co-operated in this research.

This chapter describes the characteristics of the people who bucked the trend of being reluctant subjects and willingly gave up their time to complete our survey, and the 20 individuals and couples who made an even more generous commitment to participating in in-depth interviews. As noted in the Introduction, anonymity and confidentiality were conditions for this research; unless otherwise attributed, all the quotes in this book come from our interviewees.

The sample

The sample consists of four groups:

- 40 established philanthropists, comprising half of the original sample of wealthy donors who participated in the 2002 research.
- 42 emerging philanthropists, who were not part of the original study, although in some cases they were actively giving in 2002.
- 16 people who work in the philanthropy sector, with responsibilities ranging from roles in infrastructure and support bodies to major donor fundraisers, as well as policy-makers and media commentators.
- 12 people who work as providers of philanthropy advice to wealthy clients.

The data collection began with a survey of each of the four groups. The surveys for the established and emerging donors both consisted of 40 questions and only differed slightly to allow the former group to note developments in their actions and opinions since the original study in 2002. The survey for those working as philanthropy advisers consisted of 36 questions, while the survey of those working in the philanthropy sector – 'experts' – had 20. Donors were offered the choice of completing the survey online or on a hard copy (in the latter case it could be filled in alone and posted back, or completed in the presence of an interviewer in person or on the phone). The other two surveys were only offered online, as all were working in professional environments with easy access to the internet. Table 3.1 shows the numbers and methods chosen for completing the four surveys.

Table 3.1: How respondents completed the survey

	Number	Completed online	Completed a hard copy
Established donors	40	22	18
Emerging donors	42	32	10
Experts	16	16	0
Advisers	12	12	0

The second element of the data collection involved in-depth interviews with 20 of the donors (individuals or couples, with the latter counted as one donor), comprising 10 established donors and 10 emerging donors. The interviewees were selected initially on the basis of their willingness to participate further in the research, as indicated by their response to the final question on the survey. As those willing to be questioned in-depth exceeded the number we required (29 established and 27 emerging), we selected those that gave the most representative sample in terms of gender, age and geography.

Greater detail on the methodology is provided in Appendix 1. The remainder of this chapter describes the demographic profile of the donors, together with the scale and destination of their giving.

What kind of people did we survey and interview?

This section reviews the characteristics of the people we surveyed and spoke to, including their net worth, income, feelings of financial security and source of wealth, as well as standard demographic factors such as age, gender, family size, religious affiliation and educational background.

Net worth

The most significant characteristic of the donors is that they all have a net worth and annual income that far exceeds the national average. Despite questions about income and wealth being generally viewed as intrusive, 85% of our sample gave these details (the same figure for both established and emerging donors).[1]

As Table 3.2 indicates, of those who responded to this question, none had a net worth of less than £1m, and most had a net worth of £10m or more. The emerging donors reported higher levels of wealth: over a third had a net worth of £50m or more, including six donors worth £100m or more. Among the established donors, five reported that they were worth £50m or more, including three donors worth £100m or more. The richest donor who responded to this question, worth £500m or more, was in the emerging group.

Table 3.2: Net worth of donors, by number of respondents

	Unknown	£1m-£9.9m	£10m-£49m	£50m-£99m	£100m-£499m	£500m+
Established donors	6	13	16	2	3	0
Emerging donors	6	10	14	6	5	1
All donors	12	23	30	8	8	1

Annual household income

Respondents' annual household income was also extremely high in comparison to average national earnings of £21,528[2]. Table 3.3 shows that of those who answered this question, most had an annual income of £250,000 or more, and a quarter reported an annual income exceeding £1m. Again, the emerging donors reported a wealthier profile: over two-thirds had annual household incomes of £250,000 or more, compared to just over half of the established donors reporting this level of income. Furthermore, two emerging donors reported an annual household income exceeding £10m, as against only one established donor at this level.

Table 3.3: Annual income of donors, by number of respondents

	Unknown	<£100,000	£100,000-£249,000	£250,000-£999,000	£1m-£9.9m	£10m+
Established donors	5	1	15	11	7	1
Emerging donors	5	3	8	17	7	2
All donors	10	4	23	28	14	3

Financial security

Philanthropic behaviour is known to be related to feelings of financial security.[3] Given the very high levels of household income and net worth, it might be reasonable to presume that all respondents in our sample feel very financially secure, but that is not the case. Some people – perhaps due to earlier personal or family experiences of losing a large fortune, or simply being of a more pessimistic outlook – lack an internal belief in their financial security, despite the external impression that they have reached the point where nothing can harm their standard of living. We asked our respondents where they sat on a scale of 1 to 10, where 10 = extremely financially secure; the average response across all our sample was 8.5.

We asked respondents how the recent financial crisis had affected their feelings of financial security. Despite attempts to argue that the financial crisis has been a communal event and that 'we're all in it together', our data shows that there is a section of society entirely unaffected by the turmoil. More than half our sample (54%) agreed with the statement 'It has not affected my feelings of financial security' – this sentiment was expressed more frequently by the established donors (62%) compared to less than half (48%) of emerging donors. A longer discussion of the existence and impact of feelings of financial security appears in Chapter 8.

Source of wealth

Today's philanthropists are more likely to have created their own wealth than inherited it, and our sample reflects that reality. Overall, 73% of our respondents are self-made, including a higher proportion of the established donor group (79%) than the emerging donors (68%). Some 14% enjoy inherited wealth, with a slightly higher proportion of inheritors in the 2002 cohort (16% as against 12%). Where some differentiation in source of wealth does occur is that the emerging donors are more likely to attribute their wealth to a family business (15% as against 5%), or to cite a wealthy husband/partner as their 'source of wealth' – an option not articulated by any established donors.

Age

Most (94%) respondents were willing to state their age, which ranged from thirty-something to ninety-something. Unsurprisingly, the established donors were on average older, with the youngest being in their forties and 68% aged 65 or older. Of the emerging donors, less than half (45%) were aged 65 or over. The full results are shown in Table 3.5.

Table 3.5: Age range of respondents by percentage

	Under 35	35-44	45-54	55-64	65+
Established donors	0	0	8	24	68
Emerging donors	3	8	15	30	45
All donors	1	4	12	27	56

Gender

Philanthropy continues to have a male face in the UK. Despite best efforts to recruit female donors, 73% of our respondents were men (Table 3.6). This compares with 80% in 2002. The sample included three couples (two in the established group and one in the emerging group), which helped raise the number of female donors we reached. As the survey was anonymous, we do not know the gender of five respondents.

Table 3.6: Gender of respondents by percentage

	Male	Female	Anonymous
Established donors	75	17.5	7.5
Emerging donors	71	24	5
All donors	73	21	6

Parenting

Most of our respondents (89%) have children, usually two (37%) or three (28%), with 7% having five or more offspring. A preference for pursuing philanthropic spending by people with children could be interpreted as a result of concerns about the negative impact of inheritance; and/or the desire to demonstrate good parenting and inculcate a preferred set of values in the next generation, as discussed further in Chapter 4. The adviser perspective on the role of philanthropy in establishing values and encouraging a responsible attitude to money in children is explored in Chapter 9.

Religion

We did not collect data on ethnicity, but we did ask respondents if they had a religious upbringing and whether they are currently practising a religion. In line with trends identified in the wider population,[4] the older cohort was more likely to answer 'yes' to both questions, with 74% having a religious upbringing and 51% still adhering to that religion today. Most (58%) of the newer cohort had a religious upbringing, but only 19% practise it today. Given the link between religiosity and altruistic behaviour, this sharp decline might be viewed as a cause for concern.

Education

Our respondents are generally extremely well educated. All have at least some school-level academic qualifications (one-quarter of the general UK population have no such qualifications),[5] and 90% have at least an undergraduate degree (compared to 27% of the general UK population),[6] with 8% holding a PhD (compared to less than 1% in the general population).[7] There was no substantial difference between the established and emerging donors in this regard. In addition, 57% of established donors and 42% of emerging donors have a professional qualification.

How much do they give?

As noted at the start of this chapter, securing accurate, credible data on how much people give is challenging. Some people prefer to keep the numbers private, others forget, exaggerate or lie (sometimes to win the approval of the person asking the question), while others mistakenly double-count, telescope one time period into another, or muddy the data by having a different interpretation of the key concepts. For example, at a modest level, questions arise as to whether a lottery ticket is a donation or a purchase. At the higher end of the spectrum, there is uncertainty about categorising a social investment where some sort of return is expected. For all these reasons, data on stated amounts given should be treated with care. Nonetheless, we asked our respondents to do their best to recollect accurately how much they had donated philanthropically in the previous 12 months. To minimise the impact of unusual occurrences, such as settling a large sum into a private foundation, we asked them to provide an average figure for the last three years if their giving within the last 12 months had been in any way unusual.

Ninety-one per cent of our sample provided this information. The figures ranged from £9,000 to £52m, with a mean of £1.4m, a mode of £1m, and a median of £300,000. In Chapter 5, which looks at what rich people give to, we see that charitable trusts and foundations receive the greatest value of major donations. The largest donation in our sample is in this category.

Figure 3.1: Donation size

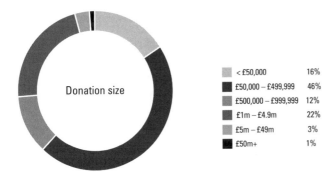

< £50,000	16%	
£50,000 – £499,999	46%	
£500,000 – £999,999	12%	
£1m – £4.9m	22%	
£5m – £49m	3%	
£50m+	1%	

How does donation size relate to capacity to give? As Table 3.7 shows, at the lower end, there is little relationship between these variables, with people in the lowest net worth band (£1m-£4.9m) making average donations larger than people in the next band up (£5m-£9.9m). Perhaps more startling is that people in the fifth band (£50m-£99.9m) made average donations almost half the size of donors in the band below (£10m-£19.9m). However, as wealth rises further, donations do seem to become more proportionate, with the top three bands of net worth showing ever increasing average donations, although these rises are not proportional. Donors in the seventh band (£200m-£499m) have, on average, more than twice the wealth of those in the sixth band (£100m-£199m), yet their average donations are only 23% larger, at £2m versus £1.6m.

However, it is important to note that as the value of the bands increases, the sample sizes get smaller, so these figures should be viewed as indicative rather than conclusive.

Table 3.7: The relationship between net worth and donation size

Net worth	Average annual donation size
£1m - £4.9m	£180,389
£5m - £9.9m	£138,410
£10m - £19.9m	£377,546
£20m - £49.9m	£837,850
£50m - £99.9m	£485,417
£100m - £199.9m	£1,600,000
£200m - £499.9m	£2,000,000
£500m - £999.9m	£52,000,000

We note for comparison purposes that giving by the population as a whole is relatively low – the UK Giving 2012 report[8] finds the median donation in a typical month in 2011/12 was just £10 per donor. If the 45% of the population who do not give is included, this obviously reduces the median donation to an even smaller figure.

In conclusion, our sample consists of an unusual group of people – they are extremely wealthy and not at all representative in terms of basic characteristics such as educational attainment, nor is there an equal gender mix. But they are all very rich people who give some of their money away – in some cases a significant sum – to benefit others, and therefore can help us to answer the question we have set ourselves: why do rich people give?

Notes

1   An 85% response rate for questions about personal income and wealth, compared with an almost 100% response to all the other questions, is not surprising, and the same concerns were encountered when researching WRPG. From that experience and our knowledge of those we surveyed we are confident that those who declined to respond are at the top end of the wealth and income spectrum. We believe that an 85% response is high for this sensitive information.

2   According to the Institute For Fiscal Studies, the media equivalised household income in Great Britain in 2009/10 was £414 a week www.ifs.org.uk/comms/comm118.pdf

3   Pamala Wiepking & Beth Breeze (2012) 'Feeling Poor, Acting Stingy: the effect of money perception on charitable giving'. International Journal of Nonprofit and Voluntary Sector Marketing, 17(1).

4   See, for example, this Office of National Statistics briefing document www.ons.gov.uk/ons/dcp171776_310454.pdf

5   http://tinyurl.com/pm8hv63

6   http://tinyurl.com/olvyt8u

7   In the absence of a published figure on the number of people holding PhDs in the UK population, this figure is arrived at by calculating the percentage of the population represented by the number of 'starters' listed in Table 1 of a report produced by the Higher Education Funding Council for England entitled PhD study: trends and profiles, available online at http://tinyurl.com/qg65x9z

8   www.cafonline.org/PDF/UKGiving2012Full.pdf p.4

4

The 'why' factor

'One should be saying 'come and join the party, it's such fun'.'

This chapter gets to the heart of the question tackled in this book: Why do rich people give? Why do some of our wealthy citizens choose to give away some of their private wealth to support charities and other organisations working to promote the public good?

Donor motivation has received more attention than other aspects of philanthropy, such as what causes and organisations people give to, or how they go about organising their philanthropy. Yet our understanding of philanthropic drivers remains incomplete, and many donors themselves find it hard to account for their actions and explain why they give. Indeed, the question 'why do you give?' often elicited in our interviewees a long pause, some seat shuffling, a nervous laugh, and eventually a comment such as: 'Well that's very hard to answer'. This was despite the fact that this question was, they knew, the focus of our study. Hesitantly, the interviewee might venture something such as 'it's deeply embedded in me', 'it's a natural desire', or 'it's just how I'm wired'.

This difficulty in excavating the rationale for giving arises in part because it is not the 'done thing' to talk in a way that might be interpreted as preaching or imposing one's morals on other people. As others have noted,[1] there is a huge amount of altruistic activity that occurs but passes without comment, because individualistic societies lack the language to describe it. Another fundamental reason why some donors find it hard to explain their generosity is because it seems such an obvious thing to do, that it does not (or should not) require a persuasive explanation. As one interviewee said:

'Why do I give? Well, I think because the alternative of not giving just strikes me as wrong. It's as simple as that!'

Donor motivation was the central theme in the first book of this series, *Why Rich People Give* (*WRPG*), published 10 years ago. In *WRPG* the following factors were identified as key to driving donations by the wealthy, as illustrated in figure 4.1.

- **Belief in the cause.** This was found to be the strongest motivator because giving decisions are often motivated by a desire to change or enhance society's systems or structures in line with a particular interest or belief.
- **Being a catalyst for change.** This includes making a real difference to society, institutions or individual lives, and getting value for money.
- **Self-actualisation.** This covers the satisfaction of personal development – applying expertise in a different sector, learning new skills, directing money that might otherwise go to government, addressing causes with a personal connection, and defining a place in history.
- **Duty and responsibility.** This is about the satisfaction of conscience, the obligations of the privileged to those less fortunate and the desire to 'put something back' into society.
- **Relationships.** This factor encompasses the fun, enjoyment and personal fulfilment of being involved with a range of people, including the senior staff of the charity, the beneficiaries and other donors.

In this chapter, we revisit these five themes to discover whether they remain the dominant factors behind giving decisions, we explore the differences in motivation between our established and emerging groups of donors, and we share five newly-identified answers to the question of why rich people give:

- Because they believe philanthropy is the right use of surplus money.
- Because they are clear about the complementary roles of government and philanthropy.
- Because they believe philanthropy is a good parenting tool.
- Because they appreciate the recognition that comes with being philanthropic.
- Because they get joy out of giving and believe that philanthropy enriches their life.

Figure 4.1: The inter-locking influences identified in the original *Why Rich People Give* study (2004)

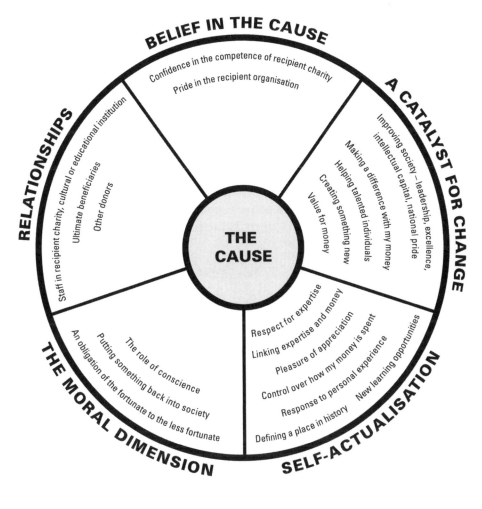

The chapter ends with a discussion of the extent to which tax breaks for giving are a motivating factor, before concluding with some thoughts on how a better understanding of motives casts light on why some people become increasingly philanthropic while others do not give at all. But first, we present the findings of our 2012 survey.

2012 survey: what rich people say about why rich people give

Our research finds that people give because philanthropy is an important and fulfilling part of their lives, and they believe they can really make a difference; because they feel giving is gaining a higher profile and becoming more valued in the political and public spheres; and because they think the possession of wealth brings responsibilities to the wider society that can be fulfilled by being philanthropic. In addition to these key factors, they are further motivated by financial incentives such as matched funding and tax breaks; by concerns about harming their heirs with over-large inheritances; by a desire to support causes to which they feel a connection; and by the attraction of getting involved in innovative and exciting projects. Every person is driven by a complex mix of motives and influences. We look at each in turn, but it must be remembered that most people are motivated by several factors at the same time.

Philanthropy is a voluntary act. People are free to give, or not give, as they choose, and free to decide how much to give. Given the supply-driven nature of this act, we began by asking our respondents about the strength of their commitment to philanthropy (including giving money, time and expertise).

The importance of philanthropy

We asked each respondent to rate the importance of philanthropy in their life today, on a scale from 1 to 10. The number '10' was chosen by a quarter (27%) of all those we spoke to, and the average was '8'. No emerging donors chose a number lower than 5.

Changes in commitment to philanthropy

As Table 4.1 shows, in almost every case respondents' commitment to philanthropy over the past 10 years has either increased (80%) or stayed the same (16%), with just 4% saying it has decreased. Among the newer donors, the story is even more positive, with 90% saying their commitment to philanthropy has increased from where it was a decade ago, and only one respondent in this category saying it had decreased.

Table 4.1: Changes in commitment to philanthropy over the past 10 years

	% of all donors agreeing with statement	% of established donors agreeing with statement	% of emerging donors agreeing with statement
My commitment to philanthropy has increased	80	69	90
My commitment to philanthropy has decreased	4	5	2
My commitment to philanthropy has stayed about the same	16	26	8

The context in which philanthropic activity takes place is clearly an important factor, and again all the indicators are positive.

The profile of philanthropy in the UK

An overwhelming majority of our interviewees feel that the profile of philanthropy in the UK has improved over the past 10 years. Seventy-eight per cent of both established and emerging donors agree with this statement, while only 15% of the older group and 8% of the newer group feel the opposite – the remaining percentage feel it has stayed about the same.

Figure 4.2: Do you think the profile of philanthropy in the UK has improved over the past 10 years?

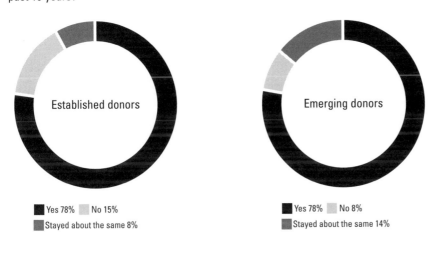

Established donors

Emerging donors

■ Yes 78% ■ No 15%
■ Stayed about the same 8%

■ Yes 78% ■ No 8%
■ Stayed about the same 14%

Donors' views that the profile of philanthropy has improved in the UK is shared by the philanthropy experts we surveyed – 80% of whom feel similarly positive. When pressed to explain why, three reasons were supported by more than half of all our respondents – both donors and experts (Table 4.2):

- People being more willing to talk openly about their giving.
- More philanthropists appearing in the media.
- Greater awareness of the role of philanthropists.

Table 4.2: Explanation for the improved profile of philanthropy in the UK

	% all donors who agree	% established donors who agree	% emerging donors who agree	% experts who agree
People being more willing to talk openly about their giving	72	70	72	67
More philanthropists appearing in the media	68	70	66	83
Greater awareness of the role of philanthropists	64	77	52	58
More public recognition of philanthropists, such as knight-hoods and naming opportunities	37	50	24	17

A fourth explanation struck a chord far more loudly with the established donors, half (50%) of whom agree that 'More public recognition of philanthropists, such as knighthoods and naming opportunities' is a relevant factor in improving the profile of philanthropy in the UK. Only a quarter (24%) of emerging donors agree with this.

Other explanations for the enhanced profile of philanthropy in the UK, supported by a minority of respondents, focus on economic factors, notably growth in wealth, awareness of the growing gap between rich and poor, and the recent economic difficulties that have highlighted the need for more philanthropy. As one donor explains:

> 'The gap between rich and poor is growing. An alternative to higher taxes on the rich is encouraging them to give money, time and expertise to help narrow this gap.'

Chapter 2 explored developments in the honours system and awards for philanthropists, as well as the growing wealth disparity in the UK and elsewhere.

Experts also noted demand-side changes in terms of charities getting better at articulating their need for support. The approach to asking, and its quality, is discussed in Chapter 7.

Two allied questions sought rich donors' views on any changes in public opinion about philanthropy, and on developments in the political climate for philanthropy over the past decade. Again, the response was overwhelmingly that things have improved.

Public opinion about philanthropy

Two-thirds (67%) of all donors feel that public opinion in 2012 was more positive than in 2002. Newer donors are more likely to feel it had become more hostile (10%) against just 5% of established donors, with the remainder feeling public opinion of philanthropy had stayed about the same.

Figure 4.3: Has public opinion about philanthropy become more positive or more hostile over the past 10 years?

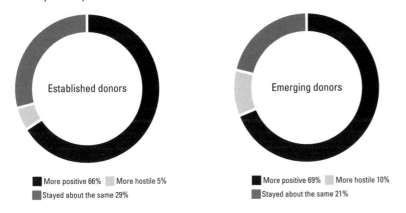

Established donors

Emerging donors

■ More positive 66%   More hostile 5%
■ Stayed about the same 29%

■ More positive 69%   More hostile 10%
■ Stayed about the same 21%

The experts we surveyed are less positive about changes in public opinion. A larger percentage feel it has stayed about the same (47%) than become more positive (40%), and 13% feel it has become more hostile. One expert says that public indifference to philanthropy makes it difficult to 'hit the public radar', while another notes:'There is still the same mix of respect, doubts about motivations and the same general lack of knowledge about philanthropy, despite greater press interest'.

Increased hostility is thought to be related to suspicions about the motives of donors and unhappiness at donors' ability to redirect tax to their favoured causes. We referred to this issue in the Introduction, and explore it in more detail in Appendix 3.

However, those experts who feel that public opinion about philanthropy has improved attribute it to greater understanding of the role private donations play in contemporary society and a recognition that philanthropists are more heterogeneous than in the past: 'It is no longer seen as the exclusive preserve of the "landed gentry" or the financial services super-rich.'

The political climate for philanthropy in the UK

Slightly less positive, but nonetheless overall favourable, replies emerged in response to the question of whether the political climate in the UK has become more or less conducive to encouraging philanthropy. Overall, 55% feel the political climate has improved, versus 10% who feel the opposite, with the rest (35%) feeling it has stayed about the same.

Figure 4.4: Has the political climate become more or less conducive to encouraging philanthropy?

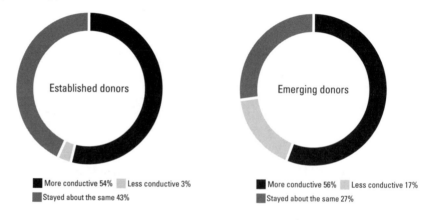

Established donors

Emerging donors

■ More conductive 54%   ■ Less conductive 3%
■ Stayed about the same 43%

■ More conductive 56%   ■ Less conductive 17%
■ Stayed about the same 27%

The experts we consulted side more with the outlook expressed by the emerging donors, in that over half (60%) feel the political climate is more conducive, but a substantial minority (20%) disagree. One explanation suggests this factor was out of the control of the philanthropy sector, because 'a climate of austerity is never going to be conducive to a culture of giving', not least because people feel less secure. We discuss this point further in Chapter 8. Others feel that enthusiasm for encouraging philanthropy is not consistent, noting that despite the genuine knowledge and concern of some members of government, 'most politicians do not have a clue'.

Overall, both donors and experts feel there has been some progress in the political climate but influencing political opinion on philanthropy remains harder than improving the profile of philanthropy or public opinion about philanthropic activity. One expert offers the following summary:

'On balance the positives just about outweigh the negatives –
though it's not been a transformational change in the [political] climate
by any means.'

In Chapter 2, we reviewed developments in the relationship between
successive governments and the philanthropy sector over the past
decade. We identified a number of developments since 2002 and
asked whether respondents feel these have had an effect (for better or
worse) on UK philanthropy over that time. The findings in Table 4.3
show that changes in demand, in terms of more obvious need and
better asking by charities, are rated as more influential factors than
changes in policy or philanthropy advice. The 'ask factors' are
discussed further in Chapter 7.

Table 4.3: Factors affecting the development of philanthropy in the UK from 2002-2012

	% of all donors who find this factor significant	% of established donors who find this factor significant	% of emerging donors who find this factor significant
More awareness of needs/ opportunities to help	71	65	76
More professional approach by those seeking funding	65	73	57
Greater government attention to philanthropy	59	63	55
Cutbacks in government funding	52	60	45
Availability of better philanthropic advice	35	28	43

Wealth-holding and responsibilities to society

Finally, we asked our respondents whether they believe the wealthy
are entirely free to do as they please with their wealth, or whether
wealth-holding brings responsibilities and obligations to society.
Perhaps unsurprisingly, given that our sample is comprised of wealthy
donors, they are found at the responsibility end of the spectrum. On a
scale of 1 to 10, where 1 is 'entirely free to use money as one
pleases' and 10 is 'fully responsible to wider society', the average
overall response was 7.7. Interestingly, this view is held more strongly
by the established donors, over a third (38%) of whom selected '10',
and whose average response was 8.1, compared to the average rating
by emerging donors of 7.2.

The obligations of wealth were linked by many to the increasing wealth disparity, reviewed in Chapter 2 and discussed above. This inequality has in turn influenced the cultural factors that were also mentioned by a handful of people. Such factors include changing expectations of what rich people should do, and increased social pressure on successful people to make charitable gestures:

> 'There's a small number of people becoming richer and richer and a large number of people becoming relatively poorer. One consequence of this growing gap is that you will have wealthy people living in gated enclaves with private guards looking after their houses and beyond that will be the masses…The way I see it is there will eventually be civil unrest if there's too big a gap between the rich and the poor. I think philanthropy is a way to stop that.'

After exploring these broad questions about wealth and philanthropy, we moved on to questions aimed at understanding more specific factors about the motivation behind philanthropic acts, starting with incentives. The top five incentives that have led donors to increase donations over the past 10 years are summarised in Table 4.4.

Table 4.4: Reasons that respondents' philanthropy has increased over the past 10 years

	% of all donors who find each reason significant	% of established donors who find each reason significant	% of emerging donors who find each reason significant
Just knowing it's the right thing to do	79	77	80
Learning about a new cause that I wished to support	56	56	56
Matched funding schemes	41	41	41
Tax breaks	32	36	29
A wealth-generating event	30	23	37

Over the past decade, much effort has been expended in efforts to make giving and philanthropy a normal part of everyday life. The aim has been to create a cultural change so that philanthropy is considered an expectation of the rich, rather than an eccentricity. As discussed in Chapter 2, initiatives to make this shift happen have been funded and supported by both government and the charity sector, including the Giving Campaign (2001-2004), the Philanthropy Review (2010-11) and the Give More Campaign (launched 2012). It is therefore noteworthy that our respondents cite 'Just knowing it's the right thing to do' as the top reason behind their decisions to donate. As one emerging donor explained:

> 'I think there are assumptions – even subtle assumptions – about philanthropy being part of the character and reputation you have to have if you want to be respected and get ahead… In the US people look down on you if you don't do this. You suddenly realise that's now the case in the UK, and then once you [become philanthropic], you then carry that sense of expectation and value.'

'Learning about a new cause' was the second most popular reason for giving, or for giving more, despite donors' stated preference for donating to causes with which they have a pre-existing relationship.

The third and fourth placed reasons take us to the heart of one of the most interesting debates in the philanthropy sector: the role that tax breaks play in encouraging giving.

Tax breaks and matched giving schemes

Only a third (32%) of our donor respondents cited tax reliefs on charitable donations as an incentive behind their giving decisions in the past 10 years, with established donors more likely to feel tax reliefs are important than the newer donors (36% against 29%).

However, both older and newer donors agree that matched funding schemes are a more attractive incentive, with 41% of both emerging and established donors agreeing they have been nudged to give as a result of an offer to match their gift. As we noted in Chapter 2, matched funding schemes have become more common in the UK over the past decade. These include two major schemes funded by government: a £200m scheme for donations to Higher Education Institutions, which ran from 2008 to 2011, and a £55m scheme to encourage the creation of endowments for arts and heritage organisations, launched in 2011.

Matched funding is offered in addition to tax relief, so the size of the original donation grows twice: once when the tax is recouped, and again when it is matched. The donation can be matched in varying proportions, from the most generous 1:1 (an extra £1 for every £1 donated), to smaller matches, such as 1:3 (£1 for every £3 donated). Academic research shows that larger match ratios have no additional impact,[2] but donors seem to prefer matched funding to tax breaks, as it is conceived as 'free money' rather than 'getting back what you never should have paid in the first place'. As one of our interviewees said:

'I think matched funding is attractive, but I'm not so sure about tax breaks. If somebody says to you: "give us so-and-so and we will double your donation", then you think: "Wow!"'

Despite most respondents disagreeing that tax breaks are an incentive to give, they happily acknowledge that such measures enable them to give more. They provide a framework for planning and developing a strategy for their philanthropy – for example, by setting up a charitable foundation – as well as increasing the value of one-off gifts. We see that while matched funding is certainly attractive, especially if it is a generous match that involves 'doubling your money', it is usually a tactical proposal linked to a specific project or cause. The match may be offered by government or by a private donor. It is a different proposition from the financial benefits and social signals created by tax breaks.

Other possible incentives, such as gaining public recognition or increasing standing among peers, attracted minimal support among our respondents, but this may be due to a reluctance to acknowledge, especially in a survey, the role such incentives play in giving. These issues are discussed later in this chapter when we turn to the data from the in-depth interviews.

Inheritance

In probing the role that inheritance plays in deciding whether or not to give, we first asked whether the presence of heirs affects this decision. As Table 4.5 indicates, the results were split fairly evenly between the options. In contrast to the stereotypical depiction of newer philanthropists as self-made people who do not wish to 'ruin' their children's lives with over-large inheritances, we find that the emerging donors are relatively less concerned about the amount of money that will be passed on to their heirs (40% against 26% of established donors). Of those who do worry about this issue, only half believe it has affected their philanthropic decisions. However, as emerging donors are on average of a younger age, this may in part be due to them either not yet having children, or not yet engaging with issues around inheritance.

Table 4.5: Attitudes towards inheritance and philanthropy

	% of all donors who agree	% of established donors who agree	% of emerging donors who agree
I am concerned about the amount of money that should be transferred to my children and immediate heirs, but this has not influenced my philanthropy	35	41	30
I am not concerned about the amount of money that should be transferred to my children and immediate heirs	33	26	40
I am concerned about the amount of money that should be transferred to my children and immediate heirs, and this has influenced my philanthropy	32	33	30

In a related question, we sought to establish awareness of one of the cornerstone philanthropic policies of the current Coalition Government. The 2011 Budget included a measure to reduce inheritance tax from 40% to 36% for those who leave at least 10% of their estate to charity. As Table 4.6 shows, most of our sample were aware of this measure (84%), but the majority claimed it would not affect their legacy plans, either because they had already written a more generous charitable legacy into their Will (17%), or for other unspecified reasons (49%). Perhaps unsurprisingly, this measure was less likely to have affected the decisions of the younger (emerging) donors, who may not yet have written their Wills.

Table 4.6: Awareness and impact of reliefs for charitable legacies introduced in 2011

	% of all donors who agree	% of established donors who agree	% of emerging donors who agree
I am aware of the new tax incentive if at least 10% of my estate is bequeathed to charity and it has affected my legacy plans	17	21	14
I am aware of the new tax incentive if at least 10% of my estate is bequeathed to charity but it has not affected my legacy plans	49	44	55
Before this measure was announced I had already written into my will that over 10% of my estate will go to charity	17	21	14
I am not aware of this measure	16	15	17

We asked donors to rank six factors that might cause them to give more. The order of priority, which was almost identical for established and emerging donors, is as follows:

Increased net worth

The factor thought most likely to lead to an increase in future donations was an increased capacity in terms of net worth – despite this factor being ranked low as an explanation for extra giving in the past decade! One donor light-heartedly noted that her giving would go up if she won the Lottery – though as we saw in Chapter 3, none of our respondents reported a net worth of less than £1m, which would be viewed as Lottery-winning levels of wealth by the majority of the population. Others pointed out that changes to the amount of wealth felt to be surplus, and therefore available for giving away, would be triggered as and when their children became more independent or if they decided to 'downscale' and live more modestly. Death also affects the capacity to give in a number of ways, whether through an inheritance, a life insurance payout, a lower cost of living upon the death of a spouse, or the donor's own death triggering a charitable legacy or final payment into their charitable trust or foundation.

Better tax breaks

The second most important factor cited was better tax breaks. Our respondents interpreted this as more than just alterations to the tax relief on charitable donations, on the basis that decreases in taxes paid (including income tax, capital gains tax and inheritance tax) would result in more money available for donations.

Discovering a new cause that I care about

The third driver felt likely to increase philanthropy was the discovery of a new cause. Despite some indications of inertia affecting giving decisions – particularly among established donors – all our sample rated the discovery of a new cause that they care about as being in the top three factors most likely to increase their giving in the next 10 years.

Better information on how donations are used
More time to think about giving

The established and emerging donors differed on the fourth most important factor. The older group selected better information about how their donations are used, whereas for the younger donors, having more time to think about their giving was chosen as the next most relevant development that would be likely to increase their donations.

Better recognition of my gifts

Both established and emerging donors feel that better recognition (such as naming opportunities) would be the least important development, though as discussed later in this chapter, in practice appropriate and enjoyable recognition does play an important role in motivating donors.

Donors also suggested factors in the external environment that would prompt them to give more, including actions and attitudes by their peers and the press:

> 'If I saw my peers increasing their giving, not as competition but as encouragement.'

> 'If I felt the public understood that we can be sincere and altruistic in our giving, rather than them thinking: "he's rich so he should give!"'

A final comment on what donors predicted would lead to increased giving echoes a central finding from this chapter – that philanthropy by the wealthy is limited more by the number of exciting opportunities than by spare cash:

> 'Giving is a way of life, it is part of the reason I think I exist. The likelihood of an increase [in my giving] is not a function of how much I have. I will give more if the projects that I believe in are present or a good opportunity exists.'

> 'Philanthropy does not depend on the size of my income or my wealth; it happens because I want to make a difference.'

These quotes brings to mind a powerful statement by Jerold Panas, author of one of the first books that sought to understand the phenomenon of 'mega givers':

> 'There is no such thing as a shortage of major donors. There is only a shortage of great ideas to raise money. A desperate need for visions and dreams… Mega givers are captivated by the opportunity, the challenge, the magic of being able to do something special.'[3]

One implication of this is the need for those seeking funding to be more effective at inspiring and asking. We explore this point in Chapter 7.

Explanations for why rich people give in 2002 & 2012

Our 2012 survey and interviews demonstrate that the five findings from the original 'why rich people give' study 10 years ago are still valid, and lead us to add five new findings that help explain why rich people give in the second decade of the 21st century.

Belief in the cause. The predominant explanation in the original study was passion for a cause, which often develops as the result of a personal encounter. Examples include support for a health charity after the donor or a loved one experiences the health problems tackled by that organisation, or support for people in a region of the UK, or another part of the world, where the donor has lived, worked or visited. The affinity between the donor and the cause underpins and reinforces their enthusiasm, and may lead them to support multiple organisations working in that cause area. There is plenty of evidence that this remains a core motivation a decade later, as these quotes from the updated research illustrate:

> 'You can only persuade people to give by appealing to an interest or a passion; it's not about the intellect. The case for support has to be personal and powerful... It's hugely important to make it personal and fundraisers have to think about this.'

> 'My donations are based on personal or life experience. For example, I am an active supporter of Asthma UK as I have had lifelong asthma.'

> 'Sometimes a new cause can just affect you. Because it speaks to something personal, you fund it, even though it's off the [general] radar.'

Being a catalyst for change. The second motivation identified in 2002 was to make something happen that wouldn't otherwise have done. This can also be expressed as 'helping to create change' or 'having an impact', and the underlying wish is to make a real difference. Respondents in 2012 also focused on the importance of this factor:

> 'People's motivation differs, but I think you need to be close enough to be able to somehow see the results. Then you get a vicarious pleasure from saying: "I helped make that happen" – that itself is enjoyable.'

> 'This sense that I could really make a difference. Seeing how it could be used effectively is a very high motivator.'

'Donors are not very interested in hearing that a university has got a gap in its finances that needs plugging. That doesn't win much money. Donors are very interested in producing an outcome that would not have been achieved by more conventional means, and I think that's probably true across all types of charitable giving.'

'We want to leave the world in a slightly better state than when we arrived and we each have different things we want to change in doing it.'

'I gave £5m to [a major art gallery]. I was told by [the director] that it was the seminal transforming gift that got the whole thing off the ground.'

Self actualisation. The third motivator identified 10 years ago refers to the personal development that comes from being a donor. This often involves giving time, expertise and contacts, as well as money. It also extends to seeing philanthropy as a way of creating a lasting legacy or, as an American study described it, 'footprints in the sands of time'.[4] This motivation remains salient today:

'It's certainly broadened my horizons… I've learned a lot.'

'Being involved in philanthropy has fostered a spirit of innovation and creativity in me.'

'It has changed my life greatly, in terms of my awareness.'

'Philanthropy gives me purpose, it gives me a sense that I'm doing something valuable that I can take pride in.'

Duty and responsibility. The fourth main motivation discussed in the original study involves giving as result of feeling a sense of duty and responsibility. When people consider the privileges that come with wealth and are aware that others are in a less fortunate position, they may decide that giving some money is the appropriate response:

'Those who are fortunate enough to be well off should share as much as they can.'

'My family give because we feel we should. If you have a certain level of wealth then you should help other people.'

'If you're fortunate and privileged, then you have a duty to give something back to society.'

These sentiments bring to mind the concept of *noblesse oblige*, which translates literally as 'nobility obliges' and implies that people of high birth and elevated status should assist those who are less fortunate. However, most of our interviewees were not born into wealthy families but rather created their own wealth. Such people can also feel a 'duty' and a 'responsibility', but it is of a different shade to that implied in the old-fashioned concept of *noblesse oblige*, as explained by this interviewee:

> 'A lot of people that I know who give are all self-made. We've come from poor backgrounds, the benefits we now enjoy were not available to us when we were younger, and certainly weren't available to the generation before us. My father was born in pretty strict poverty. So when not more than a generation away you have relatively deprived circumstances, that means you don't lose your contact with that. When you see cases of people who, through no fault of their own, are disadvantaged or lead a compromised life, then I think one feels a duty to help.'

Relationships. The fifth and final original motivation, which also continues to have resonance a decade on, is the enjoyment that comes from building relationships with a whole set of new people encountered through being a donor, such as charity staff, trustees, fellow donors and beneficiaries:

> 'Giving is contagious, infectious, whichever word you want to use – it catches, there's nothing to beat it. There is a lot of pleasure in the relationships with those involved.'

The pleasure comes from meeting people from different walks of life whose paths would not otherwise have been crossed, including inspirational people who found and run charities, brave and talented people who benefit from charitable funding, and fellow souls who support the same causes. As two of our respondents explain:

> 'I've been able to meet a whole range of people who I'd never have met otherwise, and been able to see what their lives are like.'

> 'If you give away large amounts of money… it gets you much more access, whether it's to actors in the theatre or to aid workers or to researchers in a facility, and you can get under the skin of it. People find huge satisfaction in feeling "not only have I made a difference to research into this disease but also in having interesting conversations with doctors about the nature of that disease", and that's all part of a set of stimuli and values that are interesting.'

Newly-identified reasons why rich people give

While our research finds ongoing support for the five motivations identified 10 years ago, we also find five new explanations for why rich people choose to give away some of their private wealth for the public good:

Because they believe philanthropy is the right use of surplus money. Of the respondents who shared this information, all are worth at least £1m, most are worth more than £10m, and all have large annual incomes on top of their wealth. By any measure they have surplus assets, and those who are aware of this fact often explain their philanthropic decisions as the appropriate solution to this surfeit:

> 'If you're sitting on a pile of money that you don't actively need it's preposterous [not to give].'

> 'The whole point about it, which a lot of rich people miss, is that if you help other people it doesn't in any way reduce your standard of living because there's enough money to live the way you want to live and to help other people.'

We live in a consumer society, and there is clearly no shortage of alternative ways to spend 'spare money', but many of our respondents reject the 'conspicuous consumption' model said to define earlier generations of wealth-holders,[5] and describe philanthropy as 'better' than buying material goods and services:

> 'If you've got more wealth than you need, then what's it for? I'm lucky enough to have more wealth than I need, and I have no desire to go and buy yachts and planes and all that crap.'

> 'I just feel that I have something to give. I feel that I was brought into this world to be a missionary, not to be in expensive restaurants and go on private planes. I go running in the morning and it costs me nothing!'

> 'I'm not driven by money, I'm not driven by power, I'm driven by doing the best I can.'

Others question the suggestion that 'normal' consumption is intrinsically more pleasurable than philanthropic spending:

> 'There's a diminishing return in spending money on luxuries and there's an increasing return from spending money on philanthropic giving. I profoundly believe that. Rich people find that if you spend a lot of money on properties or domestic staff, it actually causes headaches [laughs].'

The composition of the UK's rich population has undoubtedly affected attitudes towards the use of money for philanthropic purposes. The shift over less than one generation from the UK's rich being predominantly those with inherited wealth to those who are self-made (reflected in the *Sunday Times Rich List* as well as our own research) was suggested as a key explanation for the growing profile of philanthropy:

'Old money hangs on to it but new money is more willing to share!'

Those who created their own wealth often claim to be freer to dispose of it as they wish, perhaps because they feel no historic burden to maintain a position in society or because they do not wish to deny their children the pleasure of 'making it'. Apart from legal constraints (where houses, art and other assets may be tied up in trusts), some of those with inherited estates interviewed for *WRPG* also spoke about the more complex set of responsibilities associated with the maintenance of a large house and land where the same family and community have been linked for many centuries.

People with 'new money' experience a greater transformation at the moment of liquidity than those who always knew they would inherit a substantial sum, both in realising the precise value of their wealth and in a sudden freeing up of time to focus on philanthropy. The presence of these factors, in addition to attitudes regarding the 'right' use of money, is a potent combination:

'When you're building a business, 103% of your thinking is on "how do I get this thing built, what do I do, have I missed this client, is that an opportunity?" and so on... Now [I've sold my business] I look at the world and I think: "Ooh, there's a problem, I wonder if I can help with that?" and that's a real change. So it's a combination of having my time no longer totally focused on building a business and seeing the effectiveness of philanthropy and knowing what I can do. I see things, particularly in a local context, and I think: "We could help with that too". It becomes much more central in your thinking about life.'

'It was purely a realisation around the time that we floated on the stock market and realised what sort of situation we were going to be in, and we started to talk about what we were going to do. We realised there was something in the back of both our heads telling us: "you can't just hang onto this, you can't just be wealthy, you have to do something with it".'

Because they are clear about the complementary roles of government and philanthropy. While in 2002 we found a clearer demarcation of views about what should be funded by taxation through the state and what should be funded by private donors through philanthropy, this has changed somewhat in the intervening years.

The recent emergence of the Bill and Melinda Gates Foundation as the dominant institution in the philanthropic sphere has been a key factor in this development. This foundation reported assets of $35bn and spent around $2bn on global health projects in 2011,[6] which is half the budget of the UN's World Health Organization.[7] A primary focus of the Gates Foundation is health and associated issues in poor countries, which in preceding decades would have been the core concern of global governmental organisations rather than private donors. Gates' focus on health has opened the door for more modest philanthropists to feel easier about getting involved in areas that have traditionally been dominated by state funding:

> 'The big debate is the line between government provision and individual philanthropists' provision. In a sense people like Bill Gates have defied all that by seeing that not enough is being done in the medical world and giving billions to medical causes. One could argue surely that's something the UN should do, or the government should do, but actually these are people who in their own right have more [money] than some countries have, so there is no question of public/private sector – they are both! And the responsibility on them is just huge.'

Many of our respondents had thought long and hard about the appropriate role for philanthropy, whether it be alongside, or in addition to, or as an alternative to, the state. But many had arrived at a pragmatic conclusion that 'society or the government can't provide for everything', and therefore there was a role for their private, voluntary contribution:

> 'You could argue that everything should be done by government – that if they say every child has a right to such and such then they should pay for it. But I'm not interested in the politics of it. I have a very low opinion of politicians… For example, look at the NHS. Surely, people say, surely the state should provide equipment, but it doesn't, so we've given over £500,000 to the X hospital since 2003. For example, we funded a machine to deal with the alignment of knees. The state doesn't fund this. It doesn't and it can't. So should no-one do it or should someone like us who can afford it do it?'

A significant barrier to investing in cause areas that are now considered the responsibility of government is the fear that private donations will 'crowd out' state spending, or be used as an excuse to make even more severe public spending cuts. One respondent noted: 'One of the first questions you ask is: "Am I just substituting for other funding?"' and another concurred: 'Well, of course, the tricky area is whether if you do more the state will cut down.'

Some interviewees feel quite comfortable with the idea of a mixed economy, such that donations combine with taxation to provide higher levels of funding for activities and services that they care about:

> 'I'm a believer in the so-called mixed economy. Where there is a strong state support for social welfare, health, education and the arts, there can also be a role for private involvement.'

> 'Well, the state should fund whatever it's funding, that's its job, but it hasn't always got enough money to do it properly. I fund medical research – that's really the government's job, not the public's job, but there's not enough money, it's not doing remotely enough in that area, so I'm improving it at the fringes. Charities can put the icing on the cake.'

Others take a 'needs must' approach and are willing to fund activity that they feel is theoretically beyond the remit of private donors:

> 'There are certain areas I wouldn't give to because I think they are the state's obligation. But I'm also aware how much those things are now being cut back, and the difficult situation that these organisations are in.'

> 'I suspect that virtually all philanthropic activity in community development terms, whether it's education, health or just dealing with deprivation, really is the voluntary sector stepping in where governments are failing to go.'

> 'We do feel quite uncomfortable, that we shouldn't really be supporting the government... but it hasn't enough money.'

However, some interviewees feel strongly that private donations should never be a substitute for government spending:

> 'We would be extremely upset if there was a political decision made to cut all funding for things like the arts... and the money that you had given was being used for that [to make up the shortfall].'

Because they believe philanthropy is a good parenting tool. As we saw in Chapter 3, the vast majority (89%) of our respondents have children and many talked about their children when discussing their philanthropy, whether in terms of wishing to involve offspring in their decisions about what to support (particularly the younger or emerging donors), or in relation to thinking about philanthropy as an alternative to leaving all their wealth as an inheritance.

As discussed above, our survey found that a substantial minority (32%) are concerned about the amount of money that should be transferred to their children and immediate heirs, and this concern has influenced their philanthropic decisions. What was once considered to be a silver spoon that fortunate parents could bestow on their equally fortunate children has, in some quarters, come to be viewed more as a poisoned chalice.

Others see the benefits of philanthropy as a teaching tool to demonstrate through actions the values they hope to pass on to the next generation:

> 'It's a very strong signal, for example, within a family, about what your values are and what you believe in. I think, particularly for the next generation, it's a powerful message to them about your beliefs and that by giving it helps in terms of your legacy. It's all very well leaving money to the next generation but passing on the values you have is more important.'

Put more simply, a number agree that 'it's nice to be an example to your kids'.

Many donors, especially in the emerging group, want their children to be involved in philanthropy. Their involvement can make giving decisions a more enjoyable family affair and provide reassurance that charitable initiatives will continue in the future:

> 'We definitely want our family to feel proud about [our family] foundation, and we want that to go on to perpetuity. We want our children to run it after us, and then our grandchildren, and then on and on and on.'

But the overriding, and simple, motivation uncovered in this finding is that philanthropy is viewed as an aspect of good parenting, a way of showing-by-doing that they hope will be an inspiration to their children and potentially to others too:

> 'I think we have a duty to be role models to, on an immediate basis, our families and on a broader basis to society at large.'

We explore the adviser perspective on this crucial concern of wealthy parents in Chapter 9.

Because they appreciate the recognition that comes with being philanthropic. Recognition is a contentious issue – some critics of philanthropy decry it as yet more privilege heaped upon those who least need (or even deserve) it, whereas others counter that public celebration of big donors is both appropriate and useful in inspiring others to emulate their actions.

As the survey data presented above shows, our respondents do not generally view recognition as a key driver of their own giving. Yet a third (37%) believe that better recognition of donors has contributed to the improved profile of philanthropy in the UK – and this figure rises to 50% among the established donors:

> 'If you've devoted some time and energy then a bit of recognition is nice and the honours system is part of that.'

> 'If you accept that a big part of the driver is being perceived to be a reputable person in society, however you want to [define that], then it's important that in some way it's out there that you are meeting that expectation.'

Honours, from MBEs to knighthoods, are the most obvious form of recognition given to UK philanthropists, although other schemes, such as the Beacon Awards, recognise best practice in philanthropy. A number of our interviewees have received such honours, and expressed equal measure of surprise and delight that their names had been put forward:

> 'I have an MBE and I loved my day at the Palace. It was a very special day. I didn't do it for that but it was very nice to have recognition. It doesn't give you anything but it's a nice buzz. It was a surprise.'

Despite insisting that recognition was absolutely not important to him, one interviewee felt that it could be an important factor for people who are not already in the public eye:

> 'You know a lot of guys spend their lives making a lot of money but in a rather obscure way – they have a factory or they invent something or they build a conglomerate by buying one company after another and nobody knows or cares who they are except a few City editors in the financial pages. For those people it may be a bit galling that nobody knows who they are despite their incredible achievements and great wealth, so I guess it may be some people's way of saying "Hey world, I'm a high achiever".'

While no-one viewed recognition as a prime motivator of their own giving, they accepted it was a very pleasant reinforcement:

> 'Most people that I know [give] because they feel it is something they want to do. But having done it, [recognition] is something that they enjoy and like.'

> 'Of course recognition is fun; it can be lovely.'

Proof that honours are considered a pleasant by-product rather than the prime motivation is that donors continue giving large sums after they have received the award. One respondent noted:

> 'Some people expected us to stop doing it once [my husband] got his OBE!'

The husband in question confirmed that for him, as for so many, the honour was not a factor in deciding to give large sums away:

> 'In reality, it was the most unexpected thing that's ever happened to me, getting that letter [about the OBE]. I had no idea and no expectation and I still don't believe that we entirely deserved it.'

However another, more nuanced, point emerged concerning the importance of better recognition of philanthropy to inspire further gifts, and the role that recognition plays in society, as opposed to recognition of individual philanthropists:

> '[We need] continuing recognition for the role of philanthropy and the effectiveness of charitable work.'

> 'If the recognition could be useful in promoting further philanthropy, then I think it's ok. I think it's ok as a way of saying thank you and celebrating someone as a role model, and if putting your name on something can help generate further donations, then it's worth it as a means to an end.'

Moreover, it was noted that the role of recognition as a driver of giving is not only about gongs and names on buildings, but extends to having a cultural context in which philanthropy is appreciated rather than sneered at, particularly in the media:

> 'I would increase my giving if the media valued and appreciated philanthropists for their role.'

The experts we consulted agree that recognition can be a key factor in incentivising donors, because we need 'a culture that celebrates giving rather than attacks it'. Indeed, our experts rate 'better recognition' as a more important factor than 'new tax breaks', with one insisting:

> 'It is not an improper motive. There is nothing wrong with wanting to be recognised as a good guy.'

Others point out the value of the opposite scenario, noting the beneficial impact of 'cultural opprobrium if they don't give'. However, the experts also concur that the desire for recognition is not consistent across all donors. For example, one said: 'New givers are more demanding in seeking recognition for their giving'.

Because they get joy out of giving and believe that philanthropy enriches their life. The final, and most important, of the new drivers identified in this 10-year update is perhaps the simplest yet most profound. Without exception, our respondents give because in some way or other it enriches their life to do so. This need not mean it makes them deliriously happy (although this can be the case), but rather that giving brings a feeling of satisfaction at doing something worthwhile, or enjoyment due to the experiences it involves, or a renewed sense of meaning in life, particularly once children are grown up and businesses have been sold.

Some are unapologetic about the kick they get out of giving:

> 'Well, I do it because it's such fun, it's selfish, I get such enjoyment. I am privileged to be able to do it.'

> 'At a very selfish level it's something from which I derive an enormous satisfaction.'

Others are keen to clarify the deep internal benefits of giving:

> 'I always say that philanthropy makes you feel good, and I don't mean goody-goody-two shoes, righteously good, but it just makes you feel good inside. You get a buzz.'

However, citing personal enjoyment and fulfilment may be viewed as an 'easier option' than making a more value-laden argument about the 'right use of money', as one established donor noted:

> 'I wouldn't want to preach at people... To say: "I get a lot of joy and satisfaction" is an easier message than, you know, a more moralistic one.'

While that donor was concerned that the enrichment message may be in part a more palatable pill to swallow, she did end by noting:

> 'What you get out of it is a sense of being human, and we all want to feel good about ourselves.'

It was frequently noted that the satisfaction and enjoyment only comes when the philanthropy is successful:

> 'I'd say it is enriching when it's a good experience.'

> 'It's just thrilling' [to see something funded become successful].'

But the overall message is that donors gain a huge amount by giving some wealth away:

> 'It's a really high privilege to meet these students. It moves me to tears. It lifts the spirits to see other people develop as the result.'

> 'Giving and running my trust has taken the role in my life that was previously occupied by my job. I hope it gives meaning to my life for the next 20 years or so.'

Tax breaks for giving: genuine incentive or disputed motivation?

Before concluding this chapter, we pause to consider one ostensible motivation that has not yet been fully discussed: tax reliefs on donations.

It was widely accepted among our respondents that tax breaks are attractive because they make their money go further ('You have to get the tax breaks to make the money go as far as it can'). It is uncontroversial that this is motivating, because it is good to be able to achieve more with less; but none of our respondents felt it was the driver behind their original decisions to give, as these quotes show:

> 'Tax breaks do not make great philanthropists but they enable people to give more. Tax breaks are important but you need a philanthropic impulse as well. If you take away the tax incentive, the amount of money going to charities would drop considerably.'

> 'The fact is I would give anyway and I suppose it is the charities that get more money, because then [if there were no tax benefits] I would give the net amount I think I can afford.'

> 'With all the people I have discussed philanthropy, the decision to give is made first and then it's worked out how to do the tax efficiently. Tax isn't the first thing that comes to mind.'

> 'If you're going to give, you're going to give. OK, you might get a bit of tax back but that's not why you do it. You're not getting the same amount of tax back. It isn't a scam… I think people just don't understand philanthropy or philanthropists. They think: "there must be something in it for them".'

Widely-held assumptions that 'getting a tax break' is a key motivation for rich donors, who are then viewed in the same category as tax dodgers, were perceived as wrong on a number of levels:

> 'People dodging tax are not remotely connected to people giving money to charity. If you give £1m to charity and you get £400,000 tax relief then you've 'lost' £600,000 of your own money… There's something magical about saying "I'll give a million pounds" but it only costs £600,000. But at the end of the day, the end result is that £1m has gone to charity.'

> 'Well, the tax relief is not a big deal for me and I'm not sure it's a big deal for other people. No-one has ever said to me "If I give £10,000 to this charity then I'll get £2,000 back".'

In sum, and despite widespread public and media misconceptions to the contrary, rich donors value tax relief primarily because it is of such worth to the recipient charities. It increases the value of the gifts they receive and it pleases the donor to know that their money has increased by a significant sum:

> 'The tax break didn't make me give. The tax break made me give more. Because without it, by definition I would have given less to leave myself in the same position. That's the point of the tax break, it increases the value of my gift.'

However, as also noted above, tax breaks and matched funding are not alternatives – they are different mechanisms that can combine on specific projects to make private donations go further, as tax breaks increase the size of the overall pot of money available for spending philanthropically, and matched funding increases the value of a gift to a particular cause or project.

The response to threats to reform charity tax relief

As we saw in Chapter 2, tax breaks for charitable contributions hit the headlines in 2012 when the Coalition Government proposed a limit on the amount of charity tax relief that could be claimed, reversing the policy of allowing the return of all tax paid on income given away as charitable donations, which had been in place for over a decade. The 2012 Budget proposed a limit of £50,000 or 25% of income, whichever was higher, on the amount a person could donate instead of paying it in tax. The resulting furore was immediate, united and ultimately successful in rejecting the proposal.

A coalition of charities and donors campaigned in public and lobbied in private until a U-turn was announced 10 weeks after the Budget. Those campaigning against the proposal included many newly vociferous philanthropists who had not previously 'outed' themselves as major donors; for example, almost 50 people signed a letter published in the *Sunday Telegraph*,[8] fewer than 10 of whom were well-known names. Another said:

> 'It was pretty disgraceful of the Government to propose to erode [charity] tax benefit at a time of great need for more charitable giving, not less. I usually don't get involved in taking a public position or writing to newspapers, but I sent a piece about it to my local paper.'

Our interviewees expressed great surprise at this proposal, which was felt to have come 'out of the blue' from a government that had previously been uniformly positive about philanthropy:

> 'Where did that come from? Civil servants have quite a bit to answer for as they are cocooned. They don't understand donors.'

> 'Government just doesn't get it. They are never going to and we shouldn't worry about it. Government should stimulate philanthropy and then keep out. [They] must make a decision about all this and not keep changing their mind and giving different messages… They screwed up, it was very stupid.'

> 'I thought it was one of the stupidest things I've ever seen'

The confusion of those who claim tax relief on charitable donations with tax dodging, and the bad timing of appearing to criticise philanthropists at a time of public sector spending cuts, upset many donors.

'As someone who has a foundation that is funded as we go along, I was pretty panicked as I felt particularly vulnerable. The implication was that we were all "April 4th donors". We went from a situation where every signal we were getting, including fiscal signals, was encouraging, and then to be told that you were really a tax dodger was unexpected.'

The advisers we surveyed also report unprompted complaints from their clients on this matter, as we review in Chapter 9.

While the dust will no doubt settle on this particular affair, there are some useful enduring lessons, not least that rich donors are not 'in it' for the tax, but that tax is a useful tool for motivating bigger gifts and for ensuring philanthropists are receiving consistent messages from government that their actions are welcomed:

'[Tax breaks] are part of signalling what the social norms should be, that's why it matters. [The tax cap proposal] was the wrong signal to give at a time when you're saying there needs to be more philanthropy.'

Furthermore, the attention provoked by the row put a spotlight on the inherent outcome of tax relief, which is effectively hypothecation: the donor is directing money (that would otherwise have been paid in tax) to the charities of their choice, including their own foundations. This happens when Gift Aid is applied at any level of gift, but as a very small number of donors account for the majority of donations, there is a risk of a disproportionate focus on causes favoured by the rich. As the BBC commented when reporting the rescinding of the proposed measure: 'Although the donor does not personally profit from the arrangement, it means they are choosing where their money is spent – unlike normal taxpayers'.[9]

The question of whether this matters is an ongoing debate. Many people are concerned about the distribution of philanthropic funding favouring the passions and pastimes of the rich. They might be surprised to find that some of the rich agree with them, as one of our interviewees noted:

'I do sit in the opera house sometimes and reflect that my evening's entertainment is being subsidised by someone who lives in a council flat... I don't think toffs' fun ought to be subsidised by working class people's taxes... It always bother me that people who have no interest in this sort of thing, and absolutely can't afford to go, are actually paying for it.'

Indeed, there was much thoughtful discussion about the proposal, its aftermath and the implications with our interviewees, together with observations from our expert commentators:

'There should be a debate on the choices of the wealthy.'

We agree with the view expressed by many of our interviewees that there should be an informed and dispassionate review of this area, and in Appendix 3 we have added some further thoughts on this topic.

Conclusions

Ten years is not a long time in the history of philanthropy, so it is not surprising that we find no dramatic shift in the explanation for why rich people give since we last explored this question a decade ago.

We find continuing support for the five motivations identified in the first study:

- Belief in the cause.
- Being a catalyst for change.
- Self-actualisation.
- Duty and responsibility.
- Relationships.

As well as identifying five new reasons that explain why rich people give today:

- Because they believe philanthropy is the right use of surplus money.
- Because they are clear about the complementary roles of government and philanthropy.
- Because they believe philanthropy is a good parenting tool.
- Because they appreciate the recognition that comes with being philanthropic.
- Because they get joy out of giving and believe that philanthropy enriches their life.

In sum, rich people give when they feel a resonance with a cause to which they can make a tangible difference, because they feel they can – and should – do something about it, and know they will develop themselves and enjoy the relationships that emerge as a result of that gift. Furthermore, they give because they have resources exceeding their perceived needs that they wish to use well, they are comfortable with the way private donations intersect with tax-funded provision, they see philanthropy as an extension of their parenting and they are motivated by appropriate recognition. But the essence of their continuing motivation is that giving enriches their life.

Despite the significant continuity in donor motivation, there is perhaps one aspect that has changed in the past 10 years, and that is the willingness to admit – even celebrate – the enjoyment and enrichment that comes with being a donor. It would be impossible – and improbable – to argue that philanthropy has become a more enriching aspect of rich people's lives over the past decade, but it has become increasingly acceptable to 'admit' the kick that people get from their giving.

However, the 'joy factor' raises an interesting puzzle: if it's so much fun to give money away, why don't all rich people do it? The answer is that the benefits of philanthropy are only experienced by those who do it, and they are tricky – perhaps impossible – to explain to those who don't.

The causes rich people gain such pleasure from supporting are the subject of the next chapter.

Notes

1   Most notably R. Bellah et al (1985) *Habits of the Heart: Individualism and commitment in American life*. Berkeley and London: University of California Press.
2   D. Karlan and J. List (2007) 'Does price matter in charitable giving? Evidence from a large-scale natural field experiment'. *The American Economic Review*, vol 97 no.5.
3   Jerold Panas (1984) *Mega Gifts: Who gives them, who gets them?*, p.41.
4   This quote is from Francie Ostrower (1995) *Why the Wealthy Give*, p.101. The original 'Why Rich People Give' UK study was inspired by Ostrower's study of elite philanthropy in the US.
5   For example see Thorstein Veblen's acerbic study of conspicuous consumption in the late 19th century: T. Veblen (1994) *The Theory of the Leisure Class*, first published 1899. New York: Dover.
6   Both figures from the Bill and Melinda Gates Foundation annual report 2011 http://tinyurl.com/pcjmkth p.7.
7   http://tinyurl.com/nuamubz p.3
8   Published on 15 April 2012.
9   www.bbc.co.uk/news/uk-politics-18278253

What do rich people give to?

5

This chapter considers the destination of philanthropic spending, exploring how rich people decide which organisations to support and how much they allocate to different types of causes.[1] It also presents insights into how rich people decide which requests for support to consider, why they continue or stop supporting a particular cause, and what circumstances lead them to view donations with regret or with pleasure.

Where does the money go?

We asked our respondents to indicate which charitable sub-sectors they had supported in the previous 12 months (2011/12). If the past year had been unusual for any reason, we requested an annual estimate of the distribution of their donations based on the average of the past three years.

Table 5.1 shows the incidence of support for the different charitable sub-sectors, in descending order of the number (not the size) of donations made to these cause areas. It illustrates that all types of cause receive some degree of support from rich UK donors, and that there is little difference in incidence of support between established and emerging donors.

The two exceptions are 'religious organisations and causes', which is the fifth most popular cause (by incidence) for established donors, but by far the least popular area for emerging donors; and 'higher education', which attracts almost twice the number of donations among established donors.

'Charitable foundations' are slightly more popular for emerging donors, but we believe this is because the more established donors had already settled their foundations before this time period.

Table 5.1: The incidence of support for the different charitable sub-sectors

	% of all donors supporting this cause	% of established donors supporting this cause	% of emerging donors supporting this cause
Arts and culture	59	68	50
Human services and welfare (including children, older people, disability etc)	50	50	50
Education (excluding higher education)	45	53	38
Higher education	40	53	29
Health	38	43	33
Own charitable foundation	34	30	38
International development	33	43	24
Environment and animals	29	33	26
Religious organisations and causes	27	48	9
Other (e.g. human rights, domestic violence, think tanks)	10	5	14

Inevitably, these are fairly crude categories. For example, in the arts and culture sector some interviewees were concerned to explain that the focus of their support is improving access for disadvantaged and excluded constituencies, or to help young artists, rather than the sponsorship of mainstream productions or exhibitions:

> 'We don't support cultural activities *per se*, but we might support them in what they are doing to widen access and raising awareness. We support the [major venue] – but not for the work in the [main concert halls]. It's about what they do in educational terms and what they do about widening access to music in the region.'

Of course, the likelihood of supporting a cause is quite a different matter to the value of support for that cause, as a charitable sub-sector may attract a smaller number of donations that are of a high value, and vice versa. Table 5.2 provides estimates of the level of support[2] for the different cause areas.

Table 5.2: Distribution of donations by charitable sub-sector

	All donors		Established donors		Emerging donors	
	Total value	Mean value	Total value	Mean value	Total value	Mean value
Own charitable foundation	£14,000,000	£500,000	£5,830,000	£485,833	£8,170,000	£510,625
Arts and culture	£10,810,000	£225,208	£5,065,000	£187,592	£5,745,000	£273,571
Higher education	£8,565,000	£259,545	£4,235,000	£201,667	£4,330,000	£360,833
Human services and welfare	£7,987,500	£194,817	£4,210,000	£210,500	£3,777,500	£179,881
Education (excluding higher education)	£6,730,000	£181,892	£3,280,000	£156,190	£3,450,000	£215,625
Environment and animals	£5,715,000	£238,125	£2,782,500	£214,038	£2,932,500	£266,590
International development	£5,280,000	£195,555	£2,452,500	£144,265	£2,827,500	£282,750
Health	£4,697,500	£151,532	£1,410,000	£82,941	£3,287,500	£234,821
Religious organisations and causes	£1,495,500	£67,955	£1,432,500	£79,583	£62,500	£15,625
Other	£1,325,000	£165,625	£5,000	£2,500	£1,320,000	£220,000

The most popular destination for donations is putting money into a personal charitable foundation or trust, for distribution at a later date. This reflects findings from other research, such as the annual *Coutts Million Pound Donors Report*,[3] which also finds that these giving vehicles are the main recipients of major donations. However, trusts and foundations are merely a 'holding place' where money earmarked for philanthropic spending is banked until it is distributed to other causes. Indeed, many of the gifts described by our respondents will have been paid out from their own trust or foundation.

Of the operational causes, arts and culture and higher education receive the largest share, which again fits with the known pattern of philanthropic spending by the wealthy in the UK.[4] In 2012 these causes were the top two in receipt of million-pound donations. Human services and welfare causes, and educational causes (excluding universities), are supported by a larger percentage of donors but received a smaller share of the total value than higher education. This latter cause receives a smaller number of larger value gifts; this pattern is especially prevalent among emerging donors.

The two main points of difference between our two sub-groups relate to support for health causes, which received more than twice as much in total donation amount from emerging donors, and religious organisations and causes, which received from established donors more than 20 times the amount given collectively by emerging donors to this cause area.

How do rich donors decide which causes to consider?

Why do donors decide to consider some requests for donations but not others? There are currently over 180,000 charities in the UK.[5] Not all are actively engaged in fundraising (for example, grant-making organisations count as charities), but even if only half are seeking support from the general public, that it is clearly an unmanageable number to have under active consideration. Indeed, an entirely open-minded donor would need to consider more than 200 potential recipients every day to get through all of them in one year.

Of course, potential donors do not undertake such extensive research, nor are they capable of comparing the merits of every alternative recipient. Instead, people 'filter in' and 'filter out' the options, often without even realising they are doing so. In the first edition of this research in 2002, two key factors were identified as crucial to ensure a request was 'filtered in' and thus at least considered, even if a donation did not eventually occur:

- The nature of the cause, such that the donor has some prior interest or experience.
- A personalised approach, ideally being asked by someone known and respected.

Lesser, but still important, 'door opening' factors identified in 2002 were: the competence of the asking organisation; the quality of the charity leadership; whether the charity represents value for money; and the kind of involvement the donor can expect. These findings were echoed in a recent report, *How Donors Choose Charities*,[6] which studied donor choice at all wealth levels.

We decided to probe this question further in the present study, as the question of how to attract donors' attention is so crucial to those seeking funds. We asked respondents which of eight reasons are relevant when they decide which requests to consider.

Table 5.3: How rich donors decide which requests to consider

	% of all donors considering reason relevant	% of established donors considering reason relevant	% of emerging donors considering reason relevant
If I really feel that my money will make a difference	74	77	71
If I am already interested in the cause	74	74	73
If it fits with my pre-determined giving objectives	73	72	73
If I am asked by someone I know and respect	69	74	63
If I like the approach made by the fundraiser	31	31	32
If it is an emergency appeal, for example, for a disaster fund	23	31	15
If I want to learn more about the cause	21	26	17
If it is a request for a particular national appeal, e.g. Children in Need or Comic Relief	9	10	7

As Table 5.3 shows, the nature of the cause and the identity of the asker remain in the top four factors that encourage a rich person to consider a request. The two new factors are a 'fit' with pre-determined giving objectives – which indicates that more and more donors are thinking strategically and planning ahead in anticipation of being asked – and an insistence that their donation will 'make a difference'. The desire for impact is not new, but to demand evidence of impact at such an early stage in the process, essentially before the request has received any serious consideration, may be a new departure.

Showing a similar strategic approach, donors are focusing on donations that are preventative, rather than curative, in nature:

> 'I prefer to fund young people, either the very young with the parenting of the under-5s, the early years, or it's more like the teenager, the NEETs [not in education, employment or training], and helping them because I think it's more effective to help at that early stage when they have their whole lives ahead of them. You can try to prevent problems happening later on if you give them the help earlier.'

It appears that donors have taken on board the critique of 'good intentioned giving' that fails to achieve anything meaningful, and are showing a preference for considering requests that will lead to tangible and significant benefits. A further point to note is the shared attitudes of both established and emerging donors, whose answers are very similar, with two exceptions – the newer donors claim to be less influenced by the asker being someone they know and respect, and half as likely to consider requests for emergency disaster appeals.

We explore the nature of this decision-making process, and the implications for those seeking funding, in more detail in Chapter 7.

How past giving decisions affect future giving decisions

The influence of prior decisions on future decisions is known as 'path dependency', or, in more common language, 'inertia'. Using the past as a guide to the future is a rational strategy, given the limited time and energy available to make giving decisions. But it can be problematic, as past circumstances may no longer be relevant, and it may mean missing opportunities to support newly emerged causes or organisations that have not previously hit the radar. Our respondents appear alert to the risks of shutting down options prematurely. Despite the 'inertia' apparent in Table 5.3 (where three-quarters of respondents claimed to filter out requests that did not chime with a previous interest or pre-determined giving objectives), their responses to a different question indicate a more open outlook, at least among the newer donors.

We asked if, broadly speaking, they support the same causes in 2012 as they did in 2002. This question highlighted one of the most dramatic differences between our two sub-samples. Three-quarters (78%) of established donors have retained the same focus within their philanthropic spending, whereas only 38% of the emerging donors have broadly stuck to their previous giving path. Underlining this finding, a higher percentage (43%) of newer donors had made 'a significant shift' in the destination of their donations, compared to just 15% of established donors. The remainder noted that they had always supported a variety of causes from year to year. One implication of this finding might be that fundraisers should focus their recruitment efforts on the younger and newer philanthropists, yet with almost a quarter (22%) of established donors open to supporting new causes, it is still worth approaching those who might be suspected to have their giving plans set more firmly in place.

What prompts rich people to stop and start supporting a cause?

Knowing which rich donors might consider a request from an organisation they have not previously supported can literally (for once) be the million-dollar question. We therefore asked those who had made a significant shift in the destination of their donations what had prompted them to start supporting a new cause. The top three answers across the whole sample were:

- Personal experience of the cause (47%).
- Being inspired by the work of a charitable organisation (31%).
- Being approached by a fundraiser (17%).

For some people, the term 'fundraiser' includes being asked for a donation by a peer, rather than by a paid professional fundraiser. Among the established donors, a third (33%) had switched at the suggestion of a family member, but in stark contrast, none of the established donors cited family intervention as an influence. However, the newer donors were often prompted to switch because they had gained a deeper understanding of the cause, which may be related to greater efforts to bring potential donors into the heart of organisations to witness their work and meet beneficiaries. The importance and impact of seeing the work at first hand, and the difference made by philanthropic investment, is discussed further in Chapter 7, as is the question of who should ask.

People also draw on their own expertise:

> 'I was a youth counsellor earlier in my career so I was seeing these issues and have got that expertise... so I have personal experience to draw on, whereas I have little understanding of being elderly and isolated, for example.'

The opposite question: 'Have you ceased supporting any causes in the past 10 years?' generated similar answers across the whole sample. Over two-thirds (70%) had walked away from a cause, with emerging donors being slightly more likely to withdraw their funding, at 73%, against 67% of established donors. The main reason for both groups was that they found new causes they wished to support (72%), which underlines the fact that donor inertia can be over-stated. However, poor practice on the part of the fundraising organisation accounted for the next three most popular replies.

Almost half (48%) felt the organisation no longer needed their support. While it is conceivable that some did accomplish their mission and closed down, this is unlikely to be the case for a significant number.

A quarter of donors (24%) were not satisfied with how the charity used their donation, and 14% felt the organisation did not appreciate their support or communicate appropriately. For example, one stated: 'There was no opportunity for engagement', while another complained that: 'They pursued me too frequently'.

The implications of these experiences for organisations seeking funding are reviewed in Chapter 7.

Some regrets and plenty of pleasure in giving decisions

A related question asked donors if they regretted any donation made in the past 10 years. This produced more positive results as most donors (67%) had no regrets, though a slightly higher level of regret was found among emerging donors (37% against 28%), perhaps because they are still 'finding their philanthropic feet', or because they have higher expectations. The third of the sample who had regrets were probed further for the reasons; these revealed one similarity and some differences between our established and emerging donors. The commonality lay in not getting appropriate feedback (36% and 33%), whereas the emerging donors felt twice as strongly that losing faith in the charity leadership was a key factor (67% versus 36%), and regretted that their money was not spent as expected (40% against 27%). Furthermore, 13% of emerging donors regretted a donation because they did not get appropriate recognition, a reason cited by none of the established donors.

It is important to note that 'recognition' here does not usually mean public acknowledgement; but rather personalised and prompt expressions of appreciation and gratitude. The differential may be that more established donors have lower expectations because of their experiences over the years.

In contrast to asking about negative experiences, when we asked: 'Are you particularly pleased with any donations that you have made in the past 10 years?' the response was a resounding 100% positive from the emerging donors and 95% from the established group: a remarkable level of customer satisfaction. When pushed to explain the reasons for their pleasure in donating, the explanations echo answers given in other parts of this research. The top three factors behind a pleasurable gift are:

- Because I know my money was well spent (74%).
- Because of the nature of the cause (67%).
- Because I got sufficient feedback to know it was a good decision (64%).

The question of knowing that their money has been well spent is of growing significance. While many have been influenced by the work of organisations such as NPC (New Philanthropy Capital) and others who have focused on impact assessment, the question for some donors is why charities are not already using some kind of impact measurement as a management tool to monitor their own performance and to help them make decisions about the allocation of scarce resources:

> 'It was my view that charities were a very inefficient way of distributing money; now I'm more sympathetic to the organisations themselves. I can now see that charities by and large are not managed to the higher levels of professionalism – not surprisingly, because it is not why people go into charities, people don't have the breadth of experience. And on one level they are there for the staff and not for the cause... I think accountability is crucially important, as is the role of the trustees, and the management of change is essential.'

The fact that this donor is not alone in his low expectations of the effectiveness and professionalism of the charities he supports should be troubling to the sector.

Reinforcing the suggestion that appropriate recognition matters more to newer donors, 23% of this group attributed their pleasure in a donation as 'because I got pleasing recognition', whereas only one established donor mentioned this factor.

Conclusions

The giving decisions of the rich people we surveyed are similar to those identified in other research into the same subject. Rich people give the most money to their own charitable trusts and foundations, arts and cultural organisations and Higher Education Institutions. This contrasts with the giving decisions of the general population who prefer to support health causes, (especially cancer research), welfare (especially for children) and animal charities.[7]

However, there are some areas of overlap, notably international development and the lifeboats, which receive significant support from both rich and non-rich donors.

Asking how respondents decide whether to consider a cause or not generated four 'filters', two of which had been identified in the original study (prior interest in the cause and being asked by someone they know) and two that have grown in importance (belief it will make an impact, and a fit with pre-determined objectives). This development shows a more strategic approach, not only concerned with management of giving, but attempting to address societal problems at an early stage and on a preventative basis, that is particularly marked in the emerging donors.

All respondents tended to overstate the extent of inertia in their giving, yet almost half (43%) of newer donors had made 'a significant shift' in the destination of their donations over the past decade, indicating that fundraising efforts might be most fruitfully focused on emerging donors.

The top three reasons that donors embrace new causes are: personal experience of the cause; being inspired by the charity's work; and being approached by a fundraiser, including a peer. Whether or not a rich person has personal experience of an issue is to some extent a matter of chance. But fundraising organisations can take action to ensure their work is viewed as exemplary and inspirational, and invest more in ensuring they make appropriate approaches to a wider pool of potential donors, as discussed further in Chapter 7.

By raising the standards of donor care to higher levels, charities can also take action to avoid three of the common reasons that donors cease to support them, all provoked by poor practice on the part of the fundraising organisation: when donors feel their support is no longer needed; are unhappy with how their money is spent; and receive poor communication. Indeed, our data also indicate that providing donors with sufficient information so that they know their money has been put to good use, will please all types of donors, and developing ever-more appropriate forms of recognition will appeal especially to the emerging generation of rich donors.

Notes

[1] We use the terms 'charity', 'charitable organisations' and 'causes' interchangeably to refer to all organisations seeking philanthropic funding, including universities, arts organisations and NHS Trusts.

[2] The figures are approximate as the survey invited respondents to indicate their size of gift within a range that then needs converting. For example 'less than £5,000' is interpreted as £2,500, while '£10,001 to £100,000' is interpreted as £55,000. The highest bracket of '£1m+' does not allow for an easy estimate of the average size. To be conservative, we calculate this as being exactly £1m. While the figures therefore cannot precisely represent the actual donations made, this process of averaging out does allow for inter-cause comparisons, as all estimates are calculated in the same way.

[3] www.kent.ac.uk/sspssr/cphsj/research/couttsmilliondonor.html

[4] For example, the *Coutts Million Pound Donors Report* already referenced and the *Family Foundation Giving Trends* reports www.cgap.org.uk/uploads/reports/FFGT_2012.pdf both report similar findings.

[5] According to the Charity Commission website (www.charity-commission.gov.uk) in May 2013, there were 163,163 'main charities' and a further 17,128 'linked charities' on the Register of Charities, making a total of 180,291 registered charities.

[6] http://tinyurl.com/ot7k7ur

[7] According to *Charity Market Monitor 2011*, the 10 UK charities raising the largest amounts of fundraised income in 2009/10 were: Cancer Research UK (£379m), British Heart Foundation (£196m), Oxfam (£182m), RNLI (£146m), NSPCC (£124m), Macmillan Cancer Support (£118m), The British Red Cross (£116m), RSPCA (£116m), The Salvation Army (£110m) and Sightsavers International (£97m).

6

How do rich people give?

Having looked at why rich people give, and what they give to, this chapter focuses on *how* they give. We explore the mechanisms of giving and discuss whether and how rich people differ from the general public in the way they organise their philanthropic transactions. This chapter also explores the relationship between volunteering and philanthropy. We begin by reviewing the data on how most donors give.

Methods of giving by the general public compared to rich donors

According to the *UK Giving 2012* survey,[1] the five most common methods for making a donation among the general public are:

- Cash gifts (50% of donors use this method).
- Direct debits (31%).
- Buying goods (25%).
- Buying raffle tickets (22%).
- Cheque or credit card (12%).

Despite cash still being king as far as most donors are concerned, an analysis of the typical amounts given via these different methods (Table 6.1) shows that the most popular channel produces a lower average donation than other methods. The typical cash gift is £5, whereas the typical value of a direct debit is £10, so this less frequently used method results in a larger net value for charities.

Despite the hype about the role of websites and social media in driving donations, only 7% of donations were made online in 2012, and only 1% by text.

Table 6.1: Methods of giving among the general population (adapted from UK Giving 2012 NCVO/CAF)

	% giving in this way	Average amount per transaction in £s
Cash	50	5
Direct debit	31	10
Buying	25	8
Raffle	22	4
Cheques/card	12	20
Event	12	10
Fees	5	14
Payroll	3	8
Other	2	10

To establish if rich givers use different methods of giving, and to find out if these methods have changed over time, we asked our respondents to indicate how they give now and how they gave in 2002 when our study was first conducted. The results are shown in Table 6.2.

Table 6.2: Methods of giving by rich donors in 2002 and 2012

	All donors		% of established donors		% of emerging donors	
	2012	2002	2012	2002	2012	2002
Through my own charitable trust or foundation	73	55	78	73	69	38
By sending one-off donations (by cash, cheque, bank transfer)	49	49	53	55	45	43
By direct debits / standing orders	28	27	30	30	26	21
Through a CAF (Charities Aid Foundation) account	18	17	25	25	12	10
By giving shares	9	12	8	18	10	7
By writing charities into my Will	22	5	15	5	17	5
Through a donor-advised fund	6	5	5	5	7	5
Giving through payroll	4	2	5	0	3	5

It is evident from the data that many people use more than one method. The overlap between those with their own foundations who send one-off donations in some circumstances (for example, when a cause does not fit with the charitable objectives of their trust) is noticeable. Gift Aid features as a mechanism in many of these methods.[2] It is used to underpin the process of transferring cash to their foundations, for one-off gifts, and for allocating funds to a CAF account.[3]

There are some similarities between rich and non-rich donors – roughly the same proportion make cash donations (half) and use direct debits (a third). However, the biggest difference is that most rich donors set up a personal charitable trust or foundation to administer their donations. Indeed, use of this method has almost doubled over the past decade for the emerging donors, which makes sense if this is the time period in which many of them started taking their giving more seriously.

Strategic giving

Over the past decade, the overriding trend for our respondents has been towards becoming more strategic, at least in their own assessment (Table 6.3). While two-thirds of emerging donors report a shift towards more strategic giving in the past decade, compared to less than half of the established donors, this difference is likely to relate to their different starting points 10 years ago. The fact that only one respondent describes themselves as becoming less strategic shows how far this concept has come from being one option to being the only option for serious givers.

Table 6.3: Has your philanthropy become more strategic in the last 10 years?

	% of all donors	% of established donors	% of emerging donors
Overall my giving has become more strategic since 2002	56	43	68
Overall I conduct my giving in the same way now as I did in 2002	40	54	27
My giving has become less strategic since 2002	1	3	0
Don't know	3	0	5

Giving through a charitable trust or foundation

Setting up a charitable trust or foundation is the most obvious manifestation of large-scale, planned, strategic giving. Three-quarters (73%) of our respondents in 2012 have established a foundation, considerably more than the half who reported having taken this step in 2002. The benefits of establishing a charitable trust include the ability to allocate for charitable purposes a sum of money that receives tax relief at the point when it is irrevocably deposited in the foundation. There is also the opportunity to have a clearer structure for giving, a rationale for responding to applications, and the ability to create a lasting legacy if the foundation is endowed:

> 'The mechanism of the trust is good, there are tax advantages and you are one step removed from potential recipients. You can explain [to applicants] that you have to involve trustees rather than just making one-off decisions on your own.'

As we found in 2002, the fact of having a foundation itself promotes and sustains the concept of a long-term familial commitment to philanthropy, and provides a focus and structure for the involvement of children in the decision-making, including becoming trustees when they are old enough. We return to this below.

However, not all trusts and foundations are set up with the intention of existing in perpetuity. Rather than following an investment strategy that seeks to preserve or grow the value of the initial endowment and make grants out of the interest earned on this capital, some philanthropists choose to 'spend out' all of their capital over a specified period of time. We asked our respondents for their views on this model and found a stark difference in the enthusiasm of our older and newer donors regarding 'spending out', as shown in Table 6.4.

A third (30%) of emerging donors with a foundation have already made the decision to spend out, and a further third (30%) are actively considering this option. Most of the remaining third have a 'flow-through' model[4] so the question does not apply, though some have not yet considered the issue.

Only one emerging donor has firmly decided not to spend out, compared to the established donor group where a fifth (19%) have resolved against it.

Table 6.4: Attitudes towards 'spending out' among donors giving through their own personal trust or foundation

	% of all donors	% of established donors	% of emerging donors
Have had a spend out model for 10+ years	21	16	27
Changed from an endowment to a spend out model in the past 10 years	7	10	3
Still actively considering whether to change for an endowment to a spend out model	25	19	30
Have not yet considered this issue	15	16	13
This option does not arise as foundation is a flow-through trust without significant assets	21	19	23
Have decided against changing from an endowment to a spend out model	11	19	3

Why have a foundation?

Sir Alec Reed, the philanthropist who founded many charities including Ethiopiaid, WomanKind Worldwide and The Big Give, describes giving through a charitable trust or foundation as 'the Disneyland method of giving', in that the donor 'pays once at the gate and can then enjoy the rides for free!'[5]

While giving through a foundation undoubtedly 'frees up' the donor to focus on the more fun and fulfilling questions such as what to give to, rather than whether or not to give at all, it also imposes a degree of discipline on donors as they need to fulfil certain legal requirements, such as appointing trustees and providing annual reports and accounts to the Charity Commission. The governing document to establish the foundation must list its objectives, which can also bring a focus to giving. While some donors hedge their bets and cite a vague objective such as 'to promote the welfare of mankind', many put a lot of thought into deciding exactly where they wish to focus their giving (in terms of geography, cause area and/or type of recipient). This nascent strategy for giving helps decision-making further down the line. As one interviewee said:

> 'It's been easier since our categories have been up and running so we now know exactly what our criteria are.'

Giving strategically also seems to 'raise the bar' so that donations are larger than if they were made on a purely reactive basis. As one of our interviewees notes:

> 'I think people tend to give more when they're not just writing cheques because a friend asks them or because they go to something and think "oh that's interesting, why not?".'

Community foundations: local philanthropy and making 'time to give'

Many of the rich people who participated in this research also hold a fund in the community foundation that covers the area where they now live, or where they were raised or created their wealth. The suggestion that donors will give more, and will give more effectively, if they dedicate more time and attention to their philanthropy is being tested by a three-year programme (2012-2014) run by UK Community Foundations (formerly the Community Foundation Network), supported by the Esmée Fairbairn Foundation. Called the Philanthropy Fellowship, it is a £750,000 investment in nine consortia of community foundations covering most of the UK to test the idea that intensive, personalised and tailored donor education and support will unlock extra donations for local communities.

Larger donations are not only a by-product of more strategic, planned giving. We also note that recent American research finds that donors who give collaboratively, for example, in a giving circle, donate larger sums than donors who give alone.[6]

Collaborative giving

Little is known about the incidence and consequences of giving collaboratively in the UK. While the landscape of giving circles has been successfully mapped in the US, we do not even know how many such entities exist on this side of the Atlantic. However, the work of mapping and analysing UK giving circles has begun in 2013.[7]

We asked our respondents about their experiences of giving as part of a group. It was a surprise to learn that many of our respondents are already giving in this way, as shown in Table 6.5. Almost half (44%) are part of a regular or occasional group or donors. Giving collaboratively may be one of the 'best kept secrets' of the rich donor community.

A further striking finding is that the newer donors are far keener to consider giving by this method in the future. Thirty-three per cent of emerging donors who have not yet given as part of a group are open to doing so in future, compared to just 14% of the established donors.

Table 6.5: Attitudes towards collaborative giving

	% of all donors	% of established donors	% of emerging donors
I have never given as part of a group of donors and don't intend to do so	30	32	28
I have never given as part of a group of donors, but might consider doing so in future	24	14	33
I have once, or very occasionally, given as part of a group of donors	23	32	14
I have started giving as part of a group of donors in the last 10 years	11	8	14
I have been giving as part of a group of donors for more than 10 years	10	11	9

However, collaborative giving does not have universal appeal. A third (30%) of our rich donors have not, and do not intend to, give in a group. We hope further research will shed light on how well the needs of those who are giving collaboratively are being met.

Planned giving

A key characteristic of strategic giving is that it involves planning ahead, in terms of both the criteria for making giving decisions and the amount of money that will be allocated for overall philanthropic spending. For some people this is achieved by simply placing a large sum into a foundation, usually when a company is sold or an inheritance received. An alternative is regularly to allocate a percentage of income for donations. For some it is a combination of several factors:

> 'It is not a constant percentage as it relates both to needs and to taxable capacity. It is around 50% of income but does vary from year to year... Mine is more in the way of a pass-through foundation. Also, gifts to the foundation are mainly shares but also some Gift Aid.'

We asked our respondents about their attitudes towards allocating a proportion of their income for donations. Responses were split between those who are already allocating a set proportion of income for donations (27%), those who do not intend to go down this path (29%), and those who feel that having a charitable foundation makes this question redundant (41%); only 3% feel this question remains open. Among those who currently give away a set proportion, the allocated amount ranged from 5% to 50% of income.

One respondent began by committing 10% (the standard definition of a tithe) and notes: 'This started as a tithing principle but has evolved to giving as much as I can afford at any time, which may be in excess of a tithe'. None of the established donors intend to change their mind on this matter, but 5% of the emerging donors feel it is possible that at some point in the future they would arrange their affairs in this way.

When asked to explain how else they work out how much to give away, we learned of a variety of approaches:

> 'As income is not a great indicator (and what there is, is distorted by tax), I give a proportion of expenditure. Most of us do know how much we spend.'

> 'We used the Rosenberg principles [see Appendix 4] to work out how much we would need for the rest of our lives, including gifts to our children and grandchildren, and put the rest into our charitable trust.'

> 'I calculate some of my gifts as a percentage of the amount of their total appeal, for example, I might decide to give them 3% of their goal.'

> 'I redistribute my state retirement pension and winter heating allowance. I also maintain a running capital and try to donate what is above that average level.'

> 'I give away any surplus windfalls.'

The sense that charitable giving is an integral element in a range of discretionary spending is emphasised by several respondents. Philanthropy is one of several enjoyable and enriching activities – a constant theme in our interviews:

> 'I did increase the amount given when I started earning huge amounts [in my profession], but there was no mathematical relationship. At the same time that I could afford to give more, I could also buy pictures, have holidays and give money – all nice to do.'

A residual approach is favoured by some, such that philanthropic giving constitutes 'whatever I do not need for other commitments and purposes' or is the result of a calculation: 'I try to work out how much I won't need for other uses'.

However, some prefer to be driven by demand:

> 'My donations are only limited by the attractiveness of opportunities to give.'

'There is no limit or 'proportional-to-income' mentality. If the cause is right and I can trust the organisation, then I do it.'

We discuss further in Chapter 8 the issue of whether it would be possible to establish some sort of benchmark or social norm suggesting a proportion of income or wealth that might be allocated for charitable donations in order to encourage those who do not give.

A further aspect to planned giving is arranging for charitable gifts to be distributed after death. As discussed in Chapters 2 and 4, the current Coalition Government has introduced new incentives to encourage charitable legacies, yet our research finds a strong preference for giving during one's lifetime rather than through a Will, as shown in Table 6.6.

Table 6.6: When do you intend to do most of your giving?

	% of all donors	% of established donors	% of emerging donors
In my lifetime	75	68	80
Through my Will	6	8	5
I haven't decided yet	19	24	15

Perhaps curiously, the group of respondents from 2002 are less likely to have made a decision either way – with a quarter (24%) not yet decided whether to do most of their giving in their lifetime or through their Will, as opposed to 15% of emerging donors who remain undecided. This may be because Will-writing is more of a priority for the older group, whereas lifetime giving is the default option for younger donors.

Anonymity

Anonymous giving is an issue that vexes many observers of philanthropy. For obvious reasons, it is extremely difficult to count how many donations are given this way, or to quantify their collective value. This topic also prompts strong views as to whether anonymity constitutes a 'better' way to give. There is a strand of opinion, enshrined in some religious tenets, that giving without declaring oneself is the highest form of philanthropy. However, as one of our interviewees notes, there is a biblical basis for both views:

'There is this biblical tension that says: "don't hide your light under a bushel" but also: "your left hand must not know what the right hand is doing". So should you draw attention to your giving or do it quietly?'

The same interviewee is nonetheless quite clear that whether or not gifts are made anonymously: 'It mustn't be an ego trip.'

Almost three-quarters (72%) of our respondents have made an anonymous gift at some point in their lives, mostly decided on a case-by-case basis (35%), as shown in Table 6.7:

Table 6.7: Approaches towards anonymous giving

	% of all donors	% of established donors	% of emerging donors
I occasionally give anonymously	35	35	34
I have never made an anonymous gift	28	28	27
I frequently give anonymously	14	14	15
I have only once, or very rarely, made an anonymous gift	13	14	12
I used to give anonymously but no longer do so	8	5	10
I have never made an anonymous gift but might consider doing so in future	3	3	2

Despite the 'pick and mix' approach to anonymity displayed by the majority of our respondents, some want every gift they make to be executed in secret:

> 'I definitely don't want recognition and go completely out of my way to be anonymous. Especially when I'm giving to really local things where I might be involved on the management committee or as a volunteer. We live in a very tight-knit community and I don't want to be known [as a funder], and yet obviously I'm very aware of the needs there. So we go to great lengths, sending money to them via intermediaries or whatever.'

However, rich people are often willing to 'go public' when it is likely to reap wider benefits for the cause:

> 'I once asked another donor to please go public about his donation so that others would give. He agreed reluctantly and guess what? Others did give! It got covered in the *Evening Standard* and the next thing somebody phoned me and the money quadrupled. So he got the credit and the recognition but it was more important that others were challenged.'

Circumstances in which anonymous donations are made include those where people are giving in their own back yard ('since locally we wish to maintain as low a profile as possible') or wish to avoid causing discomfort ('I know the recipient and it would embarrass them'), or when giving to causes their peers might not approve of. An example of this is a donation reported in *WRPG*, when a Jewish donor contributed a significant sum towards a Christian church in the village where she owned a house.

However, some anonymous giving is motivated by pragmatic reasons, rather than a moral position on the virtue of giving in secret, as this donor explains:

> 'Some of it is to do with the fact that if your name as a trust goes on the list, then other people can see it and you get inundated by applications. We just haven't got the resources to respond to that and so we just want to remain anonymous.'

The data in Table 6.7 shows that there are changes over time. A small number of respondents (3%) are considering starting to give anonymously in the future, and a slightly larger number (8%) who previously gave anonymously have decided to stop doing so, for reasons illustrated by this quote:

> 'Some people do want to be anonymous and want to keep their head down and not run into the cynicism that still exists, like the press can sometimes be very nasty about people who give and not at all encouraging. For a long time I didn't want to talk about it, about anything I'd given, and I started to speak out because people said: "you need to encourage others" and I go along with that.'

Giving of time

In this chapter on how rich people give, the final aspect we consider is how the giving of time intersects with the giving of money.

The vast majority of our respondents (82%) volunteer as well as make donations, and tend to concentrate their gifts of time on charitable organisations that they also support with financial gifts (Table 6.8). Emerging donors are much more likely to volunteer for organisations that they do not support financially, but this could be related to their inexperience as donors and the fact they are still deciding where best to focus all the resources they have available.

Table 6.8 Volunteering – incidence and location

	% of all donors	% of established donors	% of emerging donors
I volunteer with the same charities I donate to	45	45	45
I volunteer with different charities than the ones I donate to	9	3	14
I volunteer with some charities I donate to, and some I do not donate to	29	34	24
I do not volunteer	18	18	17

The amount of time committed by rich donors is substantial, as shown in Table 6.9. Almost three-quarters commit 20 hours or more per month to volunteering, which far exceeds the rate among the general population as reported in the government *Community Life Survey 2012*[8] which found that less than half (49%) of the population volunteered at least once a month (for an unspecified duration of time).

Table 6.9: Average monthly volunteering hours

	% of all donors	% of established donors	% of emerging donors
Under 5 hours	6	6	6
5 – 9 hours	12	6	17
10 – 19 hours	10	3	17
20 hours or more	72	84	60

The most common form of volunteering involves serving as a trustee or chair of a charity, including of their own foundation (Table 6.10). Board membership is slightly more common among established donors, probably because more older donors are likely to be retired. However, this finding does not support frequently heard claims that newer philanthropists are more heavily engaged in the daily work of the causes they support. This could reflect not only the more limited amount of free time they have, but also the relatively earlier stage of their philanthropic journey:

> 'I think that a very important aspect is being closely involved in most of the organisations I support. You asked about volunteering. I do no volunteering in the normal sense but I am on the boards of several organisations, and I chair a very large non-fundraising charity which takes half my time. Also, I spend some time taking part in activities related to the promotion of philanthropy.'

Table 6.10: Most common types of volunteering work

	% of all donors	% of established donors	% of emerging donors
Board membership	79	88	71
Helping to raise funds	69	75	63
Professional advice (e.g. legal or financial)	39	47	31
Hands-on helping (e.g. listening to children read)	37	41	34

More than half of all respondents volunteer to raise funds – the most common form of volunteering across the general population.[9] Established donors are far more likely to provide free professional advice (47% against 31% of emerging donors) and to get involved in the front-line work of the charity (41% against 34% of emerging donors). Again, this could be due to having more time and greater confidence in their choices, but it stands contrary to oft-repeated claims that the newer, younger donors are more 'hands-on' than their predecessors.

Conclusions

In this chapter we show that rich people believe they are becoming increasingly strategic in their giving, most notably in their preference for organising their philanthropy through the vehicle of a charitable trust or foundation. Taking a more proactive, planned approach, such as committing to give a set proportion of income or assets, or deciding in advance which cause areas to focus on, also demonstrates a more strategic approach.

We note that donors hold disparate views on contentious issues such as anonymous giving, whether to give alone or as part of a group, and establishing a foundation in perpetuity or spending out in their lifetime. But the very fact these debates are being held in the open, and that people have considered them carefully, is a further indication of how much thought is going into contemporary philanthropic action.

We conclude that for most people, being a philanthropist involves constantly re-visiting and re-evaluating the best way to organise their charitable affairs. For many the pleasure of learning how to do it better, and the greater understanding inherent in that process, is itself enriching.

The next chapter discusses the role that rich people play in asking for money, and discusses their experiences of, and attitudes to, doing so.

Notes

1 www.cafonline.org/PDF/UKGiving2012Full.pdf
2 There is a clear explanation of how Gift Aid works on the HMRC website: www.hmrc.gov.uk/individuals/giving/gift-aid.htm
3 A CAF Account is a mechanism that enables donors to put aside money for tax-efficient giving www.cafonline.org/my-personal-giving/plan-your-giving/individual-charity-account.aspx
4 A flow-through trust is one in which all the funds are available for making donations, as opposed to an endowed trust where only the interest is distributed and the capital is retained or grown.
5 This quote appears in a case study of Sir Alec Reed on p.8 of the 2008 *Coutts Million Pound Donors Report*. http://tinyurl.com/qckaep5
6 Angela Eikenberry (2009) *Giving circles: Philanthropy, voluntary association and democracy*. Bloomington: Indiana University Press.
7 This is being undertaken as a collaboration between Angela Eikenberry, and one of the authors of this volume, Beth Breeze, and the analysis will be published in 2014.
8 http://tinyurl.com/q94qsro
9 The Cabinet Office *Helping Out* survey 2007 finds that 65% of volunteers are involved in 'raising or handling money', p.28.

7

Being asked and asking

'Charities must become much better at asking.'

Here we explore rich people's attitudes to being asked to make charitable donations, as well as their experience of asking others to give. We discuss their opinions of fundraisers and hopes for involvement with the organisations they support beyond being asked for money. We also probe their thoughts on what constitutes a 'major donation' and at what level of giving they expect to have access to the charity leadership.

We go on to review the experience of asking, and set out 10 guidelines that those who have engaged in the process identify as necessary to maximise the chances of a successful outcome. We discuss the implications of these findings for charities and conclude with a case study to illustrate the application of these principles in practice.

The importance of being asked by the right person

In Chapter 5 we highlighted that for about three-quarters of respondents, having an existing interest in the cause and a 'good fit' with predetermined giving objectives are key factors in giving decisions. An equally strong weighting is given to donor confidence that their money really will make a difference. So the top two motivators for giving, which have not changed over the past 10 years, remain:

- Belief in the cause.
- Confidence that my money will make a difference.

We also reported that over two-thirds (69%) of respondents will consider a request if asked by someone they know and respect, and this figure rises to three-quarters (74%) for our established donors. This means that faced with a large number of applications for funding, this factor is as important as an interest in the cause and a belief that the donation will have impact. While it is true that being asked by a known and respected person is less important for the emerging donors, this is only relative. It is still the case that almost two-thirds (63%) of new donors will consider a request if asked by the right person. They may not give, or give substantially, but they will consider a request from someone they know and admire. And this means someone they regard as (at least) a peer:

'The bottom line is a lot of money is raised this way, by people saying to their friends: "Oh come on".'

We are not suggesting that people *will* give because they are asked by a peer, only that it is an important factor in deciding which requests to consider. Other factors come into play, and we explore the question of taking advice in more detail in Chapter 9. But the importance of an influential 'asker' is very clear. Many expert observers of the philanthropy scene agree that peer pressure in all its forms is crucial, in particular, when it comes to making an appropriate ask:

'One reason why the rich give is that their interest is engaged by the right person in the right way at the right time. This is fundamentally important.'

None of these findings are especially surprising. Most giving is prompted, and donors support causes in which they have a prior interest, such as their former university, activities in their town, region or country of origin, or, for family businesses, charities in the local community where employees are based. They may support art forms they love and know a lot about. But what happens when donors are asked by people they do not consider as peers? And when donors have no pre-existing interest in any particular cause, or are not yet driven by a vision of how their money could make the world a better place? How can they best be asked? Do they respond to unsolicited requests and, if so, what kind of solicitation is likely to be successful? What do they hope for in their relationships with the charities asking for their support?

A number of questions in our survey tackle these issues related to asking.

Fundraising is viewed as having become more professional

We first asked about how donors regard fundraisers. As Table 7.1 shows, the majority (57%) of respondents recognise that fundraising has improved and become more professional over the past 10 years.

Table 7.1: How has the professionalism of fundraisers changed over the past 10 years?

	% of all donors	% of established donors	% of emerging donors
Fundraisers have become more professional in their approach to donors	57	67	48
The professionalism of fundraisers is too varied to say	32	26	38
The professionalism of fundraisers has stayed about the same	6	5	7
I haven't been giving for long enough to comment	2	0	5

As we see, established donors are more likely to agree that fundraising has improved, while emerging donors tend to feel that the professionalism of fundraisers is too varied to say.

Table 7.2 shows the ways in which donors believe fundraisers have become more professional. The most significant area of perceived improvement (cited by 78% of those who agreed that fundraising had improved) was in better research before donors are approached, with similar proportions of established and emerging donors believing this to be the case. But in other respects, views on fundraisers vary. The established group think that fundraisers have a better understanding of how donors wish to engage with causes and have become better at offering appropriate recognition. Meanwhile, far fewer of the younger donors think fundraisers have got better at explaining tax breaks and helping with planned giving.

However, excessive and inappropriate asking continues to occur, as this donor notes:

> 'The asking out there is prodigious. When we set up the foundation we got every month a 30cm pile of mail – the waste of paper! It was all blind asking, nobody had read our charitable objectives.'

Similarly, inadequate or non-existent research not only wastes money; it makes the whole sector look unprofessional. Donors on the receiving end of 'bad asks' do not forget the experience, and may even redirect their irritation at the whole charity sector, rather than just the organisation that approached them clumsily or acknowledged a gift inappropriately:

> 'I think there's an assumption that because people are wealthy there's less need to cultivate them. It should take 10-15 years to cultivate before asking for £100,000. There's real naïvety about this. The rich are not an easy target. It's offensive to play on guilt.'

> 'I sent £10,000 to the [X charity], and they sent a pro forma thank you letter. It still rankles 10 years later.'

Table 7.2: In what way have fundraisers have become more professional?

	% of all donors believing fundraisers have become more professional	% of established donors believing fundraisers have become more professional	% of emerging donors believing fundraisers have become more professional
Better research before approaching donors	78	77	80
Better understanding of how donors wish to engage with causes	72	81	60
Better at offering appropriate recognition to donors	33	38	25
Better at explaining tax breaks and helping to plan gifts	28	38	15

As the data is attitudinal we cannot know whether expectations are rising or there is another reason for less satisfaction among emerging donors. Either way, the data indicates that there is no room for complacency in the fundraising profession.

It is interesting to compare these donor perceptions with those of the expert observers of the philanthropy scene in our study, the vast majority of whom (83%) believe that a more professional approach by those seeking funding has been one of the significant developments in UK philanthropy over the past decade. Among those experts whose work brings them into contact with the fundraising profession, just over half (54%) believe that fundraisers have become more professional.

A marked area of contrast is that almost twice as many experts (57%) believe fundraisers have become better at offering appropriate recognition to donors, compared to just a third (33%) of donors who hold this view. However, it is unclear whether this is because experts attribute the increasing recognition of philanthropists to professional intervention by the charities, or because donors make a distinction between public recognition and appropriate direct acknowledgment by the recipient charity.

Professionalism clearly does matter, but, as discussed in Chapter 5, only a third (31%) of donors cite liking the approach of the fundraiser as a factor in their decision whether to consider a request, as compared with the importance of being asked by somebody they know, which mattered to two-thirds (69%) of donors.

This does not mean that the role of the professional 'major donor fundraiser' is unimportant. As noted above, better donor research is cited as the most significant area of improvement in fundraising over the past decade. From other work such as that reported in *Cultural Giving*[1] we are aware that many of the best approaches occur when the orchestration that underpins cultivation and stewardship is invisible to the prospect and donor: the combination of the right asker and excellent research is very powerful.

Rich donors expect to interact with the charity leadership

For many donors the approach of the fundraiser is not of primary importance because they expect to interact with the charity leadership – the chief executive, a trustee, a programme director, or an expert academic or curator – rather than with fundraising staff. (Table 7.3).

Table 7.3: Donors' expectations of relationships with the causes they support

	% of all donors	% of established donors	% of emerging donors
I am 'hands-off' with some of the causes I support but expect to be more fully involved with others	51	53	50
I like some involvement with all the causes I support, e.g. invitations to events or to view the work I fund	21	18	24
I expect to be fully involved with all the causes I support, e.g. serving on the board or being in regular contact with the charity leaders	18	11	24
I have a 'hands-off' approach but expect to be kept fully informed about how my money is being used	9	16	2
I have a 'hands-off' approach and do not wish to be involved beyond donating money	1	3	0

All of the newer interviewees and all except one in the original group interviewed in 2002 want to be involved beyond giving money. Not surprisingly, about half (51%) of all donors surveyed say that they are 'hands-off' with some of the charities they support but expect to be more fully involved with others. However, taking a hands-off approach but expecting to be kept fully informed about how their money is being used is far more common among established donors. Far more of the emerging group want greater involvement, including a quarter (24%) wanting low-level participation such as invitations to events or to view the work. The same percentage expect to be fully engaged, for example, by serving on the board or being in regular contact with the charity's leaders. This is more than twice the proportion of established donors, who may be more familiar with and so have gained greater confidence in the organisations they support. It is also possible that in some cases age or infirmity prevents extensive involvement.

Expectations of greater participation by new donors may be driven by philanthropy advisers, by their peers or by charities assuming that younger donors characterised as 'new philanthropists' will demand, for example, a seat on a committee.

As we saw in Chapter 6, 88% of established donors, and 71% of emerging donors, are trustees on charity boards. So while it may be hard to reconcile or interpret this data fully, there is nonetheless a clear message that a significant majority of donors are interested in active involvement with the causes they support. This is also reflected in the time they allocate to volunteer activities.

Rich people and fundraisers differ in their definition of major donations

Clearly, donors do not expect extensive engagement with organisations to which they give small or one-off gifts, but that begs the question: how big is a big gift? The answer is that donors perceive a 'major donation' to be far higher than the £5,000 'industry standard' – the level at which a donor tends to be taken off the general supporter database and allocated to a specialist member of staff tasked with 'managing their account' (a rather inappropriate, but nonetheless common, phrase used in fundraising departments). Indeed, for smaller organisations and those embarking on 'major donor fundraising', the definition of a 'major donor' may be as low as £1,000.

Table 7.4: How do you define a 'major donation'?

	% of all donors	% of established donors	% of emerging donors
At least £1,000	5	5	5
At least £5,000	5	8	2
At least £10,000	25	18	33
At least £50,000	33	36	29
At least £100,000	27	31	22
At least £250,000	2	3	2
At least £500,000	2	0	5
At least £1 million	1	0	2

As we see in Table 7.4, hardly any donor in our survey defines a gift worth under £10,000 as 'major'. For the vast majority (85%) of respondents, the answers lie between £10,000 and £100,000. There is some variance between the two groups of interviewees, with more of the emerging donors suggesting lower figures. This may reflect the fact that some of them are at an earlier stage in their philanthropic journey, and not making so many larger gifts. But it is apparent that for 70% of established donors and 60% of emerging donors, a major donation is worth at least £50,000 – i.e. at least 10 times the value assumed by many in the fundraising profession.

Donations and access to charity leaders

So how does this sit with donors' expectations of access to the leadership of the bigger charities they support? Is it related to the size of the gift, and is that linked to their perception of what is a major donation?

Table 7.5: At what level of gift would you expect to have access to the leadership of one of the bigger charities?

	% of all donors	% of established donors	% of emerging donors
£1,000	0	0	0
£5,000	4	3	5
£10,000	9	13	5
£20,000	11	13	10
£50,000	18	21	15
£100,000	10	3	17
£1,000,000	4	5	2
I don't expect access to the charity leadership to depend on the size of my donation	33	34	32
Don't know	11	8	14

About a third (33%) of all interviewees did not expect their access to the charity's leadership to depend on the size of their donation, and one in 10 didn't have a view on this question. That leaves over half of established donors expecting access to leadership following gifts from £10,000 upwards, with nearly half of this sub-group mentioning £50,000 and above. For emerging philanthropists the 'price' of access is higher, with nearly 20% suggesting a level of at least £100,000. What is evident is that most people who give what they define as a major donation expect a personalised and bespoke relationship at a high level within the organisation.

Major donors giving through a personal trust or foundation as a one-off rather than a regular gift also have high expectations of access:

'Because we give in fairly big dollops, it's much easier for both the recipients and ourselves to be involved and to actually see what happens. The smaller the foundation relative to the size of the organisation, the more difficult that becomes.'

Does it differ from sector to sector?

Our survey did not cover the different cause areas, but we are aware from our interviews and experience that the cultural sector offers specific opportunities for engagement with institutional leaders and experts, beneficiaries and other donors. Our interviewees who support the arts spoke of their pleasure in helping young musicians, funding a programme to bring in new diverse audiences, being part of a syndicate supporting a touring production that would otherwise not be possible, going behind the scenes at the theatre, or attending a private curator-led tour of an exhibition.

Although there are some characteristics shared with the higher education sector (for example, in the provision of bursaries and scholarships), what sets the cultural sector apart is that its core mission (whether to organise performances or exhibitions, manage an historic property or look after other national assets) itself provides opportunities for prospect and donor engagement.

Many cultural institutions create clubs and syndicates for which the annual cost of membership would not be regarded as a major donation in the terms defined above. But giving £5,000 or £10,000 to, say, an opera production syndicate at one of the national opera companies, or becoming a patron at a national gallery or museum for a similar or lower sum, certainly 'buys' access to the director and senior music/design/curatorial staff, and it is a large part of the offer, and much appreciated by donors.

Donors' experience of asking

We have seen that the role of peer ambassadors is hugely important, at least to persuade prospective donors to consider a request. Being introduced to a cause by a respected and trusted friend or colleague can make a significant difference. It is then up to the charity to persuade the prospect that the cause is consistent with their own values and predetermined objectives, and to show how donor investment will be effectively spent and make a real difference.

Asking by a peer who has already given to the cause is most effective, as those who have been through this process testify. We now look at this in some detail.

Table 7.6: Donors' experience of asking for money

	% of all donors	% of established donors	% of emerging donors
I have asked and have had some good and some bad experiences	43	54	33
I have asked and it was a good experience	33	36	31
I have never asked others for money	15	3	26
I have asked and it was a bad experience	9	8	9

Table 7.6 summarises donors' experiences of asking for money for the charities that they support. This question generated one of the sharpest distinctions between the established and emerging donors. Almost every established donor (97%) has at some point asked others to make a donation to a cause, but a quarter (26%) of the emerging group have never done so. While slightly more older than newer donors have had good experiences of asking for money (around a third in each case), roughly the same (under 10% in each group) have had only bad experiences. Most donors reported both good and bad experiences.

Many donors become involved in the causes they support, and as we see in Chapter 6, 75% of the original interviewees and just under two-thirds (63%) of new respondents cite helping to raise funds as a volunteer activity for their favoured charities. 'Helping to raise funds' may not always include asking for donations, but clearly a substantial number of rich donors recognise the importance of taking an ambassadorial role and engaging potential donors in the causes they support.

How to ask

Having explored donors' views about asking for money, we identify key guidelines as to what factors are more likely to achieve a donation, illustrating each proposition with quotes from our interviews.

- **Credibility in asking comes from giving:**

  'When I approach people, it's generally accepted that the fact I'm a wealthy man who's known for giving money to charity will influence people to give.'

  'I usually only do this for organisations that I have supported myself, and only in circumstances in which I would let it be known that I give, to get others to part with money.'

- **Donors who become askers must be passionate and knowledgeable champions of the cause:**

  'I think when one is enthusiastic and passionate it makes a huge difference.'

  'I think people respond really well when you've got a crystal clear idea and you've really defined what the proposition is and they can see clearly where the money will go and what it will achieve. I think the more precise you can be, and the more you can engage people emotionally in whatever it is you want them to give the money to, and they can see the professionalism in how the money will be spent, I think those are things that really get people willing to say yes.'

- **Just as with professional fundraisers, donors who ask must invest time in developing a relationship with those they wish to ask:**

  'It's like selling consultancy. You need a relationship.'

  'You can't do it cold. Why should I give money to something I know nothing about? It may take three or four years to build up a relationship.'

- **Askers must be prepared for rejection and not take it personally, or make it a personal issue:**

  'Nobody likes rejection very much and you know quite a lot of it will be people saying no.'

  'You've got to be quite careful because if the person says 'no' you don't want them to feel guilty for saying no, so I think we've got to un-emote these transactions.'

'Often people don't want to ask because they don't want that confrontation with somebody, but I don't really mind. It is quite difficult. You want to be tactful, you don't want to embarrass the person or yourself. You do want to pressure them to give the money but you don't want them to feel bullied or to have a bad feeling about your charity, which they will have if you go too far.'

- **Askers can take advantage of norms of reciprocity:**
  'Having asked, and been asked, you end up with a peer set that you show solidarity with. There's an element of reciprocity [that can be more important than the cause].'

  'I don't have an amount in mind when asked by someone I respect to support a cause outside my chosen areas, but I have a range. If it's Mum or Dad's favourite charity it's £5,000, if it's an important professional circle it's probably in the £25,000 range. There are people with whom you do the mutual one-shot – a million for your project, a million for mine… I'm not quite sure why we do this!'

- **Askers must realise that their efforts may produce gifts of increasing value over time:**
  'It's a small percentage of those asked who give but some of them do and they may give more over the years.'

- **Some people prefer to ask one-to-one, others prefer asking in small groups, or to facilitate situations in which the charity can make the ask:**
  'We were asked if we would be prepared to go to a private dinner to speak about our philanthropy – it was a small dinner party in another donor's house for about 12 people but they wanted to get – I hate this phrase – 'high net worth people' that don't give, don't give a penny piece. So we thought, what can we do, will we come over all holier than thou? We can say: "this is how we've done it" but it's not necessarily what other people want to do.'

  'I did have one good experience of helping a charity that we know quite well – we give to them and my husband volunteers there. I helped to put on an event. I helped to invite the guests where the charity could talk very openly and knowledgeably about the project and quite a few people were really interested to hear about it. It made a great difference for them to hear how the money would make a difference, to meet the people and to be able to ask questions, rather than just getting a bit of literature that they might or might not respond to. It was a very different and unique experience for them. And the charity did it very well.'

'I'm more happy to invite people to attend a funding circle-type thing, where the projects come and present and it's up to my friends to decide whether or not to give.'

- **Some people find asking much easier than others:**

  'I'm very reluctant to do it. I don't know why I hesitate so much. I feel I'm not very good at doing it, and yet actually I'm in a position of knowing which are the effective charities.'

  'I've always had that sort of chutzpah. If someone says to me "that's very difficult and embarrassing but it really needs to be done", then I'm your man. But overall, the bottom line is a lot of money is raised this way, by people saying to their friends: "Oh, come on".'

  'I've been in business for 30 years so I don't have any problem asking for money, making the case as to why it will make the world a better place, in however small a way, and saying: "this is a really good thing, will you help?". It's not very difficult to ask for money so that some old people can get together once a month rather than sitting alone in their cottages – that's a pretty simple story, it will make their lives a little bit better.'

- **Asking gets easier with practice and success:**

  'I've become much more direct, I used to be very embarrassed about asking for money but I'm now much bolder.'

  'You just get more confident, if you practice anything you get better at doing it.'

  'I've been round the circle [asking for money] a few times and I'm a lot more confident now because I've worked out that people need to feel there'll be a direct impact and see how they can engage; they want to see results now.'

- **Donors who ask can emphasise the life-enriching aspects of giving, because they have first-hand experience of it:**

  'When fundraising for an arts organisations you talk about the pleasure you've had from helping put on this production, or supporting talent – the pleasure of seeing a talent develop over time – and then the add-on benefits of getting to know the artists or seeing how a production is put together. So it is about the joy of the involvement and feeling that you personally made a difference.'

Conclusions

The findings presented in this chapter show that donor care, or what is sometimes called 'stewardship', is not only about looking after donors after they have given. It is also about encouraging and supporting donors in the lead up to, and during the process of, asking. Our research shows that the best experiences of being asked involve being approached by peers, and allowing time for a relationship to develop. Although the professionalism of fundraisers is thought to be getting better, there is room for further progress.

Nevertheless, the overall improvement in donors' perception of fundraisers will be pleasing to a fundraising sector that has invested heavily in professionalisation, for example, by writing new codes of practice, renewing policies, and enhancing the suite of accredited qualifications.

The development and management of the relationships with donors, who should be seen as partners in the delivery of the mission, is the responsibility of everyone – from chair and trustees to chief executive and those who head educational faculties, conduct research, direct and manage social welfare and care programmes, put on performances and exhibitions, and curate national assets. This means, as originally strongly advocated in *WRPG*, and echoed in other influential studies such as the Thomas Report (as discussed in the Introduction), that a culture of both giving and asking must be embedded in the institution.

Asking is part of the responsibility for the development and long-term management of a relationship, from the moment that someone is identified as a possible donor. This has huge implications for the role of those in the fundraising or development office. After all what does 'development' mean but the development and management of relationships for the benefit of the charity? Most of the major donors we interviewed understand that the role of the fundraiser, especially in larger organisations, is to provide the administrative infrastructure to ensure that the cultivation of the prospects (a lengthy process), the asking and the stewardship run as smoothly as possible. But they do not expect to have their key links with the fundraisers, except for practical arrangements.

There are still far too few organisations that have understood this and thought through the implications, not only for the fundraising team, but for all staff and trustees. Too many think of 'major donor development' as they think of direct marketing: a standardised process to be managed entirely within the fundraising team, only with bigger numbers.

Many fundraising organisations (small as well as large) do provide their donors with the experience that they are seeking – strong relationships and confidence that their money is well spent. But not enough have been willing to develop the corporate culture of engagement, nor invest in and oversee the institutional changes, all of which are required to underpin successful long-term fundraising from the wealthy.

In other words, the experience of becoming involved and then giving is neither as fulfilling nor as much fun for the donor as it could and should be. Undoubtedly, bad experiences are one factor in the reasons why people do not give, or do not give as much as they could. In the next chapter we review in some detail why rich people do not give.

Before that we offer practical examples of the successful application of the principles and processes our research shows are so clearly needed to secure major philanthropic gifts.

Notes

1 www.theresalloyd.co.uk/Publicationsandarticles/CulturalGiving/tabid/98/Default.aspx

Key ingredients for securing large philanthropic gifts

Caroline Underwood, The Philanthropy Company

I had the privilege of working with Save the Children between 2008 and 2011. During that time we were able to treble income from high value donors to support Save the Children's work with children and their families in over 70 countries.

So how did this come about? And what are the lessons about philanthropy that can be learned from Save the Children and other charities?

In my twenties I was lucky enough to be part of a start-up team for the Museum of Contemporary Art (MCA) in Sydney. There was no dedicated and internationally-focused centre for contemporary art in Australia and no government funding for such a venture. My role was to set up the direct marketing and membership programmes to engage people in the not-yet-opened MCA and, as a consequence of their subscriptions, raise funds.

Interest was high; we won direct marketing awards; but it also quickly became apparent that there was a group of people who were passionate about contemporary art and creating a space in Australia where both Australian and international artists could be shown in carefully curated exhibitions. Thanks to the leadership of Director, Leon Paroissien, and the board's investment, I undertook a substantive research tour to examine best practice in giving among US art museums. We then established structured gift levels and a programme for patrons tailored to the Australian market to build on the passion and knowledge of donors. This resulted in substantial philanthropic gifts, which have continued to grow as the MCA has developed

I was to see this passion again among audiences and writers at the Royal Court, where plans for a capital appeal were in play. Was it really possible to raise £26m (a sum that may seem small now but was then perceived as astronomical – the Royal Court was the first theatre to receive a grant from the National Lottery requiring matching funds) for a small theatre outside the West End with a reputation for raw plays performed among 'bedsit' scenery? Audiences, while not obviously wealthy, were engaged and enormously loyal. The leadership and vision of Stephen Daldry as Artistic Director was compelling; the Chairman was the engaging Sir John Mortimer and the Chair of the Development Committee, the simultaneously scary and charming Gerry Robinson, and then the energetic Elisabeth Murdoch. All were committed to the Royal Court and this trio, together with the extraordinary networks and personal generosity of Joyce Hytner, made up a magnificent team.

My job was to cajole, prompt, support and shepherd this team into focusing on raising big funds and we were able to raise the £26m for this much-loved theatre within three years

When I was part of a team looking at the potential for the Royal Festival Hall and the impact this might have on the transformation of the South Bank, we developed a business plan for fundraising that featured incremental growth, a donor 'pyramid' showing possible and expected gifts, and an income timeline. Critical to this was the experience and commitment of Dame Vivien Duffield DBE and her leadership gift to the campaign.

It may now appear obvious that a campaign to raise over £100m would need a business plan showing income – but it was not common practice until the substantive capital campaigns of the late 1990s. The business plan also included a joined-up communications strategy where the marketing and audience development was integrated with fundraising. Again obvious, but many organisations find this approach difficult to achieve, sometimes due to structures or a lack of will to make the strategic decisions to support fundraising.

Meanwhile, universities were achieving substantial philanthropic gifts. Years of cultivating alumni were resulting in generous and far-sighted gifts for buildings and academic leadership. Involvement with CASE (Council for Advancement and Support of Education) brought me close to the next generation of fundraisers who are committed and determined, and who offer a pool of talent and expertise in what is needed to raise significant donations.

So – passionate supporters. Compelling and persuasive leadership. Vision. Business plan and substantial investment. Talented fundraisers with enough track record and confidence to think big about major gifts. These aspects emerged time and again with a wide range of organisations seeking to raise funds. The same key elements are needed to drive an organisation forward, to attract talented staff, to achieve great things that attract philanthropists to give their personal support.

This model was to work again at Save the Children.

The more I looked at the powerful footage on the Save the Children website and the more I read about the impact it was having for children in some of the toughest places in the world, the more I could not understand how philanthropists were not getting involved. Clearly, there was huge public support, and the need was desperate. But the more I looked, the more I also saw how difficult it would be for someone who might want to make a major donation to find out how to do that. Who would they call? How could they find out which projects they might support? What if they wanted to understand the wider impact of a project on, say, the country government or policies?

I believe that many charities inadvertently put off major donors. Our big UK charities are outstanding at achieving small regular donations. And the public respond; millions and millions of pounds are raised every week in the UK through small regular gifts. But the challenge of securing more significant gifts from a small number of people remains a mystery for many charities.

Chief Executive Jasmine Whitbread and trustees of Save the Children took a bold leap and created my role of Director of Philanthropy and Partnerships – 'Philanthropy' in recognition of the new kinds of donors we wanted to attract and 'Partnerships' to reflect the new approach to working with corporates and trusts – not approaching them as a 'supplicant' begging for gifts, but as equal and strategic partners working towards specified aims. This was the first role with this title in the UK charity sector and many others have quickly followed.

The staff at Save the Children, as at so many charities, are enormously bright and committed. But nevertheless, the first year of Philanthropy and Partnerships was tough. Securing major gifts takes time; usually at least 24 months to build key relationships. Scepticism ran high. It is also difficult to measure the impact of particular initiatives; charity appeals for mass-market donations can be quickly analysed and scaled up or down to recognise return on investment. It is more difficult to do this with major gift fundraising. Gifts over £100,000 rarely emerge unexpectedly; they take time to secure.

Little by little we grew the staff team to support corporate, trust and major gift fundraising. Importantly, we placed real emphasis on our prospect research team and on a talented team of proposal writers who could liaise with the field staff to find out more about potential projects and, critically, research and prepare reports to donors. While this team is harder to justify in financial terms, it is a critical part of engaging and securing gifts from major donors. Fundraisers often spend 95% of their time trying to develop projects and just 5% fundraising.

So what are the elements needed to secure large philanthropic gifts? I would simply say that it takes a genuine need where philanthropy can make a difference; passionate supporters; compelling leadership, with both executive and volunteers prepared to be closely involved; vision; significant investment for several years; attitude; talented and well-cherished staff; business planning; and financial rigour with clearly articulated income targets. Rocket science? No. Sound strategy that results in philanthropic income? Yes.

Caroline runs the Philanthropy Company, a consultancy specialising in helping organisations improve their philanthropy programmes and ultimately grow their income.

8

Why rich people don't give

'I think we'll leave saving the world to you.'

What do we know about people who are not givers at all, or give very little? In this chapter we explore this crucial issue in depth. As our sample comprised rich people who do give, unsurprisingly, they were not able to answer this question directly. As one said:

'I really don't know – I just don't get it... It never occurred to me that I wouldn't make some contribution, it was just a question of working out how. I do not understand the mind-set that says: "we won't give".'

We base this analysis on the views, experiences and informed speculation of our interviewees, as well as existing research on this topic. We include suggestions from our expert observers, and examine the reasons given for not responding to requests. We go on to explore ideas of what can be done about it.

Why people don't give

There is no simple answer to the question 'why don't people give?', but the dominant reason seems to be because:

- **They feel financially insecure.**

Other reasons include:

- They lack empathy for potential beneficiaries.
- They don't feel it is their responsibility to help.
- They were not brought up or socialised with philanthropic values.
- They have fears about the consequences of starting to give.
- They lack faith in the capacity of charities to spend their money wisely.

150

We discuss each of these explanations in turn, illustrating them with quotes from our research. We explore the issue of lack of trust in the effectiveness of charities in some detail, since those who do give also express reservations about this. We consider whether there should be a suggested level of giving, whether people are giving as much as they can, and what might be done to address this. We also discuss the influence of tax incentives, and whether lifetime legacies can address feelings of financial insecurity. We end with a discussion about what might be done to encourage those who don't give to give.

- **Feeling financially insecure.**

  'Wealthy? £50m is the point at which you don't have to panic any more.'

As we noted in Chapter 3, feelings of financial insecurity are a key characteristic of many wealthy people, including some who nevertheless are donors. This factor featured prominently in *WRPG*, and prevails equally today.

Figure 8.1: Feelings of financial security

How financially secure do you feel on a scale of 1 to 10?
Where 1 = not at all financially secure and 10 = extremely financially secure
Figures within circles indicate number of donors choosing this option

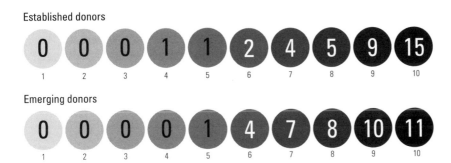

As in 2002, we asked respondents how financially secure they feel on a scale of 1 to 10, where 1 indicates 'not at all secure' and 10 means 'extremely secure'. There was not much difference between our two sub-samples, but the lowest response recorded (4) came from an established philanthropist, despite this group showing a slightly higher average of 8.7 than the emerging philanthropists, who rated their financial security as 8.3. There were respondents in both groups who answered '10' and the average across the whole sample was 8.5.

We also asked respondents to state the minimum level of net worth they would need to have in order to have answered '10' on the question posed above: i.e., in order to feel 'extremely financially secure'. More than half the respondents rose to the challenge of addressing this rather difficult question, though some suggested that an answer was impossible, for example noting that: 'It depends on age and stage of life'. Others disputed the possibility of attaining total financial security: 'No amount – it would never be 10 because of acts of God'. Someone with inherited wealth offered an interesting explanation for their inability to answer this question, on the basis that being financially insecure was simply beyond their experience:

> 'My current net worth is already in excess of what I would need to feel extremely secure, so I find it hard to set a figure for what the minimum would be. Having grown up with this income I don't have a counter-factual.'

For those who did feel able to name a figure, the range was very large, from as low as £1m to as high as £1bn. The figure suggested most frequently was £10m (by six donors – three established and three emerging), followed by £5m (which got four 'votes', three of which were from established donors).

However, we find that some respondents' feelings of financial insecurity are inconsistent with their stated actual wealth holding. An established donor claimed to feel a '6' out of '10', and that the amount needed to score '10' was 'possibly £4m-£5m'. Yet when asked a few questions later to state their net worth (the order of questions was intentional!), they placed themselves within the band '£5m-£9.9m'. This phenomenon, albeit demonstrated by a small minority, also featured in 2002.

Some of our sample can also appear out of touch with objective assessments of wealth and financial security. Another established donor, who describes their net worth as being £5m-£9.9m, only rated themselves a '5' on our financial security scale of 1 to 10. When asked how much they would need to score 10, they replied: 'Much more than is thinkable', perhaps unaware that a fortune of over £5m is already beyond the reach and imagination of most people.

Clearly, assessing one's own financial security is a subjective question, and the answer depends in part on temperament and outlook. While four donors whose net worth was 'only' in the second lowest bracket (£1m-£4.9m) rated themselves as feeling entirely financially secure (10 out of 10), a handful of respondents believed that no amount could ever achieve a '10' on the scale, because the world is too uncertain. As one emerging donor said: 'You never get to 10 because you never know what the future holds'.

The inability accurately to assess one's own wealth, to act in accordance with one's own definition of financial security, and the insistence that financial security is unattainable, all create genuine challenges for the encouragement of philanthropy. People will not give if they do not feel financially secure, even if objectively, and by their own definition, they do indeed have enough money to face whatever the future holds for them.

Feeling financially insecure is a major barrier because the people concerned consider that they have no surplus wealth to give away. This is not necessarily an unrealistic sentiment. As Martin Brookes, then chief executive of NPC (New Philanthropy Capital), stated in the 2010 Barclays Wealth report *Barriers to Giving*: 'Many feel it can be a bit premature to give away large amounts of money if they don't know how much money they need or have actually got.'[1]

Leaving aside the interesting position of not knowing how much money one has 'actually got', the question of how much people feel they can 'afford' is crucial. Believing that they could 'afford to give' was cited by 50% of those interviewed for the *Barriers to Giving* report.

Many of the donors in our survey have first-hand experience of peers (family, friends and colleagues) who claim not to be able to afford to give:

> 'I think one of the principal reasons why a lot of people who could give don't give is just the sense of basic insecurity… that somehow disasters are going to strike or their whole life is going to fall apart, or they may have liabilities that they didn't have. And that actually includes a huge number of people who are getting through several hundred thousand a year.'

> 'Some people can't reasonably afford to give or they think they can't reasonably afford to give. They need more for their own purposes. It's because people's aspirations has been driven up and up by what others have, consumerism, brand worship.'

We know that to many these feelings are no less powerful for being apparently irrational. In other words, there is a perceived psychological cost of giving that is far higher than the actual cost. This phenomenon of feeling insecure while holding assets that the vast majority of the population would regard as 'more than is thinkable' was discussed in *WRPG* and reiterated in the academic literature.[1]

Efforts to increase feelings of financial security

It has been suggested that the best medicine for feelings of financial insecurity is to consider seriously what is needed to maintain whatever they regard as an adequate lifestyle, and build in a healthy margin. The rest can then be accurately viewed as surplus that is available for giving away. At least one of our interviewees has done this:

> 'I'm lucky enough to have more wealth than I need, and I have no desire to go and buy yachts and planes and all that crap. Years ago, I did the Rosenberg exercise and built in a large margin for living too long and being too sick. I decided what I'd give the children, and then set the rest aside in a charitable trust which I add to periodically, and that's for giving away. We set it aside into a trust and the next step was to find a strategic way of doing it.'

The 'Rosenberg exercise' is a reference to an influential book designed to help the wealthy calculate their capacity to give. It was written in 1994, but remains relevant today. (An extract is reproduced in Appendix 4.)

Rosenberg said:

> 'I am trying to convince people, especially wealthy people, that it is very much in their interest to give away much more and to create a society where they can live safer, happier, better lives... They just need to change how they think about how much they can afford to give.'[2]

We now explore some of the other key reasons for not giving that are identified in our research. The experts we surveyed offered several other ideas on why rich people don't give, and interviewees with experience of asking also reported a wide range of explanations and excuses. We discuss these in turn.

- **They lack empathy for potential beneficiaries.**

As Rousseau suggested nearly three centuries ago, the lives of the rich are so far removed from the lives of the poor that they lack any common fount of shared experience:

> 'Why are kings without pity for their subjects? It is because they count on never being human beings. Why are the rich so harsh to the poor? It is because they do not have fear of becoming poor.'[3]

We know that some do indeed fear becoming 'poor', and also that, as we have reported, many rich donors support pro-poor organisations. Nevertheless a knowledgeable observer suggests that some of today's rich don't give 'because they have no connection with society and their experience of life is so different, and there is no civic or communal engagement. Where are the exemplars?'

Yet nowadays, there are many exemplars on a global, national and local basis. A number of books and reports, including this research, the *Coutts Million Pound Donors Report* and *Giving is Good for You*,[4] provide first-hand accounts of the experiences and pleasures of giving, as well as the frustrations and lessons learned. Regional papers around the country publish stories of local giving. But the very fact that this lack of role models is identified as a constraint is an indication that more needs to be done. We would certainly like to see more regular and mainstream reporting of major philanthropy and return to this in our recommendations:

> 'No sense of a desire, interest or obligation in helping others less fortunate than themselves, giving opportunities or making the world a better or more beautiful place; perhaps a less generous spirit, or a less developed sense of a commitment to the community in which they live or work; perhaps a lack of understanding about the personal motivation or pleasure that might come from giving, set against a very clear understanding of the personal reward and pleasure gained from making more money or spending it rather than giving.'

As we noted in *WRPG*, under-giving by some rich people may be due to a lack of empathy, rather than meanness or financial illiteracy:

> 'I think a lot of wealthy people in society may live in a bit of a bubble, I don't think they're really exposed to it. You have to go and see the real problems there are in society. It's not enough to read about it in a newspaper. Unless you make it your job to do that, you can easily get into thinking that everything is fine in the world – especially when you live in a super-wealthy conurbation like London and you spend your holidays jet-setting off. But of course it isn't.'

One solution for those 'living in a bubble' is to be introduced to a project, shown the way and inspired, probably by someone they know. Earlier chapters explored the importance of the right person opening the door and asking. This remains as true now as it was 10 years ago.

- **They don't feel it is their responsibility to help.**

Allied to a lack of empathy is the feeling that 'It's not my responsibility'. Several people referred to those who feel that they are doing their bit by setting up and running a business, employing people and paying taxes, and have no further obligation or responsibility to wider society:

> 'I think also some people feel they've started a business, employed a whole lot of people and that's enough, they're entitled to enjoy the benefits of that.'

People may also think that there is already enough money going to that cause/organisation, or that funding the project in question is the job of government:

> 'It doesn't occur to them; they believe there is little incentive to; they believe they've paid their taxes, and therefore it's the state's responsibility to support health, education, culture, overseas development or whatever.'

> 'Some people don't give, because even when they are concerned [about an issue] they think the state is responsible.'

Linked with all the sentiments expressed in this section are attitudes regarding the role of the state and the appropriate partnership with private philanthropy. We explore this issue in more detail in Chapter 4.

- **They were not brought up or socialised with philanthropic values.**

Many observed that non-givers lacked a sense of duty to wider society:

> 'I think it's because they were not brought up to give.'

> 'People raised in the Sixties have a sense of putting something back into the community. People raised in the Nineties don't. It's about a sense of entitlement. It's about spending the money that they've made themselves. There's a whole psychological aspect to this.'

However, even those 'brought up to it' within the same family may make very different decisions:

'Some members of my family who got the same inheritance have got less involved than me, and there's a knowledge gap about how to do it in a satisfying way. And there's this fear of being pursued and asked and put in a difficult situation where you don't know how to say 'no'. They need to build up confidence. I tell them that the more you sit down and work out what you do want to give to, and have that clear in your mind, then you can legitimately turn around and straightforwardly say: "I don't give to that because it doesn't fit with my remit" or whatever. People need the confidence to say no to things they don't want to support without feeling guilty about it, because that stops people giving at all.'

Here again, we see the importance of getting started: 'building up confidence'. This is unlikely to happen if people are not asked by the right person in the right way. This was identified as a key factor by many of our expert observers, and confirmed by those with experience of asking among our donors, as we explore in Chapter 7.

Those who decline when asked, or give a reciprocal gift at the minimum level, are considered not to be making a philanthropic commitment, but giving what they can get away with:

'Greed. Where people think they can "get away" with not giving, many will.'

As our experts with fundraising experience and others have commented, some rich people will also hide behind the giving of time to excuse not giving money as well. This is true of too many trustees of organisations seeking funding. They do not feel they should give when they are asking others for money, even if they can afford to give. We discuss the giving of time by our interviewees in Chapter 6.

- **They have fears about the consequences of starting to give.**

For people who are not in the habit of giving, getting started may be delayed by a fear of the consequences. These include unleashing a plethora of applications, and adverse attention from the press:

'If they've never tried [it's because] they don't want to be pestered or bothered.'

Fears held by non-donors are also sparked and reinforced by problematic media coverage of philanthropy and philanthropists. As we also identified in WRPG, the negativity that surrounds philanthropy, often in the form of cynical and critical reporting about giving, is unhelpful:

'Reforming the press is a hopeless cause. We won't be able to change their negative approach. You need to accept from the outset that whatever you do will be rubbished in newspapers because that's what they're there for. If you are giving money away people will think you are doing it for self-aggrandisement.'

The adverse coverage is perceived to be both about wealth creation and wealth-holding, and about giving money away:

'The mindless media sledging of the wealthy and the successful is the biggest single deterrent to increased giving.'

In 2002 and also today, too many people working in the UK media attribute negative motivations to rich people's philanthropy, assuming that it is driven by social aspirations, desire for political access and hopes of obtaining privilege. Illogically, many are also convinced that the tax breaks available for charitable gifts can somehow make the donor better off.

Despite the ongoing cynical tone of much media coverage, in Chapter 4 we report the perception among most of our interviewees that the climate has generally become more positive for philanthropy:

'As more people have talked openly about their giving it has encouraged others to think about their own philanthropy at all levels.'

However, for the expert observers (some of whom are journalists), this is a nuanced and complex area:

'If philanthropy is to become mainstream and accepted as a part of everybody's life, we need more people talking about it. Media has a role to play here. They are not always interested in good news stories. But somehow philanthropy must become more media-friendly. Philanthropy needs a rebrand and a new image that makes it an aspirational and exciting activity.'

There may be more interest but still not unqualified approval, and some think the situation is just as bad, or at least as muddled, as it was:

'I don't think that public opinion has shifted... There is still the same mix of respect, doubts about motivations, and the same, general, lack of knowledge about philanthropy that there was in 2002, despite the greater press interest in philanthropists.'

- **They lack faith in the capacity of charities to spend their money wisely.**

A further group of reasons for not giving revolve around the issue of trust, and confidence in charities to do a good job. There can be an implication that the charity does not merit their money or time. A number of expert observers raised this question of confidence, but as with several other factors, it is often mixed up with other explanations:

> 'I think some people feel that philanthropy is soft, that it's intellectually soft. They've been in rigorous commercial environments, where there is an incentive for efficiency and all costs need to be justified and rationalised by the pursuit of those commercial goals and here is something that is in a different universe, and they can't make the jump.'

> 'The 'justifications' they give include un-evidenced and often prejudicial attitudes to charities, their 'costs' and their beneficiaries. Some of the most hostile of these attitudes may be voiced so fiercely because of an underlying sense of guilt about their lack of generosity or altruism. Others have very different attitudes to different types of giving – for example, they will happily donate large sums at a charity auction among their peers, but respond entirely negatively to a direct appeal from the same charity.'

Over half of our respondents (53%) believe that charities are inefficient in managing donations. Although some disquiet about charities may be based on a lack of understanding of how charities operate and the need to cover core costs or invest in fundraising, this belief is clearly a barrier to giving:

> 'There's also a trust issue. A lot of charities are run by good-hearted people, and that's wonderful, but they're not necessarily efficient or good at getting value for money.'

The 2010 Barclays Wealth research *Barriers to Giving*,[5] found this lack of confidence to be even more widespread. Efficiency and the amount spent on administration are cited as the most important factors when selecting a charity (89% and 88% respectively).

Current donors are obviously sympathetic to the charities they support, but if even supportive donors have these reservations, they are unlikely to be able to reassure others they are trying to introduce to a cause.

We note that one response to this situation is the small but significant trend for new entrepreneurial philanthropists among our emerging donors to establish and run their own non-profit organisations, sometimes raising money from others. Some in turn develop strategic partnerships with existing non-governmental organisations (NGOs). Others design, test, refine and implement an operational model. Yet others are working in partnerships with governments. Often, this is not only because they want to be hands-on, and see themselves as social entrepreneurs, but also because they do not respect the way they think traditional charities operate.

However, only a very small minority establish new entities. The great majority of those interviewed support existing charities, including in sectors where they are unlikely to set up their own institutions, such as universities, arts organisations, hospitals and hospices, and local community activities. This does not mean they have complete confidence in their efficacy. The implications for individual charities, and for the sector as a whole, are clear. We return to this in our recommendations.

Other research has examined this question of trust, and suggested a response. In 2012 STARS Foundation[6] undertook research[7] on the perceptions of trust, risk and collaboration within international funder-charity relationships. The results indicate a need to change the way organisations are funded, with more focus on collaboration between the charities and their funders to develop projects and solutions together. This would encourage innovative thinking and sustainable funding, and signals a shift away from overly prescriptive funding models. In other words, these strategic relationships rely on building trust and understanding between funders and the organisations they fund.

Are people giving as much as they can?

'Oh no, no, no, not by miles.'

The Barclays Wealth research on barriers to giving was based on a survey of 500 high net worth individuals in the US and UK, including 150 with investable assets of over £3m. It found that only one-third gave more than £10,000 a year – less than 1% of their net worth. These figures seem to demonstrate a culture of under-giving. To quote one of our interviewees when asked are people giving as much as they can:

'Of course they're not.'

One interviewee gave a thoughtful response, attempting to understand why so many people give less than they can afford:

> 'I think there's a level at which you're comfortable giving money away, and it's probably different for everybody. It's like there's an amount of money you're comfortable spending on a bottle of wine at a restaurant and there's no particular logic to it, at some point the price of a bottle of wine in a restaurant just seems unreasonable and it isn't really to do with whether you can afford it, it's to do with whether or not you think it's reasonable. I think people have a level of giving where they think "I can afford that but I can't really go above that without having to worry about where money's going to come from for other things". And I would guess it's about 2.5% of income. Let's say somebody's making £1m a year in the City, he would give £25,000 a year to charity but he might think £50,000 is a bit much. It's not meanness, it's just a psychological thing.'

But as we have noted, it is extremely unlikely that someone earning £1m a year would give £25,000; it is more probable that it would be significantly under £10,000. It is important to acknowledge that there is no sense of smug complacency among those we interviewed. An extremely generous donor, at the top of our scale, said:

> 'We're not giving as much as we can. Even I'm not giving as much as I can. I mean, I'm not. There's some comfort in knowing that if everything goes pear-shaped I have enough to cushion me through that unknown. At some point I could say: "I can live very well on £1m a year, there's no need to give anything to my kids, therefore I will only keep £60m".'

The need for wholesale changes in attitudes to money, both within families and across society, was echoed by another interviewee:

> 'We need a change of values. We need to start with those who are making large sums of money. Many of them still don't get it. The culture has to change.'

Is it worth suggesting a percentage of income?

> 'I suppose it's fine if it suits some people, but it wouldn't work for me mathematically. I know what we're giving away and right at the moment I'm giving away something like 35% of my income.'

Despite the fact that using a percentage of income as a guide may not be appropriate for those whose wealth lies in assets (both liquid and not), thinking about giving as a percentage of income is an easily-understood marker. In Chapter 6 we explored the attitude of our interviewees to the idea of allocating a percentage of their income or wealth for philanthropy, and found that while this idea does not appeal to some people, others were adopting it as an approach or think it might be a useful guide in the future:

> 'It is such a private area and it isn't spoken about very much so it probably is quite useful that people get a sense of how much to give away.'

Yet outside the concept of tithing related to religious traditions there is little sense of a benchmark or goal. The decision to set The Giving Pledge, discussed in Chapter 2, at giving away 50% or more of wealth has proved a useful catalyst to stimulate ideas about how much one might commit to charitable giving:

> 'I think The Giving Pledge – which hasn't been talked about nearly as much in the UK as in the States – is about the really wealthy. But I think more people are asking questions – does that mean you have to sell your business in order to do that? So your heirs won't inherit your business? I really believe The Giving Pledge is a way of raising people's sights and encouraging them to give more. It is a fantastic opportunity for people to ask themselves and their families what the wealth is all about at the end of the day.'

The Giving Pledge may indicate some kind of aspiration for the super-rich – but what about those who are less wealthy but very affluent nonetheless?

Over the years, various suggestions have been made for what we might call a secular level of tithing. The Giving Campaign suggested a level of 1%, with the marketing slogan: 'Can you afford to live on 99% of your income?' In May 2004 Chair of the Campaign Lord Joffe said in the House of Lords:

> 'If the level of giving is to increase significantly, it is the well off who must substantially increase the level of their donations. Do we want a society where the wealthy focus solely upon self-gratification, buying yachts, personal jets and other play things, or a caring society where everyone contributes as generously as they can to make a better society for all?'

Lord Joffe proposed a benchmark for charitable giving in the UK, and developed his ideas from the 1% of the Giving Campaign. He proposed that individuals should be encouraged to consider their giving in relation to their income and wealth, giving an average of 1.5% to charity. This benchmark could be on a sliding scale according to each individual's wealth, with the well-off aiming to give a minimum of 2% each year and the particularly wealthy a higher percentage, going down to virtually nothing for those on annual incomes below £10,000. The overall target should be for individual donations to double over the next 10 years. He suggested that it is the wealthy, rather than the poor, who should lead the way. However, as of mid-2013 none of these ideas have been taken up.

We asked our donor interviewees what they feel about a benchmark of 1%. Some slated the idea for setting the bar far too low:

> 'How can anybody be satisfied with that and be prepared to say it? It's shameful.'

> 'I think that's pathetically low! That would mean a person earning a million pounds a year would give away ten grand, that doesn't make any sense, it's far too low.'

> 'I can't see any harm in trying it, let a thousand flowers bloom. But I wouldn't want it to be seen that the acceptable amount is 1% of income, I think that's pathetic. I think the old zakat[8] was 10% wasn't it?'

Some suggested that it might be useful as a starting point:

> 'If everyone gave 1% it would be a huge step forward.'

> 'I think part of it is to encourage people to start giving, and you'll generally start low, and then to encourage them up. So if it helps to get them started then that's fine, but not as an overall rule.'

But many felt that the idea of a percentage is unhelpful, too prescriptive and fundamentally unambitious:

> 'I don't believe in quotas and percentages. What matters is that people give something.'

Several people pointed out that calculations based on a percentage of income are far too simplistic and fail to account for 'lumpier' one-off donations that constitute a larger absolute amount than giving away a steady trickle each year:

> 'We put 40% of the money we made when we sold the business into our foundation but that was years ago, so in any given year we would not appear very philanthropic.'

Are more or simpler tax breaks the answer?

The question of tax breaks and the simplification of the tax system is complex. Better tax incentives were thought likely to increase the level of donations by about a third of those interviewed for *WRPG*, with a further small number suggesting that better information about tax benefits would be beneficial. The Barclays Wealth research reports that over half of their respondents (52%) say the most effective way for the state to encourage donations would be to increase tax breaks. Yet it is clear that some tax reliefs still go unclaimed and there is scope for greater education about the availability of existing fiscal incentives for those who do not give, or give little. These include not only tax-efficient donations out of income, including payroll giving, but also gifts of shares and other appreciated assets, a much-underused mechanism of giving.

It is unclear whether ignorance of tax breaks is being used as an excuse, or whether people are genuinely unaware of the existing opportunities. Greater involvement of advisers might address this, as we discuss in Chapter 9.

It is also apparent that, as discussed in Chapter 7, donors are not impressed with the way that charities explain tax breaks or help with planned giving. There is huge room for improvement.

As we pointed out in *WRPG*, and many people have since, including the Thomas Report[9] and the Philanthropy Review,[10] one way of addressing feelings of financial insecurity and incentivising giving in the lifetime of the donor is the creation of lifetime legacies.[11] These are a form of split interest trust, much used in the United States since the late 1960s. They allow a donor to make an irrevocable gift to a charity during their lifetime, of shares, property or cash, while retaining the benefit of the income or use of the gift for the term of their life. In other words, they don't actually part with it until they die. The donor can make deductions against capital gains tax at the time of the gift and its value is not counted as part of their estate for the purposes of inheritance tax.

The Lifetime Legacies coalition (an ad hoc group of lawyers, tax experts, advisers, charities and others) believes that many people who do not currently feel able to make a significant commitment of support to charity, because of their existing or anticipated commitments, would take advantage of this opportunity. It would also allow charities to grow support in a new community of donors. We support this initiative.

What (else) can be done to encourage those who don't give to give?

As we report in Chapter 4, the key drivers for those who give include belief in the cause, making a difference, and believing philanthropy is the right use of surplus wealth. Donors are also clear about the complementary roles of government and private philanthropy, and believe that family engagement in philanthropy helps to instil desirable values in their children. They appreciate the recognition that comes with being philanthropic, and, most of all, they get joy out of giving and believe that philanthropy enriches their life.

How to inculcate these crucial elements? Several of our interviewees expressed concern about the decline in values and family traditions of charitable giving:

> 'It struck me how important it is to hit the wealthy children with this; why aren't boarding schools – who are themselves charities – promoting more about philanthropy in the classroom so that children from quite a young age get an understanding of what philanthropy is about?'

There was a widespread emphasis on reaching and teaching the next generation:

> 'Encouraging philanthropy is very much about teaching children in school. Each school should allow three hours of volunteering a week and create a structure for young children to volunteer. Role models are also important, but it's not about celebrities, it's about real role models that people can identify with.'

Some philanthropists are supporting this through projects such as the Youth Philanthropy Initiative:[12]

> 'So taking a long view is important to aim at the 25-year-olds. It is they who will be instrumental in forming philanthropy in the future.'

Others think it is the job of government:

> 'It's like playing football and nobody's bringing the team together – and that's got to come from government. If the government taught philanthropy to schoolchildren, it wouldn't change everybody but if it changes 5% or 10% of the population, that's worth doing.'

But not all agree:

> 'I wonder if we are too obsessed with telling governments that they have to do something. I think they largely should stay out of it. We as charities have to get better at saying why help is needed, why we are the best way to connect capital with social needs, and we of course need philanthropists to use their convening/peer power.'

However it is done, a combination of teaching and role models is essential:

> 'Better education at a younger age – and there are some great schools programmes – is also key to normalising giving, particularly in a secular society.'

> 'It's a combination of role models, teaching and then making sure that people understand about research and due diligence on the charities. This generation doesn't have a clue so it has to be re-thought. It's about how to be passionate if you like. It's an art as well as a process, so the role models have to be people whose lives have been transformed by becoming philanthropists.'

But as we have already discussed, in our review of feelings of financial insecurity, what can be 'afforded' is only one factor.

Getting going

It is hugely important that the early experiences of serious giving are positive and reinforcing. The journey must be enjoyable from the very beginning:

> 'So often a particular opportunity or a call on you comes at a time when you can do it but I think the big journey people go on is discovering the joy in giving. And there is a joy in giving if you're sufficiently close to see the results. I don't think everyone has to be a hands-on donor, asking for reports on exactly what's happened, I think people's motivation differs, but I think you need to be close enough to be able to somehow see the results. And then you get a vicarious pleasure from saying: 'I helped make that happen' – that itself is enjoyable. I have a line that I use in speeches that there's a diminishing return in spending money on luxuries and there's an increasing return from spending money on philanthropic giving. I profoundly believe that.'

Once people have engaged on the philanthropic journey, other factors kick in:

'I don't think people get rich and then immediately think: 'I should give some away', I think it's a much more gradual process than that. Learning about it and becoming comfortable with it, and that comes about in a variety of ways.'

'I remember when I was earning quite a lot of money and being asked for £1,000 a year and that seemed like a huge sum of money – and although it is a lot of money to some people – at that time it actually it wasn't to me. But it's a question of people getting used to it [having the money to give].'

'There may well have to be a stimulus for getting into serious giving.'

Conclusions

While our research describes and celebrates the fulfilment of giving, too few wealthy people are sharing that experience. However irrationally, many feel that they cannot afford it; they feel insecure. In addition, some live in a 'bubble' and are thought to lack empathy for potential beneficiaries; they do not feel that it is their responsibility to help – they pay their taxes. For some this is compounded by the absence of the philanthropic values that are so manifest among our interviewees.

The situation is not helped by fears that once they start giving they may be inundated with requests, and be pilloried by those elements in the media that appear to despise wealth creation and will question their motives. And some (including those who do give) express concern that charities are ineffective and do not account well for the monies they receive.

We report a mix of views on suggesting a prescriptive level of giving. Many feel that 1% of income is too low, and too simplistic an approach for the very wealthy with a complex portfolio of assets. Others feel it is better than nothing, and may help to establish some kind of social expectation or norm.

Tax incentives are used by our donors, but are not well understood by the wider world. This is also not helped by media misrepresentations, but there is a need and an opportunity for advisers and beneficiary organisations to be more effective at explaining them. The introduction of lifetime legacies would help address feelings of financial insecurity and enable people to enjoy giving while living.

There are several players who should contribute to encouraging the wealthy to give more, including government (through tax incentives and challenge funding, and investing in education of the next generation), and the media (celebrating role models and raising awareness of opportunities for giving time, expertise and money). But unless the crucial matters of personal feelings, values and the early experience of giving are addressed by organisations seeking funding there is a risk that any interest aroused is likely to be short-lived. In particular, the sense of personal fulfilment gained through giving reinforces commitment and involvement.

Notes

[1] P. Wiepking and B. Breeze (2012) Feeling Poor, acting stingy: the effect of money perceptions on charitable giving. *International Journal of Nonprofit and Voluntary Sector Marketing,* vol 17, issue 1, pp.13-24.

[2] Quoted in his obituary published in 2008 by the Stanford Graduate School for Busienss. http://tinyurl.com/pzeh6kc

[3] Rousseau cited in Nussbaum, 2001:263,259.

[4] John Nickson (2013) *Giving is Good for You.* London: Biteback Publishing.

[5] Barclays Wealth (2010) *Barriers to Giving.* Prepared by Ledbury Research.

[6] www.starsfoundation.org.uk

[7] http://tinyurl.com/omejfoq

[8] Zakat is a Muslim obligation to give away a portion of wealth. In fact it is not a standard 10%, but varies depending on the amount of wealth and the type of assets the individual possesses. Other religions also advocate tithing wealth or income for charitable purposes.

[9] http://tinyurl.com/pdu5dec

[10] http://tinyurl.com/3v7ck55

[11] For an explanation see www.ctrg.org.uk/campaigns/lifetimelegacies

[12] An initiative started by the Canadian Toscan Casale Foundation. It now has UK backers including the Pears Foundation, the Wood Family Trust and the Paul Hamlyn Foundation, as well as government support via the Cabinet Office and the Social Action Fund. www.goypi.org/partners-donors.html

9

Who advises the rich on giving?

One of the major developments in the world of philanthropy over the 10 years since our original research has been the growth of an increasingly professional infrastructure to support and advise donors on their giving. From being an add-on to the traditional work of lawyer or accountant, philanthropy advice has become a dedicated service offered by many of the major banks, law firms and tax advisers. In this chapter we discuss the findings of our survey of philanthropy professionals, who together have a combined experience of over 110 years supporting the giving of rich people.

We start with a review of the position in 2002, and go on to describe the very significant developments of the past decade. We consider the extent to which donors are taking advantage of this increased supply of professional expertise, and who else they ask for advice. We explore the experience of advisers, whether and when they take the initiative in raising the topic of philanthropy with their clients, and the kind of advice that is required. We look at the causes they advise on and consider the concerns raised by donors.

Advisers observe that an increasing number of their clients are giving in their lifetimes, despite the fact that feelings of financial insecurity forms a recurrent theme; and that tax planning is an important way of maximising the amount that can be allocated to charitable causes. We also report complaints made by clients about suggestions they are dodging tax and even somehow making money as a result of giving it away. We then look at changes in adviser services, often in response to market developments such as the growth in the number and range of investment products that are socially responsible or have social impact. We conclude with advisers' views on the broader factors that they believe influence the values and philanthropic decisions of their clients.

First, we review the situation when we last conducted this research, before presenting the new findings and discussing their implications.

Philanthropy advice in 2002

Ten years ago, the profession of 'philanthropy adviser' was embryonic in the UK. The key organisations in this space, notably the Institute for Philanthropy, NPC (New Philanthropy Capital) and Philanthropy UK, were all in their infancy. The Association of Charitable Foundations provided (and provides) practical advice on setting up trusts, as well as a range of guidance to members, and a small number of community foundations helped individuals with the development of their charitable giving. A few firms of lawyer and accountants, and some banks (mostly of US parentage), were providing advice to clients, but usually in the context of tax planning and wealth management, rather than specialist philanthropy advice.

Not surprisingly, the experience and perceptions of the advisers at that time reflected the range of attitudes and concerns reported by wealthy people themselves. Advisers believed that the factors that made rich people more likely to give were being self-made/entrepreneurial, aged at least in their forties or fifties, and coming from a strong faith tradition. They felt that some who had inherited wealth and came from a family with a tradition of philanthropy might also give, but this was less likely when combined with the responsibility and maintenance cost of an estate and collection being held for the next generation.

Other factors felt to encourage charitable giving were a desire to avoid tax, a reluctance to pass on too much to the children, and a wish for involvement in a cause, with accompanying recognition. Some advisers observed that attitudes to leaving money to children might change as people aged: a combination of family pressure, a realisation that the children are able to handle wealth, and a sense that 'blood is thicker than water' may account for this.

Advisers reported that feelings of financial insecurity were unrelated to actual levels of wealth, but rather linked to a lack of confidence that lost or diminished assets could be replaced. Entrepreneurs were less likely to share that worry. Estimates by advisers in 2002 of the level of wealth needed for financial security varied, but the most common range (reflecting client actuality) was £30m to £50m. A few advisers were aware of the theories of Claude Rosenberg, discussed in the previous chapter, and advocated their application as part of a general programme of awareness-raising in the UK.

Ten years ago, few advisers saw the active promotion of philanthropy as part of their role, but nearly all felt a responsibility to advise their clients of the available options, mechanisms and benefits, both in terms of tax and for the family. Some observed that a lack of understanding by their clients of their real level of wealth combined with the absence of a tradition or expectation of giving and, in some cases, perceived complexity of giving, led to inactivity. This was reinforced by uncertainty as to the appropriate level at which to give and a lack of time to devote to the question.

Adviser views on the minimum wealth required to set up a charitable trust ranged from £100,000 to £10m. Nobody suggested using a trust as a mechanism to channel regular transfers of income. There were also comments about the absence of tax incentives to encourage gifts of capital in the lifetime of the donor, such as those available in the US.[1]

Ten years on, what do we find?

As we saw in Chapter 2, the philanthropy landscape has undergone some very significant developments in the past 10 years. But in relation to the availability of advice, the situation has been transformed. We have seen:

- The growth of a stronger and larger group of specialist providers of philanthropy advice, and services such as donor advised funds and the provision of administrative support, to a range of wealthy individuals, families and corporates.
- The creation of expert departments within banks with a growing number of clients drawn from their high net worth customer base.
- Leading legal firms providing expert technical guidance and support.
- The strengthening of the nationwide network of community foundations.

- An expansion in the number of other networks linking funders with shared interests, ranging from the very private to more open and accessible groups.
- A more serious interest in the provision of professional education to practitioners, for example, through the STEP/Philanthropy Impact Philanthropy Programme,[2] and the launch of the STEP Philanthropy Advisers Special Interest Group.[3]
- The availability of free online advice from a number of sources.

These developments demonstrate the widespread perception, by a range of experts, of the importance of a facilitating infrastructure comprising people and organisations to which the rich can turn for advice, reports and recommendations, introductions, education and administrative support. This is backed by significant investment in expertise and training, including the establishment of specialist departments by banks and wealth managers, legal firms and accountants, and the proliferation of specialist philanthropy advice firms.

However, the experts we surveyed were equally divided as to whether the availability of better philanthropy advice has in fact made much difference to UK philanthropy over the past decade.

Are more donors taking up philanthropy advice?

Although the number of those who seek advice is growing, the advisers we surveyed reported that fewer than half of their wealthy clients raise the topic of philanthropy without prompting. A key factor to track going forward is whether and how this changes in the next decade.

As we saw in Chapter 4 (Table 4.3), a third (35%) of all donor respondents believe the availability of better philanthropic advice has been a significant development in UK philanthropy in the past decade, with emerging donors more likely to hold this view than our group of established donors (43% against 28%).

As Table 9.1 shows, just over a quarter (28%) of our respondents have sought advice, and in most cases (24% of the total) that advice influenced their giving plans.

Table 9.1: The incidence of seeking philanthropy advice

	% of all donors	% of established donors	% of emerging donors
I have not sought philanthropy advice on my giving from a professional adviser	56	73	40
I have sought philanthropy advice and it has influenced my giving plans	24	14	33
I have not sought philanthropy advice but might do so in the future	16	11	21
I have sought philanthropy advice but it did not influence my giving plans	4	3	5

Seeking advice is far more common and acceptable among the newer donors. While three-quarters (73%) of the established group have not sought advice and only 11% might do so in future, a third (33%) of emerging donors have already sought such advice and a further fifth (21%) see it as a viable option in the future. This is not to write off the older donors as potential clients of philanthropy advisory services, as some report extremely satisfactory results:

'It helped to make us more professional in our giving and also made us really think about what kind of projects we wanted to support and what we did.'

All who reported a good experience of seeking advice emphasised that the support 'helped me to be more strategic in my giving'. One enthusiastic newer donor reports:

'It helped me to focus on the most appropriate area and find a way into the debate about the best way to fund.'

However, donors who do not seek professional advice still involve others in their giving decisions. As Table 9.2 indicates, donors consult a range of people – two-thirds (67%) consult their partner, and over half (57%) ask trustees of their foundation. Nearly a quarter (22%) discuss it with their children, and one in seven consult colleagues. Others 'might ask knowledgeable people' or 'might phone other donors who are already engaged'. These 'consultations' sometimes solicit views on the leadership of the potential beneficiary and how successful it has proved at delivering outcomes:

'I consult regularly with the other donors in my sector and foundations that share my objectives. We share information on the effectiveness of grantees.'

Table 9.2: Who do you consult before making a major donation?

	% of all donors	% of established donors	% of emerging donors
My partner	67	66	68
Trustees of my trust or foundation	57	58	55
My children	22	16	29
Professional advisers	17	13	21
Colleagues	13	16	11
Other family members	9	8	11
Friends	8	8	8

Some interesting differences emerge in this finding: both sets of donors consult their partners or fellow trustees to a similar extent, but newer donors are twice as likely to involve their children. They are also more likely to consult 'experts'.

Several emerging donors mentioned either NPC or the Institute for Philanthropy as a key influence at an early stage:

'The Institute for Philanthropy workshop inspired me to set up my social enterprise.'

Some have maintained their relationship with their adviser over many years:

'My adviser and I work together both strategically and tactically. It is a close working relationship that has run several years. My adviser has been very influential in shaping my philanthropic activity.'

The range and nature of the advice sought varies, from how to get started to ongoing support:

'It influenced the type of grant made – to core costs or project, and one-off or multiple year – and where it went, looking at effectiveness and the impact of the organisation and its sustainability, and type of cause – social change or preventative.'

And several credited their adviser with helping them to become more effective:

> 'When we first set up the trust we were well meaning, but very disorganised and fairly unfocused in our giving. We then met with NPC to help try to focus our giving. NPC helped us to think about the gaps in the sector we are interested in... for example, transition to adulthood for disabled children. We [trustees] commissioned NPC to do some research into transition and this has shaped much of our funding since that time [past five years].'

However, not all the help comes from professional advisers. Skills transferred from the business and entrepreneurial sectors were mentioned more than once:

> 'I think as trustees we have got better at choosing good charities because of our association with a professional entrepreneur who has focused on commercial models until recently. He's now a trustee and has helped us to extend more commercial principles to our charitable aims. As a result our giving plan is more effective. I also completed an MBA about five years ago at London Business School. One of the courses I did was on social entrepreneurship and the adviser on the course also helped us to improve our giving plans.'

Not all of our donors wish to consult or collaborate with others: one (older) respondent's reply, in emphatic bold print, was 'NONE'! However, the advisers we surveyed feel that overall, social norms, including family expectations and peer group pressure, do influence their clients' philanthropic decisions. This is discussed further below.

Even if they do not take advice on their philanthropy, many donors, if not all, take advice about structuring their finances in a way that optimises their tax position and ensures the most effective management of their charitable funds. Some attend events related to charitable giving organised by their bank or law firm.

Who are the advisers now, and what is their experience with their clients?

While the advisers who responded to our request to participate in this research are self-selected, the same was true 10 years ago. We note a more complex and expert range of providers, reflecting changes in the broader marketplace.

Of the 14 advisers interviewed in 2002, 10 were partners in professional legal firms, two were partners in accounting practices, and two were senior bankers providing private wealth management services to high net worth individuals.

The categories of advisers interviewed in 2012 show a completely different profile. We see that of the 12 who participated, six are experts within banks and/or wealth managers, two are partners in leading law firms that include a philanthropy practice as well as tax planning, three are senior people within an independent professional organisation providing philanthropy advice, and one is a sole trader with similar expertise. Of the 12, two are full-time philanthropy advisers while the others provide philanthropy advice as part of the other services they offer, such as banking or legal work. But all had substantial experience – nine have been providing advice for eight years or more and none had fewer than four years' experience. It may be that those who had been advising for some time were more willing to share their knowledge and understanding by responding to our survey.

This shows that there is now a far wider range of sources of expertise, many of which have emerged in the past decade. Lists of advisers and the services they offer are available in the *Guide to Giving*, available on the Philanthropy Impact website.[4]

We asked about the proportion of their professional lives spent giving philanthropy advice, and the average was over 70%, with a minimum of 9% and a maximum of 100%. Clearly, this reflects the fact that most of the 12 are primarily focused on providing advice, whereas 10 years ago it was likely to have constituted a much smaller portion of their working day.

Half of the advisers surveyed *only* talk to clients about philanthropy, being specifically invited by colleagues or the client to do so. And seven out of 10 say that they would raise the issue if the client did not mention it first. Reasons include: if they believe the client would be interested in incorporating philanthropy into their wealth management; if they thought the client's personality indicates this would be of interest; if they were aware that the client had made substantial gifts; and if they felt the client had assets that could be put to philanthropic use.

When the topic has been raised, advisers report positive responses in two-thirds of the cases. Just over a fifth report 'neutral' reactions, and a small number have had negative reactions, but do not necessarily attribute these to a rejection of the idea. A 'neutral' reaction might mean that people might be interested, but not yet, and there are a few who wish their philanthropy to be very private: 'It does not mean they are not giving.'

Advisers believe that wealthy clients have become more open to talking about philanthropy in the past 10 years. Seventy-five per cent of our sample think that the responses are more positive than in the past, while the rest feel the response is too varied to pinpoint. Nobody suggests a more negative climate. We asked advisers to consider why this might be the case:

> 'There is definitely a greater interest among our clients around the world in philanthropy and more specifically in being more thoughtful about their philanthropy. This is due to the tremendous wealth creation around the world in the last 15 to 20 years; and the fact that much of this wealth is self-made.'

This sentiment was echoed among both the adviser and the donor community:

> 'My perception is that it is more normal for people with wealth now to think about how they use part of it to contribute through philanthropy. This is definitely becoming more normal in continental Europe... I also really notice a change in internal culture – colleagues now ask new clients about philanthropy interests as a matter of course. When I joined in 2008, it was thought by at least a few colleagues in the UK to be something embarrassing to raise. I don't know the extent to which the change has been caused by having a philanthropy adviser in-house and getting used to raising the question, and how much it has been caused by external changes in thinking around philanthropy.'

Several people identified greater awareness and, indeed, expectation among their clients that the issue would be raised:

> 'Clients generally are more aware that the issue might be raised and therefore more comfortable when discussing fees around philanthropy or the need for strategic advice.'

Despite donors' concerns about the negative impact of the media on perceptions of philanthropy, as discussed in Chapter 8, the media can play a useful role in raising awareness about improving philanthropy and the role of advice in making it more effective.

This is complemented by the activities of the advisers themselves:

> 'We are bringing it to them proactively, hence the ever-increasing number of clients who respond positively and then want to meet to discuss it.'

Some advisers also feel that along with the expectation that the wealthy should give, there is an increased awareness of need during the era of austerity prevalent at the time of this research:

> 'I think that, post-recession, people generally appreciate more the role they can play in the so-called 'Big Society' and the responsibilities we all have to do our bit to contribute. We are becoming a little more Americanised in expecting to make a philanthropic contribution, however large or small.'

We also asked which kinds of clients were likely to raise the issue of philanthropy unprompted. While it is, of course, difficult to generalise, the advisers we consulted said their client base in 2012 leans towards people who are over 45, self-made and feeling financially secure. Religion appears to be far less of a factor than it was 10 years ago.

What kind of advice do clients want?

The form that philanthropy advice takes is very varied, as shown in Table 9.3.

Table 9.3: Type of philanthropy advice requested

	% of adviser respondents being asked for service
Personalised discussion of their philanthropic interests, with tailored solutions on how their giving might be structured	75
Signposting to materials produced by other organisations, such as Philanthropy Impact, NPC or the Association of Charitable Foundations	67
Introductions to other donors who share their interests	67
Management of clients' philanthropy, including relationships with beneficiaries, project visits, assessment of feedback reports etc.	58
Recommendations of books and articles	50
The provision of training on strategic philanthropy	42
Introductions to external philanthropy specialists	33
Suggestion as to which charities they might support within their areas of interest	25
Introductions to potential beneficiaries	25

What are the causes on which donors seek advice?

It is plausible that donors seek advice for their giving to some causes but not for others. For example, a donor may not feel the need to consult an expert when deciding whether or not to donate to their old school or university, but may want help in deciding other projects to support, where they lack 'insider knowledge'.

As Table 9.4 shows, the top three causes advisers discuss with their clients are international development, human services and welfare, and education. Assistance with clients' own charitable trusts may well be required, but some causes barely hit the adviser radar, including environment and animals (which research shows is not a very popular choice for rich donors).[5] Religious organisations and causes and higher education, both of which normally attract a disproportionate share of the donations made by richer donors, are seldom discussed with advisers. We suggest this is due to familiarity with such causes on the part of the donor.

Table 9.4: Likelihood of philanthropy adviser being involved in clients' donations to cause areas

	Likelihood of philanthropy adviser being involved
International development	Very
Human services, and welfare (including children, older people, disability etc.)	Very
Education (not universities)	Very
Client's own charitable trust or foundation	Quite likely
Health (including medical research)	Somewhat likely
Arts and culture	Somewhat likely
Environment and animals	Not likely
Higher education	Not likely
Religious organisations and causes	Not likely

Other activities and services required from philanthropy advisers include:

- Administrative support.
- Involving the next generation.
- Creation of new charitable foundations.
- Advice on grant-making policies.
- Introductions to families who run their own trust and have experience of grant-making and impact assessment.

What are the biggest client concerns?

Advisers were asked what concerns matter most to their clients (Table 9.5).

Table 9.5 The main concerns of clients seeing philanthropy advisers

	% of clients having such concerns
Maintaining the value of their assets	85
The right amount to leave to children and other heirs	69
Ensuring enough for a comfortable old age	62
Having enough to provide for dependents	54
Increasing the value of their assets	38

As we see, the overarching concerns are the maintenance of their wealth and confidence in the future value of their assets, leaving the right amount to children and ensuring enough for a comfortable old age. Other concerns include legacy planning in such a way that 'does not spoil the kids' and 'using funds for good while I'm still alive, not waiting for death'.

The question of maintaining asset value is related to feelings of financial security, which, as we have established throughout this book, is a necessary condition for major giving:

> 'The more financially secure clients feel, the more likely they are to start to consider philanthropy.'

There was a wide range of views from advisers on how financially secure their clients felt in the turbulent economic period from 2008, with an equal proportion feeling their clients have become more secure as felt they had become less secure:

> 'The very wealthy have remained wealthy but overall as the economy has downturned people are generally more conscious of ensuring they have ways of securing their wealth and adding to their assets.'

> 'The financial climate has obviously affected clients' approach, but we still set up over 200 new charities last year – many of them new school academy charities, but a significant number promoted by individuals.'

We suggest that this consistency between the expressed priorities of donors and the perceptions of advisers on what concerns their clients reflects more openness and willingness to talk about these matters than was apparent 10 years ago. Provision for old age and death, how much to leave to children, and matters relating to inheritance – and inheritance tax – are recurring concerns.

Given the importance of these issues, it is interesting that few clients had discussed inheritance tax with their advisers. Only four say that their clients occasionally raise this topic, and just one says that it is often raised. It is more likely such issues would be discussed with a lawyer rather than a specialist philanthropy adviser. This quote reflects the nature of the adviser and the level of wealth concerned:

> 'A few very wealthy clients have already planned to leave most of their estates to charity and have made significant gifts to charity in their lifetime. One of the reasons they cite is that they do not want their money to go to the taxman in inheritance tax or income tax. There is little doubt in my mind that most people give more because of the tax reliefs available to them.'

We explored the views expressed by those clients who raised the question of inheritance tax rules, and how that relates to philanthropic decisions:

> 'The prevalent view is that money that has been taxed in one's lifetime (whether as income or capital gains) should not then be subject to another tax on death.'

It is not surprising that advisers note a link between tax planning and philanthropic decisions, not least because they are providing guidance on the most effective management of donor assets to achieve a range of goals and address the multiple concerns expressed by their clients:

> 'Some clients have expressed a desire not to leave all their wealth to their children but to leave it to charity. Some say they do not believe that the government/tax law should enforce rules: it should remain a personal/family decision. Most people do not give to save tax but hope to make any giving tax-efficient.'

Passing money to children

One of most significant and recurring issues for wealthy people is the question of how much money to pass on to their children. This concern goes across many cultures and levels of wealth:

> 'It is now more widely talked about that giving can be a way of offsetting money left to children. The damage that too much money can do to children is also discussed more openly.'

Half of the advisers say their clients are concerned about the amount of money that should be transferred to their children and immediate heirs, and this has influenced their philanthropic decisions:

> 'Some clients have expressed a desire not to leave all their wealth to their children as it is not healthy and does not educate them, but to leave to it to charity. They have gone on to establish a trust in their lifetime. Others have expressed views that while they will not leave all their wealth to their children, it should remain a personal/family decision and as such have involved their children in the process of giving/establishing donor relationships.'

In Box 9.1 we look at the example of Warren Buffett, one of the richest men in the world at the start of the 21st century, who has pledged to give away the bulk of his fortune, much of it via the Bill and Melinda Gates Foundation.

Box 9.1: Warren Buffet

Warren Buffett has famously said that the perfect amount of money to leave your children is 'enough so that they would feel they could do anything, but not so much that they could do nothing'.

Buffett, who has pledged to give virtually all of his $44.7bn fortune to charity, celebrated his 82nd birthday in 2012 by giving each of his three children $600m in the form of Berkshire Hathaway stock for their chosen charitable foundations.

It is interesting to note the report[6] in May 2013 that at the recent Berkshire shareholder meeting, an estate planning lawyer asked Buffett for advice on how his clients should determine how much is too much to leave their children.

Buffett said that parents' behaviour is probably more important than the size of any inheritance, because parents are the primary teacher for their children. But Buffett says he has been getting more generous towards his children as he ages, so every time he revises his Will he tends to leave them more.

None of the donors we study is as wealthy as Buffett, but the issues are the same.

Two-thirds of our advisers say that in the past 10 years (or since the adviser has been working in their field) their clients have become more concerned about leaving their heirs too much money, and none said that their clients have become less concerned:

> 'I think there is an increasing view that children should not be too 'feather-bedded' and should need to establish themselves in life. That in turn opens up the clients to being more generous with their philanthropy – "charity begins at home" is not so prevalent a view as it used to be.'

However, this factor should not be over-exaggerated:

> 'They still ensure their heirs have money and they still want to engage them in philanthropy.'

Advisers report that donors see the practice of philanthropy (and education in that field, such as attending training courses) as a way of enhancing values in their children, developing a respect for money, and ensuring an effective approach to the distribution of charitable donations.

Some clients do not want their children to inherit substantial wealth too young and look to defer the age at which their children become entitled to money. They also wish to educate their children to handle wealth responsibly. This often drives them to set up charitable foundations with the intention that their children will become involved in the decision-making and management.

The practice of philanthropy is not only an end in itself; it is also a means to a complementary goal:

> 'Philanthropy has become a positive solution for clients who want their children to develop a social conscience as well as understand the value of money.'

While most of our donor respondents have children, data from the UK Office for National Statistics shows that a fifth of women now reach the age of 45 without having a child.[7] This has implications for those seeking funding, not least in the form of legacies:

> 'It is of course often the case that the next generation or, more to the point, the lack of a next generation. may encourage greater philanthropic giving – that was certainly the case for the largest charity that I have been involved in establishing and running, where the founders had no children, were not on good terms with their wider family, and so decided to dedicate all their wealth to charity.'

But most people do have children, and concerns about how they will manage their lives, and their money, remain of paramount importance. As advisers note:

> 'A concern has developed in recent years concerning the next generation – they have not had to struggle hard to build up capital as previous generations and parents are more and more considering establishing charitable trusts and involving children in giving away money rather than passing it on. This leads to increased philanthropy and wiser money management, and hence more money for future generations to give.'

Giving while living

> 'Clients say that they want to see their money working, whether in business or in their philanthropic endeavours. They are often control freaks and want to keep control of how their money is spent. Both these factors are drivers for lifetime giving rather than giving on death.'

While the recurring question of passing money and values to children relates to the welfare of the children, giving while living addresses quite different impulses: having a hold over how the money is allocated and enjoying the pleasures of giving, described in Chapter 4.

Half the advisers (50%) report that the majority of their clients expect to do most of their giving in their lifetime, and 90% claim that over the past 10 years their clients have become much more likely to give in their lifetime. However, feelings of financial insecurity can still hold some back:

> 'I think that clients are receptive to the view that they should get the pleasure and enjoyment of making lifetime gifts, whether to existing charities or to foundations that they set up. The big deterrent to lifetime giving is, of course, the unknown cost of care home fees and whether they will need to provide for that.'

Some advisers suggest their client base is roughly evenly split between giving in their lifetime and giving after death, while others say their clients haven't decided yet. None believe the majority of their clients plan to do most of their giving in their Will. But of those who do plan to do most of their giving as legacies, advisers believe that two-thirds will give to charities their clients are already supporting, and one-third will set up a charitable foundation.

As we have seen, tax planning is an integral element in the range of adviser services. Tax reliefs enable donors to give more. In Chapter 4 we discuss at length the response of donors to the government proposals in the autumn of 2012 to cap tax relief – now withdrawn. Three-quarters of the advisers report that their clients raised this issue with them:

> 'The vast majority of my clients raised the issue with me. They were totally dismayed and could not believe that the Government would even suggest such a foolish move. They were adamant that this would lead them to drastically reduce their philanthropic giving.'

> 'A large percentage of clients were angry and felt the Government was mistaken and did not correctly understand philanthropy, or even how the tax incentives correctly worked!'

> 'They felt that the implication that they only gave to avoid tax was very misleading and unfair.'

Advisers report that their clients do understand that there is an issue, both in terms of the misuse of charitable structures and the question of the hypothecation of tax – dedicating the revenue from a specific tax for a particular expenditure purpose (for a full explanation, see Appendix 3):

> 'Clients understood the concerns but were disappointed with the debate in the media equating 'philanthropists' with 'tax dodgers'.'

> 'Some of our clients were angry that they were made to feel like tax dodgers when they were giving often vast sums away.'

What other changes have advisers seen?

Advisers also report significant changes in the broader field of the provision of advice. Bearing in mind that it is a small but heterogeneous and very experienced group of advisers, Table 9.6 shows how those we consulted feel the field has changed in the past decade.

Table 9.6 Changes in the world of philanthropy advice over the past decade

	% of advisers noting this change
Increased number of people and organisations offering philanthropy advice to wealthy clients	85
Increased number of clients of philanthropy advisory services	77
Increased professionalisation of the philanthropy advice field	69
Clients seeking more extensive and strategic advice	69
Clients seeking philanthropy advice at a younger age	69
Clients seeing the engagement of their children in decisions about charitable giving as a way of inculcating values	62
Clients seeing the allocation of funds to charitable causes as an integral element in the long-term management of their assets	54

We noted in Chapter 4 the overriding importance of 'making a difference' – as valid today as it was 10 years ago. The findings presented in this chapter show that many donors are taking steps to ensure they do make a difference, by seeking appropriate expertise and capacity building, and by putting in place mechanisms to assess effectiveness and impact.

People with this approach are more likely to be self-made and, as we have seen, a growing number are establishing their own very actively engaged grant-making foundations and sometimes operating charities – thus creating new organisations that will in turn embark on fundraising, often from the very individuals who, like them, want to do their 'own thing':

> 'I recall one very wealthy client who gives in order to realise strongly-held views, for example, funding a new faculty within a big university to explore an area the client considers needs greater resource in this country. We deal with a lot of individuals who come to us to set up special-purpose service-providing charities, rather than generalist foundations. An example is a recent case where the donors believe that there is not enough done to support carers of the terminally ill, and so established a charity specifically to promote support for carers.'

As we saw in Chapter 8 when exploring why some people do not give, or do not give much, the perception of need is sometimes combined with a lack of trust in the capacity and competence of existing charities to provide cost-effective solutions:

'People from non-philanthropic families tend to be people who have made money, for example, by the sale of a business or via private equity. They often have no experience of giving but want to make a difference. They are often focused on venture philanthropy, wishing to provide skills as well as money and keen that any charity/cause runs on a sou.'

The interest in what might be called alternative business models is not necessarily ideological, but rather a practical issue. This is another feature that has changed in the past decade. As we reported in *WRPG*, 'most people relied on the reputation of the charity and the fact that someone they respected was involved, and had confidence in the underlying regulatory system; if concerned they would check in advance. Although there were reservations about certain generic areas (for example, overseas development), knowing that the donation had made a difference was more important.'

Ten years on, donors are seeking advice about the competence of their potential beneficiaries, particularly in international development and in the areas associated with government spending – welfare and schools.

Donors are also increasingly seeking advice on socially responsible investments (SRIs). When we explored SRIs in 2002 this was a small emerging topic, and many rich donors were adamantly against the idea because they wanted to pursue investment strategies that generated the highest possible return on capital, and hence increased the amount available for distribution as donations. Furthermore, a decade ago the term SRI was mostly associated with avoiding investments in specific products such as tobacco, arms, or pornography. Even when the concept of social investment was more fully understood, it was felt to be a complex issue that needed time for consideration. Some were more ambivalent, but the perceived complexity was a deterrent – and perhaps the excuse. For people holding this view, there was a sense that the worlds of business and charity should remain completely separate, with no appreciation of the concept that pursuing lower financial returns may be the better strategy if it achieves a higher social return in the areas of interest to the donors.

We are aware that the assessment provided here is subjective and qualitative, and provided by a very small base. Nonetheless, our respondents suggest that matters have moved considerably in the area of SRI. Over half of our advisers report that some clients are interested in socially responsible investments for their family foundations, and a quarter report that some are interested in such investments for their family assets. However, to date it appears to some advisers that it is mainly the larger trusts that are exploring the opportunity.

There is a gap in the marketplace, and, as we discuss in Chapter 2, an identified need for qualified independent advice and structures that would encourage banks to include products that deliver a social as well as a financial return in their portfolios:

> 'Many clients are very interested. We are lacking decent independent advisory services and the market is not developed enough for us to offer a really good service within the bank. Additionally, clients view this very much as 'mission aligned investment' – so an alternative to their philanthropy. On the whole, people want to invest in companies/funds that tackle the issues they would otherwise be tackling with their philanthropy.'

More than one observed the immature state of the marketplace for social investment, the lack of understanding of the products and the lack of regulation:

> 'It's complex, unregulated and unknown. There is interest but it needs to have further clarity around it and probably more regulation.'

What factors do advisers think influence the values and philanthropic decisions of their clients?

Standing back from the immediate questions and processes, we invited advisers to explore their experiences of talking to wealthy people about their concerns and why they give. Since most of our sample have been providing advice for at least eight years, we received some very thoughtful and nuanced responses.

We invited advisers to offer an informed speculation on the importance of social norms – for example, family expectations or peer group pressure – as an influence on philanthropic decisions. On a scale of one to 10, where 1 was 'no effect' and 10 was 'extremely important', the average was nearly 6, with a range from 2 to 8. In other words, this very experienced group feel that family and societal expectations can be very influential:

> 'The 'Gates effect' has been very powerful, as has the example of other local philanthropists. Individuals have an increasingly strong feeling that they can be a real part of a solution. I don't know whether this is caused by the obvious failings of European governments, the wide and troubling gap between rich and poor, both locally and globally, or other reasons, but these big issues, combined with media reports and books about the impact that individuals have had on social issues, has created a prevailing view that philanthropy is important and can work.'

We see here several strands reflected elsewhere in this research:

- The importance of a respected example.
- The macro social and economic environment.
- The confidence that one can be part of a solution.
- The influence of media coverage.

The fact that their peers may be giving, and clearly getting something out of it as well, is also important:

> 'Many of them are very independent individuals, having built a business. But there is little doubt that people come to us having heard their friends or peers are doing more giving (and enjoying it) and wanting to try it out for themselves!'

It can also be a matter of status:

> 'It is becoming much more accepted that one should do something, possibly including setting up one's own foundation, and in that way keeping up with their peers.'

And yet again, as we explored in Chapter 7, the importance of who asks is crucial:

> 'People give to people and that influences their giving and often which charity's fundraising dinner they attend. They are often giving because they are asked by somebody!'

Advisers were asked who they believe are the main influences on their clients' ideas about the obligations of wealth. The strongest weighting was given to friends, with 70% thinking this category important – more than parents or wider family, each selected by half the sample. A third identified religious figures and business associates as equally influential. One or two mentioned the media and academia, and the influence of role models such as Bill and Melinda Gates and initiatives such as The Giving Pledge:

> '[There is the question of] the media and the influence of thinkers and academics on philanthropists. In my experience philanthropists are just the same as the rest of us: that is to say, their ideas and passions are formed by learning from the world around them, and that in turn is a process that is highly dependent on the absorption of ideas and information from the range of media. This is especially true for environmental issues, where many philanthropists who support climate change do so because of what they have read.'

It is interesting to juxtapose this with the fact that advisers also point to the core influences of religious tradition and family values on some donors:

> 'In the main, philanthropic decisions are personal and are affected by incidents during a person's lifetime. That said, people who have grown up in a community with a strong culture or a religious belief in philanthropy and giving do so [give] as a matter of course.'

However, as we report in Chapter 3, religious affiliation is less important for emerging donors than for those we interviewed 10 years ago.

Also as we found 10 years ago, there is a distinction between people who grow up with an expectation that they will give, whether or not they are wealthy, and others. Advisers observe that this is still the case:

> 'Many clients talk about the work their parents did and their commitment to the community – whether or not it was philanthropy. For example, working as a social worker, medical professional or teacher often comes up. Family values are the key.'

But equally some donors come to the whole subject of philanthropy afresh:

> 'Most of our [individual donor] clients are first generation philanthropists – mostly it's about them feeling lucky to have made so much money and wanting to give it back thoughtfully. The families that have a long history of giving are generally the less strategic ones – and more reluctant to spend money on philanthropy advice or changing their ways.'

Clearly, this is a diverse landscape. Another adviser said:

> 'People growing up in philanthropic families tend to be involved from an early age. We have seen a shift in recent years from just continuing with a replication of what their parents did to wishing to restructure family giving – wanting to understand the impact of their giving and to be more involved in projects.'

Given their extensive knowledge of donors, what do advisers believe are the triggers for giving? We have already seen a reference to 'feeling lucky' – a theme that emerged in 2002 – and it has not gone away:

> 'Mostly they give because they want to, feel blessed to have wealth, and want to try to make a bit of the world a bit better because of it.'

'There is a general theme of "giving something back". They realise that they have been very fortunate to amass the level of wealth they have and want to use some of it to help others – but in a targeted way. Some give because of religious commitment, others give, for example, to educational causes because they have "got where they are today" because they were able to benefit from a good education.'

Everyone has a mix of motives – some more 'pure' than others, perhaps, but all part of being human:

'There are personal motives – for example, health, being asked by somebody, being educated as having a responsibility, as well as "keeping up with the Joneses at the charity dinner circuit".'

We explored the question of desire for recognition in Chapter 4. This is rarely mentioned by advisers – the very people who have the most personal and private conversations with their clients. This finding lends weight to donors' claims that few of them are motivated by public acclaim.

As we have noted, a significant development over the past 10 years has been the willingness of people to be far more open about their philanthropy. Many of those we have interviewed have featured as donor case studies in the *Coutts Million Pound Donors Report*[8] and in John Nickson's book *Giving is Good for You.*[9] Advisers also report this trend:

'While many of our conversations are still confidential, larger numbers of people are now willing to discuss their giving. There is still a sense of wanting to put something back when compared to the rest of society when they have been fortunate. The state of society and the economy has increased an interest in philanthropy at the higher end of giving.'

Conclusions

The past decade has seen a rapid expansion in the provision of philanthropy advice, which has become an integral part of the offer of many banks, law firms and tax advisers. Complementing these has been the development of a range of specialist providers.

We found that in 2012, one-third of the newer cohort of interviewees had sought professional philanthropy advice, compared with one in seven of the established donors. Furthermore another 21% of the emerging donors might seek advice in the future, compared with 11% of established philanthropists. However one looks at it, the increase in supply of expertise is occurring in step with an increased interest from the market.

The three most popular issues on which donors ask for professional advice include personalised discussion of their philanthropic interests, signposting to materials produced by other organisations, and introductions to other donors who share their interests. These are closely followed by the provision of a practical management service, including relationships with beneficiaries, project visits, and assessment of feedback reports. Other issues of interest to a significant minority include the provision of training on strategic philanthropy and suggestions as to which charities they might support within their areas of interest.

All this is in the context of the concerns that are most likely to be raised by clients: the maintenance and increase of their wealth, and the level of assets that should be transferred to children. We see how the strands of wealth-holding, inter-generational wealth transfer and philanthropy come together in a process in which children are involved in the philanthropic decision-making as a way of inculcating values.

Philanthropy advice services are changing, in response both to client demand and market developments such as the growth in socially responsible investment and a range of products that offer a social and financial return. These in turn are emerging in a landscape of recession and increasing inequality on a global scale. The importance and responsibility of the role of the adviser can only be strengthened in these circumstances.

This chapter brings to an end our analysis of the material from our surveys and interviews, complemented by findings from other reports and research. In the final chapter we draw on our conclusions from this research, and make recommendations to strengthen the culture of philanthropy in the UK.

Notes

[1] We note that the campaign to introduce lifetime legacies, recommended by a number of reports after WRPG in 2004, including the Philanthropy Review in 2011, had still not succeeded by summer 2013.

[2] www.philanthropy-impact.org/the-philanthropy-programme

[3] www.step.org/philanthropy-advisors

[4] www.philanthropy-impact.org

[5] See for example the report on *Family Foundation Giving Trends 2012* from CGAP which showed that 3.4% of grants by causal area went to Environment and conservation, or 6.2% if the Wellcome Foundation figures are excluded. http://tinyurl.com/olvadol

[6] http://tinyurl.com/pey5kfw

[7] http://tinyurl.com/nz7q5ej

[8] Available online at www.kent.ac.uk/sspssr/cphsj/research/couttsmilliondonor.html

[9] John Nickson (2013) *Giving is Good for You.* London: Biteback Publishing.

10

Recommendations

We have summarised our conclusions on each aspect of our research at the end of each chapter. In this final chapter we set out a series of recommendations, linked to key findings for different sectors and audiences.

As no individual or organisation is 'in charge' of philanthropy in the UK, our recommendations are aimed at all those with influence – or simply a determination to make things better – in government, in charities, in the philanthropy infrastructure bodies, among philanthropy advisers, in the media and within the donor community itself. Some of these ideas are already 'live' and being taken forward by individuals, charitable organisations and sector umbrella bodies working in partnership. We hope that our evidence will add further weight to the collaborative endeavours currently taking place, as well as sparking new efforts where needed.

Recommendations to government

It is evident that a level of cynicism about the conflicting messages that come from government long predates the ill-thought out (and eventually withdrawn) proposals announced in March 2012 to cap tax relief for charitable giving. However, that episode highlighted the point that while there had been a number of welcome initiatives that might be described as 'pro-philanthropy' (described in detail in Chapter 2), the commitment was partial and inconsistent between government departments. The disappointment is compounded by the fact that, over the course of the past decade, a series of independent reports by highly reputable people, some commissioned or partly-funded by the government, have consistently recommended courses of action that are then not taken forward.

We make eight recommendations to government:

Clarify government strategy on philanthropy.

Working with others, those responsible in government for policy relating to philanthropy need to instigate, and fully participate in, the necessary debates to clarify the role of philanthropy in 21st century society. These include:

* How the contributions of philanthropists, the voluntary sector and public funding interact.
* How the fiscal system will support and incentivise voluntary giving.
* The issues of hypothecation and tax reliefs explored in Appendix 3.
* Ensuring that all government departments, including HM Treasury, adopt a coherent approach.

Ideally, these efforts will be arrived at with cross-party consensus, so that philanthropists and those seeking funding can operate within a consistent policy environment over the long term.

Implement the charity tax relief known as 'lifetime legacies'.

This is probably the most consistently and widely canvassed proposal. It was recommended in 2004 by *WRPG* and the Thomas Report, and at various stages since by an active coalition of organisations, and by the Philanthropy Review.

For the reasons we discuss in Chapters 4 and 8, regarding why rich people do and do not give, not least the constraint of feelings of financial insecurity and the reinforcement of enjoying the pleasure of giving while living, we reiterate our support for this mechanism.

Extend the concept of matched funding.

Donors at several levels have responded positively to matched funding schemes. These include that run by HEFCE[1] to promote giving to higher education, and the Catalyst programme run by the Arts Council and Heritage Lottery Fund and UK Aid Match, run by the Department for International Development. We recommend that this type of scheme should be extended to other cause areas in which, following clarification of government strategy set out in the first recommendation above, there would be the hope and expectation of greater philanthropic engagement. These new matched funding initiatives might include (but not be confined to) aspects of social welfare such as children, elderly people, disability and homelessness; healthcare and hospices; as well as projects related to the environment and conservation.

Invest in schools training.

Many of our respondents identified the importance of training the next generation. We have reported on some of the activity in this area and suggest that further investment would be extremely beneficial in the long term. This would be a collaborative process with grant-making trusts and organisations such as the Citizenship Foundation and UK Community Foundations.

We also recommend matched funding for a scheme focused on sixth-form pupils, linked to in-school teaching about the role and purpose of charity in modern society. This could be complemented with the involvement of local philanthropists as both funders and role models to visit schools to share their experiences and show how giving has enriched their lives.

Fund the Charity Commission adequately.

Although not a central question in our research, the role and quality of the work of the Charity Commission relates to many of the issues raised by our respondents, and some made direct comments about its activities. Funding cuts imposed by the Coalition Government have caused the regulator's staff to shrink by a third in three years and further reductions in its budget are scheduled in the years ahead.[2] Concerns about the Commission's ability to fulfil its role in the face of these cuts have been sparked by genuine problems, such as the Cup Trust saga,[3] and exacerbated by the ill-founded suggestions reported by the media that some funded organisations are 'dodgy charities'. While, no doubt, there is a tiny minority of rogue schemes and fraudulent organisations whose existence does massive harm to the sector as a whole, and provides excuses for those who don't want to give, it is deeply harmful to suggest that corruption is endemic within charities.

We therefore recommend that the Charity Commission should be funded adequately to do its job as charity regulator, with the resources and authority to deal with those who break the letter and spirit of the rules around charitable giving.

Instruct HMRC to co-operate with those researching philanthropy.

There are widely expressed concerns at the lack of robust data surrounding giving by the wealthy. Very little reliable information is available on the proportion of higher-rate taxpayers that give, how much they give, and to which causes. We share these concerns and recommend that government takes further action to improve both the quality and the quantity of relevant data.

We acknowledge that the challenge is to identify a source of accurate data on giving. As major donors often support several organisations, it is not possible for individual charities to assess the total donations by any given philanthropist.

We therefore support the suggestion made by those involved with the Philanthropy Review and others that, subject to appropriate anonymising of data, the HMRC, with the support of academics, should produce an analysis on an annual basis to enable both the charity sector and government to monitor changes in giving behaviour, particularly whether more higher-rate taxpayers are giving, whether they are giving more, the proportion of giving coming from very large philanthropists and the causes they typically give to. While this would only encompass giving on which tax relief is claimed, it would produce far better information than we have now, and over time provide an accurate basis for analysis and policy-making.

Ensure that the honours system respects and recognises significant and sustained philanthropy.

We have reported on the development of the honours system and the new focus on philanthropy as a criterion for recognition. We recommend that this is developed to its maximum potential, with a particular focus on long-term and strategic commitment.

While those making very large donations deserve recognition, we also recommend that greater efforts are made to recognise other types of excellent philanthropists, such as those funding more challenging causes, those who succeed in inspiring others, and those who help to popularise new methods of giving.

Consider the simplification of the tax system surrounding charitable giving.

We also note the suggestions to simplify the tax system. It is clear that few people understand how Gift Aid works, and that even fewer people (even some charities and advisers) understand processes such as gifts of shares. At the very least, an injection of government funding and effort could help to explain very clearly how charitable tax reliefs work, to challenge the misconception often promoted by critics of philanthropy that one can somehow make money by giving it away.

Recommendations to charities

Our research generates clear messages for charities. Some can be addressed by charities acting on their own, and improving how they deal with prospects and donors. Other activities will be strengthened if charities act together.

Many fundraising organisations (small as well as large) do provide their donors with the experience they are looking for – strong relationships and confidence that their money is well spent. But not enough have been willing to develop the corporate culture of engagement, nor invest in and oversee the institutional changes required to underpin successful long-term fundraising from the wealthy.

We therefore make five recommendations to charities, and other non-profit organisations seeking philanthropic funding:

Charities must become far better at asking.

Everyone in charities – including trustees, senior management, programme experts and support staff – must understand the importance and processes of developing long-term relationships with donors for the benefit of the charity. This means understanding that philanthropists usually wish to engage with organisational leaders, such as trustees, as well as those who deliver the mission, and not only interact with fundraising staff. We recommend that the leadership of each charity takes steps to ensure there are appropriate opportunities for this to happen.

We also recommend that charities invest more resources in essential activities such as prospect research and planning a sustained process of engagement for each donor, tailored to their specific interests, which may take some time, before asking for money. In essence, we recommend that charities take a long view in their relationships with major donors.

Efforts to improve 'the ask' should involve the following elements:

- Ensuring that the case for support emphasises the long-term impact on the lives of beneficiaries and the wider community, and responds to donors' interest in preventative approaches to addressing societal problems.
- Developing a personalised plan to involve the prospective donor, ensuring there is a match between the lead contact on the relationship, who must be a respected peer, and/or senior executive, and the person who is being approached.

- Ensuring that the fundraising staff dealing with major donors have the necessary status, resources and training to underpin long-term relationship management.
- Ensuring that everyone who comes into contact with major prospects understands and can explain tax reliefs and planned giving.
- Ensuring that all those likely to interact with prospective and current donors can explain the case for support, the business model and funding mix, as well as the need and rationale for core costs.
- Having a commitment to a feedback approach that is integrated with the management process, demonstrates transparency and accountability, is honest about failure, and is able to show how the institution learns from it.
- Not 'bombarding' donors (particularly those who give through the mechanism of a trust) with inappropriate applications.

Experiences of serious giving must be positive and reinforcing.

To ensure that donors' experience of giving is positive, and one they will wish to repeat, charities should:

- Develop a bespoke programme of engagement that works in the way that the donor wishes, rather than adopting a one-size-fits all approach.
- Offer opportunities to visit projects and learn about the underlying issues.
- Offer opportunities to meet other donors, if desired.
- Provide feedback in a format and frequency that the donor requests.
- Understand that some initial gifts are made as a reciprocal gesture because of who asked, and not because of an underlying commitment to the cause.
- Provide appropriate thanking and recognition. Always ensure that letters are personal, rather than a standard response; they should be signed by the most senior person available, and where possible they should be handwritten with a form of address that is not over-familiar.

Integrate legacy promotion with other forms of relationship development.

We note the government scheme to encourage charitable bequests by reducing inheritance tax for those who leave at least 10% of their estate to charity, the increasing trend in childlessness, and the discussion on the topic of inheritance. There are clearly implications for those seeking funding, especially in the form of legacies, and we recommend that charities consider investing more in the promotion of legacies as part of their engagement with wealthy donors. This might include the formation of 'clubs' for those promising legacies.

A generic approach to raising awareness of the opportunities and benefits of bequests could complement promotion to individual donors on a personal basis. Such promotions often work well in partnership with other charities, such as the 'Remember a Charity' campaign, and with the support of solicitors, for example, 'Make a Will Week'.

Consider matched funding schemes.

We report in Chapters 2 and 4 on the value of matched funding schemes as an incentive to increase philanthropy. These were offered through government schemes but can be equally effective if the challenge grant is made by a private donor. We recommend that charities pursue the concept of a matching fund or a challenge grant with donors, particularly for specific projects or fundraising campaigns, and ideally promoted by an existing major donor.

This might be particularly appropriate for endowment fundraising, which is widely viewed as one of the most difficult 'asks' to make.

Charities must address the lack of confidence in their competence and efficiency.

Our findings show that even donors who generously support charities are not always confident that those charities operate as effectively as possible. Individually and collectively, charities must make the case that their mission is necessary, that they are adopting the best approach to addressing it, underpinned by the most appropriate business model, and allocating resources efficiently.

They must explain that they are rigorous in their management processes, and exist for the beneficiaries, not the staff. There should not be a 'race to the bottom' in terms of the proportion of costs allocated to administration, governance, fundraising and central overheads. Instead, charities must explain why and to what extent this expenditure is necessary to sustain the mission.

199

Recommendations to philanthropists

A significant change in the UK over the past decade is that more people are speaking publicly about their philanthropy, and inspiring others. Along with the need to galvanise people who have made their money is the imperative to educate and inspire the next generation. We also report the importance of peer asking, with the emphasis that the asker must themselves be a giver. It is also clear that there is an ongoing debate about the role of philanthropy and the application of private wealth to societal problems.

We therefore make five recommendations to donors:

Philanthropists should talk more openly about their giving.

People making large donations should, where possible, be willing to speak to the media about their philanthropy. This will help to support charities in their efforts to publicise major donations, will provide public endorsement of the project or programme, and will encourage others.

Be willing to act as role models for the next generation.

Major donors should consider taking steps to become more public role models, for example, by visiting schools and universities to talk about their giving. This will ensure the younger generation has first-hand knowledge of philanthropy and could reap significant future benefits if philanthropy is presented as an aspirational act to young minds.

Invest in trustees and senior management of charities.

Donors who are also trustees or committee members of a fundraising organisation need to accept that it is the role of every board member to ensure that fundraising is professionally run with adequate resources, and that the task of raising funds is seen as the responsibility of the whole institution. To achieve this goal, philanthropists should consider providing financial support for the training of board and committee members, as well as senior management, of the organisations they support.

Encourage other donors.

Every trustee can be involved in looking after prospects and donors, even if not every trustee feels able to get involved in directly asking for money. Given the reliance on peer recommendations, major donors may be the very best person to inspire others. In addition to making their own gifts, persuading others to donate may be the most helpful contribution that rich donors can make to their favoured cause.

Contribute to public debate.

Much of the discourse around private philanthropy, the role of the state and the part played by tax incentives is ill-informed. We recommend that donors contribute to the debate on a local and national basis to make their voices heard and increase understanding of how private donations make a real difference to wider society.

Recommendations to advisers

Philanthropy advice is a rapidly expanding field, which we expect to see develop further over the coming decade, and exert greater influence over the quantity and direction of an increasing number of donations. Yet there is no standard code of practice for people working in this field, and in Chapter 9 we note a number of opportunities for the growing philanthropy adviser profession.

We therefore make six recommendations to those working as advisers to philanthropists.

Develop a code of practice.

This should include input from individuals and organisations working in this field, and be strengthened by consultation with key players such as the community foundations, umbrella bodies and infrastructure organisations.

Be more confident in raising and addressing feelings of financial insecurity.

We realise that this is highly sensitive and do not expect advisers to lecture their clients about the morality of wealth-owning. However, where there is a perceived opportunity, advisers should feel confident in helping people to calculate how much they can afford, for example, by using the Rosenberg approach described in Appendix 4.

Incorporation of philanthropy advice and services in routine dealings with clients.

We are aware of the investment in training by STEP, and the growth in the size of in-house philanthropy advisory teams. There is also an increase in the number of independent advisers, and increasing capacity in UK Community Foundations. We applaud this expansion, but there is still room for further development. The more that philanthropy is seen as an integral strand in the effective holding and management of wealth, and a way of making a difference to society, obtaining personal fulfilment and engaging the next generation, the more likely it is that people will participate.

Greater promotion of social investment products.

We are aware that some advisers would like to promote social investment products to their clients in a responsible manner, but even within the current constraints more could be done to alert donors to the opportunities offered by this type of mechanism, whether Social Impact Bonds or schemes such as Kiva.

Track the advice donors are seeking.

We suggest advisers find a way to track how and on what topics donors ask them for advice, so that this information can be shared though portals such as Philanthropy Impact.

Test attitudes on paying for advice.

We recommend further research into the question of fees and the willingness of philanthropists to pay for advice. There is some anecdotal evidence but this requires more structured exploration.

Recommendations to the media

We are aware that 'the media' covers a very diverse set of broadcast, press and online communications. There is no overarching body to influence the behaviour of individual entities, let alone set standards in this area. However, with some honourable exceptions, our respondents spoke often (and in general terms) about the media's malign influence, citing contradictory attitudes to wealth and wealth creation, cynicism about motives, and a lack of understanding, even in the financial press, of the basic mechanisms of tax relief for charitable giving.

Given the powerful authority of the media, particularly in the face of declining alternative influences on social norms such as religion, we make four recommendations:

'Normalise' philanthropy.

We recommend the media presents philanthropy as a regular part of a rounded life for the rich and not-so rich. Profiles and obituaries of individuals such as leading business people and entrepreneurs, footballers and entertainers, bankers and lawyers, artists and scientists, should highlight their engagement with wider society and their philanthropy. Where philanthropy has enriched the lives of the people being discussed, this should be celebrated.

Be accurate in discussions of charity tax reliefs.

Journalists have a responsibility to get their facts straight and to avoid over-complicating how tax reliefs on charitable giving work. Appendix 3 is aimed at assisting journalists in this task.

Regular and routine highlighting of philanthropy in quality media, whether broadcast, print or online.

We believe that the serious and business press, and business pages of all print and online media, have a particular role to play in this field. They are read by key constituencies including the wealthy themselves, those who manage wealth, and those who provide services to the rich, as well as policy-makers and other opinion-formers.

Occasional profiles of donors and features about ways of helping good causes are helpful but may contribute to the marginalisation of philanthropy by implying – however unintentionally – that only certain 'types' (such as the very richest members of society) are expected to give. We therefore recommend regular features about donors in a range of sectors. Examples are:

- Features and columns on the causes seeking donations, similar to the regular columns that highlight which car or which wine to buy.
- A 'Donor of the day' feature in a national newspaper, following the model established by the *Wall Street Journal*.[4]

Local papers tend to be much more sympathetic than the national press when reporting on charitable giving, but more could be done to celebrate and sustain local philanthropy. For example, community foundations often struggle to get coverage of their work – each local paper should offer regular space to highlight their work and the achievements of donors who give in the area they cover. A local version of 'Donor of the day' could be an excellent addition to any regional newspaper.

Be more responsible and proactive in educating and convening opinion on philanthropic matters.

There are some 'live' and important issues, highlighted in this book, such as the appropriate extent and nature of charity tax reliefs and the usefulness of public benchmarks for giving (e.g. 1% of income). These can be discussed in various settings, such as meetings hosted by Philanthropy Impact or other membership or umbrella organisations, as well as online. But the media has a particular ability to educate the public on contentious issues, to air opposing views, and to help achieve progress towards a consensus.

Further research

We are fully aware of the limitations of our research and recommend that further research be undertaken to continue strengthening the knowledge base, in the following areas:

Giving by the wealthy

In addition to the recommendation above, that government needs to commit to allowing access to and interpretation of HMRC data on giving by all taxpayers, we need further investment to obtain better research into giving by the wealthy. For example, at present there exists no study (neither one-off nor annual) of giving that falls between 'ordinary giving' and 'mega-giving': the representative survey methodology used by the annual *UK Giving* survey means it cannot capture major gifts and rates a monthly gift of £100 or more as a 'higher donation', while the annual *Coutts Million Pound Donors Report* only covers gifts worth a minimum of seven figures. Clearly, many donations fall in between these extremes, and a regular analysis of this 'middle range', from the £100s to the £100,000s, is much needed.

The attractions and potential of collaborative giving

While collaborative giving does not have universal appeal – a third (30%) of our rich donors have not, and do not intend to, give in a group – the questions and concerns of the other two-thirds, who are either already giving this way, or open to trying it, are worthy of further exploration to ensure their needs are being catered for.

The question of fees and willingness to pay for advice.

As noted above in the recommendations to advisers, research on who is willing to pay what, for which kind of advice, can contribute to further developing the philanthropy advice sector.

Why Rich People Give/Richer lives

Finally, we wish to inform readers that the detailed research underpinning this book, in the form of a cohort analysis, will be undertaken again in 2022.

We invite readers to make contact through our website **www.richerlives.org** if you think we missed important questions in our surveys or have other ideas for further research.

Further reading

As noted throughout this book, there is a growing body of research and expertise in the field of philanthropy, and our research has been inspired and informed by a wide range of authors and colleagues, both academics and practitioners. The stories told by the philanthropists themselves are the most insightful and inspiring. The sources we use are referenced throughout this book, and in Appendix 5 we list further recommended reading, as well as websites, regular newsletters and other sources of free information for donors, advisers, charities, policy-makers and the media. We also provide information on a selection of magazines, research and policy reports and lectures, along with biographical and autobiographical stories of philanthropists and their beneficiaries.

There are frequent additions to this body of knowledge, which create an ever-growing opportunity to increase awareness of the experiences, opportunities and issues surrounding major philanthropy.

Notes

1   The Higher Education Funding Council for England.
2   According to the Charity Commission website, it has 303 FTE (Full Time Equivalent) staff in June 2013, which is down from 466 FTEs in 2009-10. The 2013 Comprehensive Spending Review included a further reduction in the Charity Commission's budget of just over 6% for the financial year 2015-16 amounts. www.charitycommission.gov.uk/news/spending-review-settlement
3   The Cup Trust was given charitable status in 2009 and received £176m in income, yet gave away just £55,000 to charitable causes. A report by the Public Accounts Committee (PAC) said the Charity Commission had failed to carry out sufficient checks on the charity. See www.bbc.co.uk/news/business-22758191
4   See http://topics.wsj.com/person/W/melanie-grayce-west/6185 for examples of this feature.

Appendix 1: Methodology

This research is based on four methodologies, as follows:

- Four different surveys, mostly completed online but conducted in person or on the telephone where necessary:
  - A survey of 40 established donors, defined as those who participated in the study undertaken in 2002.
  - A survey of 42 emerging donors, defined as those who did not participate in the 2002 study, although they may have been actively giving at that time.
  - A survey of 16 'experts' who work in the philanthropy sector in a variety of roles, including policy-makers, major donor fundraisers, researchers, journalists and people from umbrella and infrastructure bodies.
  - A survey of 12 people whose work is fully or partially concerned with providing advisory services to philanthropists.

- Twenty interviews, 10 with established donors and 10 with emerging donors – in both sets of 10 we interviewed some couples, who are counted as one donor. The interviewees were selected initially on the basis of their willingness to participate further in the research, as indicated by their response to the final question in the survey. As 29 established donors and 27 emerging donors were willing to be questioned in depth, exceeding the number required, we selected on the basis of creating the most representative sample in terms of gender, age and geography.

- A literature review drawing on academic and charity sector publications. This literature is referenced in footnotes where appropriate, and/or listed in Appendix 5.

- Secondary analysis of primary data that has previously been published by sources such as HMRC, Office of National Statistics and in the *Sunday Times Rich List* and *Giving Index*. Data and information were also contributed by individuals and organisations, as noted in the acknowledgements.

Sampling

The key challenge facing those seeking to study rich donors is that there is no list of UK philanthropists to be consulted, and too few of them in the general population to make standardised random sampling methods a viable option. It is therefore necessary to identify and approach them one by one but, as discussed at the start of Chapter 3, it is not easy to recruit philanthropists to participate in research studies. Rich donors are clearly not obliged to explain their philanthropic acts to anyone, including curious researchers, and may choose not to engage with research for many reasons, including: modesty; a reluctance to appear egotistical or overly-pleased with themselves; a lack of time (particularly for those still creating their wealth); a desire to avoid to advertising their wealth in case of security implications for themselves and their families; and a reluctance to become known as a major donor for fear of being bombarded with requests for donations.

We therefore used a combination of convenience sampling (which involves recruiting people who are willing and available to participate in the study, in most cases because they have a pre-existing relationship with the researcher) and snowball sampling (which involves those who have already participated in the study helping to recruit additional participants from among their acquaintances, so the sample group appears to grow like a rolling snowball). Both convenience and snowball sampling are non-probability sample techniques, but they are viewed as appropriate approaches in certain situations, such as when standardised random sampling procedures cannot be followed, for the reasons set out above.

However, extensive attempts were made to make the final sample as representative as possible, by paying attention to the composition of the sample as it grew and seeking out under-represented groups, such as women, people outside London and younger people.

Confidentiality was guaranteed to all those who participated in the survey and interviews. While the level of concern about this varied, for some it was undoubtedly very important.

The surveys offered a mix of multiple-choice questions, together with opportunities to add free comment on a number of topics, and to elaborate on the reasons for certain answers. For a copy of the questions used in all three of the surveys that we conducted, please see our website www.richerlives.org

The schedule of questions used in the interviews is set out in the box below.

1. Thank you for completing the survey prior to being interviewed today. We know that some people found the format and range of questions a bit limiting. Were there any issues relating to your philanthropy that you would like to say more about before we start the interview?

2. The title of our research project is: Why do rich people give? How would you answer that question?

   Supplementary question, if a long list is offered: What would you say are the most important reasons why people choose to be philanthropic?

3. Many people deny that an interest in public recognition or honours is a driver for their philanthropy, but admit to enjoying such recognition when it is given. Often they are persuaded by fundraisers that their endorsement and public association with the cause will validate it and encourage others. What is your take on this whole complex question of recognition?

4. Can you offer any insight into the opposite question: Why do some rich people not give?

   Supplementary question, if a long list is offered: What would you say are the most important reasons why people choose not to be philanthropic?

5. How do you feel philanthropy fits in to the wider scheme of things, in relation to the public and private sectors? Are there some causes that philanthropy should not be expected to fund? Or some areas where philanthropy should have a larger role?

6. What do you think about the furore that greeted the Government's proposal in the 2012 Budget to cap tax reliefs for charitable giving?

   Supplementary questions if these issues don't arise naturally:

   (a) Did you feel this affair revealed anything about government and public understanding of philanthropy and what motivates donors?

   (b) What role do you feel tax breaks play in encouraging giving?

7. Do you feel that most people are giving as much as they can?

    If not: What do you think is the best way to encourage more wealthy people to give?

8. In November 2012 a senior politician said: 'I give away 1% of my income every year, which seems fair and right.' What is your response to that?

9. Do you have experience of asking for money for causes with which you are involved?

    If yes: What has your experience been? Why do you think some people do respond and some people do not respond?

10. Clearly, we are talking to you because you are a committed donor and enjoy your philanthropy. How can that experience of the fun of giving, the pleasure of the relationships with those involved with the organisations you support and the knowledge that you are making a real difference to the causes that you care about be presented to others in a way that will make them realise what they are missing?

11. How has giving changed you, and the way you look at the world?

12. Is there anything else you would like to discuss?

Analysis

The 82 donor surveys were completed over an eight-month period from August 2012 to March 2013. They primarily generated numeric data, which was analysed using SPSS software. This acronym means 'statistical package for the social sciences' and is a commonly used application that performs statistical analysis on data. Where the surveys generated text data, this was held in a text dataset and analysed in a similar way to the dataset containing interview data, as discussed below.

The 20 interviews were conducted over a five-month period between November 2012 and March 2013. 18 interviews were taped on a digital recorder, and for two interviews verbatim responses were recorded manually. All were then transcribed in full to create a text dataset of almost 40,000 words, containing the content of all 20 transcripts. This dataset was then analysed using the same qualitative techniques as used to analyse the data presented and discussed in the original *WRPG* study.[1]

The 2012 analysis process began with re-organisation of the data by question (i.e. all the answers to question one, followed by all the answers to question two and so on), so that themes relating to the same topic could more easily be identified. A content analysis was then undertaken to identify themes present in the whole dataset and to explore the relationships between these themes. Content analysis is a method that has been developed to explain how meanings are exchanged within complex webs of social interaction with the ultimate aim of yielding significant insights into human behaviour.[2] The dataset was coded by hand using an open-ended strategy to identify the main themes that emerged in the interviews; these codes emerged inductively as significant variables and patterns were noted in the course of reading, re-reading, organising and re-organising the data. Cross-referencing the codes highlighted the repeated presence of a number of distinguishing features within the dataset (such as the importance of asking and the role of recognition), which are presented and discussed in this book. Interview data was constantly cross-referenced with the survey data, to bring to bear quantitative support for qualitative findings where possible, thus making our findings more robust through triangulation.

Notes

[1] This process is described in J. Ritchie and J. Lewis (eds) (2003) *Qualitative Research Practice: A guide for social scientists*. London: Sage.

[2] K. Krippendorf (2004) *Content Analysis: An introduction to its Methodology*. London: Sage.

Appendix 2: Philanthropy networks

Over the past decade there has been a significant growth in the number of networks supporting donors with particular interests, or who want to give either through intermediaries or in collaboration with others. Here we describe some of the key networks.

Giving through intermediaries

Firstly, we note the strengthening of the nationwide network of community foundations,[1] which offer a range of services to promote philanthropy, including the provision of general and bespoke training, donor-advised funds, and networks of donors with similar interests. Community foundations are independent registered philanthropic institutions serving geographically-defined territory. They act as grant-making foundations, giving grants to support local projects, and their mission is to improve the quality of life in a community. They are supported by a broad range of private as well as public donors and seek philanthropic contributions primarily from people connected to the community served. They are governed by local boards and build capital endowments with the aim of ensuring funding capability in perpetuity.

The national body supporting local community foundations is UK Community Foundations (formerly the Community Foundation Network), which is itself a registered charity with a commitment to build thriving communities in the UK. With more than £309m in endowed funds from over 3,000 donors, it provides about £70m in grants a year.

As we note in Chapter 4, some of our interviewees have a fund with a community foundation to support causes in that area, as well as giving directly to other national and international charities. Some use a community foundation to administer all their donations, including giving outside the area served by that community foundation.

Secondly, the last decade has seen growth in the scale, scope and reach of the Charities Aid Foundation (CAF).[2] CAF provides a wide range of services for donors, including the administration of donor-advised CAF Charitable Trust accounts, advisory services, savings and investments and access to CAF Social Investments. There are now more than 2,500 CAF Charitable Trust accounts holding between £10,000 and £100m+, and over 85,000 CAF Charity accounts, designed for individuals who donate less than £10,000 per annum. Donations through these accounts totalled £160m in 2012, and the availability of these services supports the practice of giving among the more affluent.[3] One aspect of the service is the provision of charity chequebooks for CAF account holders. A small but growing number of banks, such as C. Hoare & Co., are also offering this service, albeit requiring a significant minimum deposit. The provision of such a facility by banks was recommended by the Philanthropy Review, discussed in Chapter 2.

Thirdly, and closely related to developments in both community foundations and CAF, there has been growth in the number of donor-advised funds. These are charitable giving vehicles administered by charities or commercial entities, created for the purpose of managing charitable donations on behalf of an organisation, family, or individual. A donor-advised fund offers the opportunity to create an easy-to-establish, low cost, flexible vehicle for charitable giving as an alternative to direct giving or creating a private foundation. In some ways it is like a grander version of a CAF account. Donors enjoy administrative convenience, cost savings, and tax advantages by conducting their grant-making through the fund.

Finally, there has been growth in the provision of expert technical guidance and support from leading legal firms, including help with structuring trusts, tax and cross-border giving, together with event hosting for clients, often in association with the broader advice network. This is complemented by an interest in the provision of professional education to practitioners, for example, through the STEP/Philanthropy Impact philanthropy programme.[4]

Donor networks

There are several networks linking funders with shared interests. These range from extremely private networks (often associated with the very wealthy, and sometimes linked to family offices) to more open and accessible groups.

The Association of Charitable Foundations (ACF) hosts and organises a range of issue-based networks for members, including those for people interested in: Asylum, refugee and migration issues; Corporate foundations; Capacity building; Children and young people; Disability; Faith-based projects; Financial inclusion; Gypsies and travellers; Housing and homelessness; investment strategies; Mental health; Monitoring and evaluation; Northern Ireland; Older people; Operational support; Penal affairs; Race equality; Smaller funder; Technological innovation; and Violence against women and girls.[5]

Outside ACF, examples of issue-based donor networks include the Environmental Funders Network,[6] an informal network of trusts, foundations and individuals making grants on environmental and conservation issues with a mission to increase the overall level of financial support for environmental causes and to help environmental philanthropy to be as effective as possible. Ariadne is a similarly structured European network for funders interested in supporting human rights.[7]

The Network for Social Change[8] is a low profile group of about 110 members providing anonymous funding for progressive social change, particularly in the areas of justice, peace and the environment. Together they give around £1m per year to a variety of projects and organisations. As with other networks and groups, many members use a variety of mechanisms, and the Network for Social Change includes experienced philanthropists with significant charitable trusts, who value the Network as an efficient way to fund cutting-edge projects.

Another example is The Funding Network (TFN).[9] Founded in 2002, it was the UK's first public giving circle and has been described as the 'Dragons' Den' for small or emerging charities with a focus on social change. TFN now forms a community of givers who have together raised more than £5m for over 670 diverse local, national and international projects, through TFN groups in London, Bristol, Leeds, Oxford, Devon, Norfolk and Kent. As with community foundations, many TFN supporters also give directly to a range of other causes.

The Funding Network has created the independent City Funding Network that runs giving events for a younger audience based on TFN's successful model. The first event in July 2012 raised more than £25,000 in an hour for three charities. There will be two events a year until 2015. These will be supplemented by educational events.

A more recent innovation is The Philanthropy Club, a members-only club of City professionals aspiring to be philanthropists. The idea behind the Club is to inspire a culture of philanthropy and to channel giving in a way that is strategic, effective and sustainable. These are among the programmes of City Philanthropy,[10] a three-year initiative (2013-15) funded by the City of London Corporation's charity City Bridge Trust (CBT). It comprises a number of constituent elements funded by CBT to achieve a two-fold mission: 1) to embed a culture of effective philanthropy in the City of London (including Canary Wharf), particularly among a younger generation of professionals; and 2) to promote London as a global centre for effective philanthropy.

Fundernetwork,[11] launched in 2013, is a website coordinated by ACF to provide a 'safe space for online learning and sharing among funders'. This has been funded by a number of organisations, including the Big Lottery, leading grant-making trusts and NPC, and provides funders with a range of freely available reports, as well as opportunities to share concerns and ask questions on a wide range of issues and causes. This is another example of the increasing provision of readily accessible free online research and advice.

Notes

[1] http://ukcommunityfoundations.org

[2] www.cafonline.org

[3] While this research has focused on the very rich we are aware that there are some 8 million people classified as 'mass affluent', with liquid assets between £50,000 and £5m (a level that overlaps with those at the lower end of our cohort). This constituency is also of interest to the UK Community Foundations.

[4] www.philanthropy-impact.org/the-philanthropy-programme

[5] www.acf.org.uk/networkingevents/ibns/?id=308

[6] www.greenfunders.org

[7] www.ariadne-network.eu

[8] www.thenetworkforsocialchange.org.uk

[9] www.thefundingnetwork.org.uk/about-us

[10] www.cityphilanthropy.org.uk

[11] http://fundernetwork.org.uk

Appendix 3:
The tax relief debate

In Chapter 4 we explored the reaction to the Chancellor's 2012 Budget proposal that, from April 2013, a cap would apply to all unlimited tax reliefs, including donations to charity.

It took some time for the implications to be fully appreciated but, once understood, there was a vociferous backlash from charities, philanthropists, professional advisers and most commentators. A campaign to exempt charitable giving from the cap garnered widespread support and the media carried extensive articles and editorials on the subject. Apart from a small number of dissenting voices, the majority of observers called on the Chancellor to reverse the decision. Unfortunately, the Government's initial defence of the proposal inflamed the issue, as questions of fairness in taxation were conflated with tax avoidance.

After extensive consultations with charities and philanthropists, the Chancellor announced on 31 May 2012 that the measure would be withdrawn and charitable giving would not be included in the cap on unlimited tax reliefs.

As we report, many of those we surveyed were among those who strongly disagreed with the proposal and felt insulted by the way it was presented and defended. However, many of the same people are also aware that there is a legitimate debate to be held. A particular focus is the question of 'hypothecation'.

What is meant by hypothecation?

The hypothecation of a tax (also known as the ring-fencing or earmarking of a tax) is the dedication of the revenue from a specific tax for a particular expenditure purpose. An example in many European countries including the UK is a television licence. All users of television sets are obliged to pay the government an annual fee to use their televisions. The proceeds of this levy are then used to fund public broadcasting.

By extension this term has been applied to the process by which gifts to charities attract tax relief. The most common form of tax-efficient giving is through Gift Aid, available to donors who are UK taxpayers.[1]

With donations from basic rate taxpayers, charities can claim back the tax the donor has paid. In other words, charities take the after-tax donation and reclaim basic rate tax (currently 20%) on its gross equivalent. A higher rate taxpayer can themselves claim the difference between the basic rate and the higher rate (currently 40%) on the donation. Those paying additional rate (currently at 45%) can claim the difference between the basic rate and the additional rate.

The principle in tax law is always that the donor is treated as if they had never become liable to tax on their gross gift, as they have 'deprived' themselves of that income. The tax system therefore does not recognise hypothecation in relation to charitable gifts because no tax has been collected that can be hypothecated. Hypothecation therefore becomes a philosophical argument adopted by some commentators.

The argument goes like this: When a donor makes a (gross) gift to charity, the tax code demands that they deduct basic rate tax before paying it over to the charity. The charity is then entitled to reclaim the amount deducted. Because the donor has effectively decided where the tax on their donation goes (i.e. to a specific charity or charities of their choice), they are said to have 'hypothecated' that tax, rather than it being added to the funds available for general government spending.

The contrary argument, recognised in tax law, is that the gross amount given is not recognised as taxable in the first place.

We look at how this works with examples.

> Case 1. If a UK basic rate taxpayer gives £1,000 to a charity, the charity can claim £250 in Gift Aid, bringing it up to £1,250. (This is the gross sum that the donor would have had to earn to be left with £1,000 after paying tax at the standard 20% rate).

> Case 2. If the donor is a higher rate (currently 40%) taxpayer, they can then make a claim themselves for tax relief for a further £250 (20% of the gross). The charity ends up with £1,250 and the cost to the donor is £750. In effect the 40% that would have been paid in tax on gross earnings of £1,250 has gone to the charity instead of being collected by HMRC.

Case 3. If a basic rate taxpayer would like the charity to receive a gross sum of £1,000, they can make a Gift Aid donation of £800, and the charity would claim £200.

Case 4. If a higher rate taxpayer would like the charity to receive a gross sum of £1,000, they can make a Gift Aid donation of £800, the charity would claim £200, making a total of £1,000, and the donor would themselves claim tax relief of a further £200, so the net cost to the donor is £600.

Case 5. If a higher rate taxpayer decides that they could afford £1,000 out of post-tax income (as in case 1 above), they would make a gift to the charity of £1,333.33. The charity would claim Gift Aid (25%) of £333.33, bringing the value of the gift to the charity to £1,666.66. The higher rate taxpayer donor claims a further 20% of the gross, bringing the net cost of the donation down to £1,000.

It is likely that many, if not all, of those we surveyed pay additional rate tax at 45% on taxable income over £150,000 a year. In that case we might add three more scenarios:

Case 6: If a 45% taxpayer gives £1,000 to a charity, the charity can claim £250 in Gift Aid, bringing it up to £1,250, as in cases 1 and 2 above. The donor can then make a claim themselves for tax relief for a further £312.50 (the balance of 25% of the gross, 20% having been claimed by the charity). The charity ends up with £1,250 as before and the cost to the donor is £687.50 – i.e. £1,000 minus £312.50).

Case 7: If a 45% taxpayer would like the charity to receive a gross sum of £1,000, they would make a Gift Aid donation of £800, the charity would claim £200, making a total of £1,000, and the donor would themselves claim tax relief of a further £250, so the net cost to the donor is £550.

Case 8: If an additional rate taxpayer decides that they could afford £1,000 out of post-tax income (as in cases 1 and 5 above), they would make a gift to the charity of £1,454.50. The charity would claim Gift Aid (25%) of £363.50, bringing the value of the gift to the charity to £1,818. The additional rate taxpayer donor claims a further 25% of the gross (£454.50), bringing the net cost of the donation down to £1,000.

In all these cases the donor is 'hypothecating' the tax that he or she would have paid and instead directed it towards the charity of their choice. The amount that is hypothecated ranges from £250 (in case 1), through £666.66 (in case 5) to £818.00 (in case 8).

The additional benefit to the charity – and loss to government – of receiving the donation that costs the donor £1,000 net is £416.66 (£666.66 less £250) from the higher rate taxpayer, and £567.50 (£817.50 less £250) from the additional rate taxpayer.

Some have suggested that donors who are higher or additional rate taxpayers should not be able to reclaim the difference between the basic rate and the higher rates for themselves, but rather that all the tax relief should go to the charity. The counter-argument is that donors would simply adjust the size of their donation to take account of this change, so a donor who decided that they could afford £1,000 net would give that amount, not £1,333.33 or £1,454.50, and the charity would receive (after claiming Gift Aid) exactly the same amount as with the gift from the basic rate taxpayer, i.e. the charity would receive less than under the present system.

It is worth setting these examples out in detail because it was apparent from the sometimes heated debate that followed the 2012 proposal cited above that some commentators and journalists, including those in the financial press, do not acknowledge that basic rate taxpayers also enjoy the benefits of hypothecation.

Some people believe that the greater powers of hypothecation available to those who pay more tax, combined with the scale of the current budget deficit, point to an argument that all charity tax reliefs should be abolished, and all donations be made out of post-tax income. Others, while accepting the figures, argue that tax should not be paid on income that is never enjoyed but rather has been given away for the public benefit. A further point made by those in favour of retaining tax reliefs for charitable giving is that the cost to the Exchequer in lost taxation is more than offset by the greater sum made available for spending on the public good (i.e. in the example above the £1,000 that would otherwise have been retained for private consumption). In addition, it could also be argued that the large volunteer work force utilised by charities means that, taking the sector as a whole, charities have a cost efficiency advantage over similar or identical services, were they to be provided for by government. So, there is a multiplication effect for the economy over and above the £1,000.

A final argument is that even where a cost to the Exchequer can be identified, for example, when a donor contributes to a cause on which the government would never have spent public funds, the tax relief is still an appropriate strategy to encourage social capital and a pluralistic society.

These are the contours of the debate that needs to be had – and in which, as our study shows, rich donors are willing to participate.

Wealthy donors, on the whole, make use of tax reliefs, so presumably they do want government to promote philanthropy through the tax system. But what they also want is clarity and consistency, and they feel government should be decisive and clear in the messages it sends out.

Further information on Gift Aid and its application can be obtained from the Guide to Giving,[2] on which we drew for some of the examples.

We are most grateful for the assistance of Kevin Russell ACA, CTA, Vice Chair of the Charity Tax Group and Technical Director at the charity Stewardship, who reviewed the initial draft of this appendix and made very helpful suggestions.

We are also grateful to Graham Elliott CTA, MBA of Withers Worldwide who commented on the final text.

Notes

1 80% of donors who give more than £100 a month use Gift Aid, according to the *UK Giving Report 2012.*
   http://tinyurl.com/c882uuj
2 http://tinyurl.com/n2svhzp

Appendix 4:
How to calculate how much you can afford to give

This appendix contains an extract from Wealthy and Wise, *a book written by Claude Rosenberg Jr, published in 1998, which helps people calculate how much they can afford to give.*

As an investment manager for over 40 years, I have observed that too many people, including many of those with considerable wealth, find their money more a source of worry than pleasure. Many needlessly deprive themselves of personal amenities. Others wish to invest in their community and help address its needs and problems, yet they unnecessarily deprive themselves of this pleasure too.

But there is a solution to all these problems: by adopting a more generous approach to charitable giving, donors can experience an exceptional sense of personal satisfaction and fulfilment while improving society. This is certainly true of myself and my wife. Other than our love of one another and our family, philanthropic activities have represented the high point of our lives. The same is true for countless individuals I know personally, from varying levels of wealth. I have also seen how planned giving strategies can strengthen family bonds, while conveying essential values and social responsibility to children and young adults.

Further, charitable involvement can prove extremely stimulating and simply be a tremendous amount of fun. In sum, philanthropy can truly add joy to your life and to others around you. *Wealthy and Wise* and its newtithing approach has already helped make positive changes in the lives of many donors and recipients. The door is wide open for many more donors to duplicate such achievements.

How to begin: meet your personal needs first

Throughout my career, I have seen at first hand the understandable fears and concerns that plague people about their finances. We all want to live comfortably, right through our senior years; we want to protect ourselves against catastrophic illness that could threaten our prosperity; we want to plan our estate well, provide the best education for our children, and enhance our family's way of life; we want to prudently nurture our investment assets, and not jeopardise the income they produce.

Given these desires, my strategy first requires that you do some basic financial planning to cover such essentials as housing, health coverage, income needs in retirement, and estate plans. This is crucial for determining how much philanthropy you can undertake. Only after you have addressed these issues can you gauge your disposable income and the abundance of your investment assets.

Know the current value of donations past and present

Our perceptions of the value of money become easily outdated. We often fail to acknowledge the shrinking purchasing power of money and the growth rate of our own investment assets. This misperception may distort into ineffectively low sums how much we think we can spend, or how much we think we can give to charity.

When I was young, a pack of chewing gum sold for a nickel. The same pack costs 50 cents today. Does this mean that gum is now expensive? Of course not.

Our incomes and other assets have likely grown along with inflation. In fact over the long term, they probably have even exceeded it.

For example, the stock market for the past 20 years has risen at far more than three times the inflation rate over that time. So as donors, it's important to adjust our thinking to the passage of time. For example, when someone asks us today to donate $1,000 we may be taken aback. We may only relate to what $1,000 used to buy, making the request seem audacious in what it asks us to forego. In truth, assuming the $1,000 is more like what $100 was in my childhood, the request probably isn't that bold at all.

Similarly, if you give consistently to charity, remember that donating the same dollar amount year after year actually means you are contributing increasingly less money in terms of buying power, while the value of your own investment assets may well be rising.

Table 1 depicts the declining buying power of $1,000 over the past 23 years. If you already give to charity, are satisfied with your recipients' accomplishments, and have seen your own assets beat inflation and meet your obligations, the 'ravages' of inflation' documented here may give you good reason to adjust your giving upward.

Table 1: The effects of inflation

If you donated...	in....	an equivalent donation in 1998* would require
$1,000	1997	$1,030
$1,000	1990	$1,246
$1,000	1985	$1,525
$1,000	1980	$1,933
$1,000	1975	$3,003

OR...

If in 1998 you donate..	it is equivalent to a donation of	back in...
$1,000	$971	1997
$1,000	$803	1990
$1,000	$656	1985
$1,000	$517	1980
$1,000	$333	1975

*For 1998, a conservative 3% inflation forecast was used.

The advantage of *newtithing* – a modern, reliable formula to determine prudent giving levels

Affordability is the single biggest issue for most individuals as they explore charitable giving. Ironically, people's assessments of how much they can afford to donate is often significantly flawed. First, people typically misjudge their affordable giving capacity by forgetting to consider the tax deductions that reduce the actual cost of a gift. For example, if you are in the 30% tax bracket, a gift of $1,000 doesn't actually cost you $1,000. After the charitable deduction, it really costs you just $700. If you are in the 50% bracket, the net cost is only $500. And if you donate an appreciated security rather than first convert that security into cash, the capital gains tax savings further lowers your cost by perhaps another $100 to $250.

Second, throughout history, the typical approach to charitable giving has been to base donation amounts on gross income alone. Consider the custom of 'tithing', normally defined as donating 10% of one's yearly income. Although tithing constructively encourages philanthropy, its financial 'formula' is actually outmoded in two significant ways:

- **Tithing does not distinguish between *gross income* and the far more important sum 'surplus income'**,[1] i.e. the income available after you have paid taxes and met living expenses.
- **Focusing exclusively on income, tithing ignores a significant portion of most people's financial wherewithal: their *investment assets*** – the savings accounts, money market funds, bonds, stocks, real estate and other investments that may generate additional income or capital appreciation.[2] Clearly, we need to change our attitudes about our money and its usage. We need a more realistic gauge of our surplus funds.

How to employ *newtithing*

How secure you feel about your level of investment assets significantly influences how much you are comfortable spending or donating, a decision also influenced by your annual income, financial obligations, and capital gains or losses. You can make your financial assessment retrospectively by surveying your standing over the past year, or by projecting into the coming year.

Assume you want to know what a comfortably affordable donation would be for an individual or household with an annual reported salary income of $100,000 and with $500,000 of investment assets yielding an additional income of $30,000. The following five steps of newtithing enable you to track your net worth and gauge how much you can comfortably afford to spend or donate now or in the future.

1. **Determine your 'surplus income'** – *your income minus living expenses and income taxes*. To determine your surplus income, subtract from your total income of $130,000 (salary plus investment income) your living expenses (estimated at $75,000) and income taxes (estimated at $30,000). This leaves surplus income of $25,000, which will likely land in an investment vehicle, thus adding to your investment assets.

2. **Determine your 'discretionary funds'** – *your surplus income plus the amount of change during a year in your investment assets*. To conservatively estimate your discretionary funds, we have assumed the following average results that produce new end-of-year investment asset totals: a) fixed income investments (savings accounts, money market funds, bonds, etc), representing 30% of capital, will not appreciate at all in price; and b) equity investments (stocks, as well as real estate, private investments, etc) representing the other 70% of

your portfolio, will at least appreciate enough over the long-term to exceed inflation. Regarding these equity investments, we have assumed annual 7% gains in value, leading to a conservative 5% increase over your start-of-year $500,000 in investment assets, for an increase of $25,000 in surplus income plus $25,000 in expected capital appreciation. Eureka! An increase of $50,000 over your start-of-year investment assets.

3. **Determine your 'total available assets'** – *your discretionary fund plus start-of-year investment assets.* Combine your $50,000 in discretionary funds with your $500,000 in start-of-year investment assets, for a total of $550,000 of total available assets.

4. **Calculate the true cost of your potential donation(s)** – *your potential donation minus its tax savings.* Determine an appropriate donation level for the year (to illustrate, say $10,000). Assuming that you make your donations in appreciated securities, factor in the resulting tax savings from your contemplated donation. In the 30% marginal tax bracket, the savings on a $10,000 charitable donation is $3,000, making the next cost of your donation only $7,000.

5. **Determine how much better (or worse) off you are after your donation** – *your total available assets minus your after-tax donation.* A $10,000 gift costing you only $7,000 would reduce your $550,000 in total available assets to $543,000. This sum amounts to an 8.6% increase over your start-of-year investment wealth, well ahead of expected inflation and allowing for additional expenditures. Compounding your investment assets at 8.6% for the next five years would raise your asset wealth to $820,000 in half a decade. Not a bad outcome for a generous soul.

What if disaster strikes? Won't I regret donating anything?

If you were to sustain a drastic financial loss – say 90% of your earning assets – I can't guarantee that you won't be sorry about many things. But your charitable contributions probably won't be one of them.

To illustrate this, compare two individuals with initially identical financial profiles: (See Table 2). One of them, the 'donor', makes a charitable gift that costs $50,000 after the tax deduction, while the other, the 'non-donor', gives nothing.

Table 2: Charitable contributions and drastic financial loss – $

	Donor	Non-donor
Original investment assets	1m	1m
Less donation after tax saving	50,000	0
Investment assets before loss	950,000	1 million
Less 90 percent loss	(855,000)	(900,000)
Remaining investment assets	95,000	100,000

Source: Newtithing Group, San Francisco

Note the tiny difference in remaining investment assets between the donor and non-donor after the loss – just $5,000, a miniscule half of 1% original investment assets and approximately 5% of the remaining sum after the loss. Clearly the charitable gift is neither the culprit of financial loss nor the straw that breaks the camel's back.

Newtithing guidelines

To suggest possible giving levels for various taxpayer groups, we examined IRS (Internal Revenue Service) categories of adjusted gross income, and conservatively projected disposable income and investment assets for each taxpayer level. A distilled version of suggested levels appears in Table 3.

To create conservative calculations for preserving your financial security, our findings purposely underestimated investment assets[3] and potential growth figures, and overestimated personal expenses.

While we do not suggest donation increases for the two lowest IRS taxpayer categories, the average individual in the next five higher taxpayer categories can afford to give substantially more to charity. Certainly, the higher the taxpayer category, the far greater is the potential for increased charitable giving. Around two-thirds (or nearly $100bn) of increased donations could come from the top taxpayer bracket alone. In *Wealthy and Wise*, I offer specific suggested donation amounts for more than 130 different financial profiles of adjusted gross income and investment assets.

Our suggestions strive to account for the respective needs of each taxpayer group. For the groups represented by the four lowest levels of income ($94,400 of average reported salary or less) and investment assets shown in Table 3 (below), the donations suggestions assume that individuals need their investment assets to grow as much as is realistically possible. For the next two higher levels, however, the suggestions emphasise more moderate asset growth. And for the top level, suggested donations are recommended (simply for illustrative purposes) so as to maintain asset wealth roughly even with inflation. Not surprisingly, people in the top taxpayer category are the very ones who should be considering far more generous deployment of their wealth. Their abundant investment assets qualify them as excellent candidates for 'capital reduction' through substantially increased charitable donations during their lifetime.

Table 3: Possible affordable donation levels

Average reported salary [4]	Average investment assets [5]	Discretionary funds [6]	Average actual donations [7]	Possible affordable donations [8]	Cost of possible affordable donations [9]
29,910	55,820	2,000	660	660	555
50,090	104,290	9,300	1,250	1,250	883
69,060	182,210	18,800	1,970	2,900	2,018
94,400	474,160	44,100	3,010	8,800	5,386
173,310	1,548,530	129,300	7,460	33,800	17,846
337,520	4,449,400	350,400	17,190	140,000	73,640
811,990	19,945,880	1,495,700	101,700	1,337,000	869,127

Source: Newtithing group, San Francisco

Notes

[1] i.e 'disposable income'.

[2] Investment assets do not include one's home or related possessions that do not produce income and that normally should be considered 'untouchable' during one's lifetime.

[3] Securities, real estate, and private investments using 1995 IRS income data extrapolated through year-end 1997. To produce conservative estimates, values of personal housing, IRAs, 401Ks, etc, were omitted, as were increases in values of real estate and private investments from 1995-1997.

[4] From year-end 1995-1997; conservatively estimated since it excludes income growth of 11.8% (Table B-27, Economic Report of President, 1998).

[5] See footnote 3 above.

[6] Composed of: surplus income and current-year capital gains for each asset group (for commons stocks, a 20-year annualised total return was assumed 9.29%).

[7] The average of: IRS itemised donations and Giving USA's estimate of donations made by non-itemising filers.

[8] Based on 'average investment assets' and 'discretionary funds'.

[9] Assumes donations of appreciated securities. Assumes the wealthiest group's donations exceed the maximum level for allowable tax deductions, thereby reducing their average tax deduction rate to 33%.

Appendix 5: Further reading

There is a growing body of literature on and about philanthropy, covering topics such as donor motivations, the practice of philanthropy, differences between countries and traditions, the place of philanthropy in society and how it complements the role of the state.

In addition to a developing academic sector, an increasing number of organisations that provide philanthropy advice also commission reports on various aspects of philanthropy practice. Usually they make these freely available beyond their client or member base.

The purpose of this appendix is a focus on practical application. We set out here a selection of accessible and readable books, reports and guides, and websites that are regularly updated and offer e-bulletins, newsletters and other information, that we believe are of use to those seeking funding, those who are donors, and those who advise them. They are also relevant to policy-makers, journalists and others with a serious interest in developing a culture of giving in the UK.

Books about philanthropy and philanthropists

Zoltan Acs (2013) *Why Philanthropy Matters: how the wealthy give, and what it means for our economic well-being.* Princeton and Oxford: Princeton University Press.

Matthew Bishop and Michael Green (2008) *Philanthrocapitalism: how the rich can save the world.* New York: Bloomsburg Press.

Laurence Brady (2013) *Seven Pillars of Philanthropy* (eBook).

William Damon and Susan Verducci (2006) *Taking Philanthropy Seriously: beyond noble intentions to responsible giving.* Bloomington, Indianapolis: Indiana University Press.

Angela Eikenberry (2009) *Giving Circles: philanthropy, voluntary associations and democracy.* Bloomington, Indianapolis: Indiana University Press.

Pablo Eisenberg (2004) *Challenges for Nonprofits and Philanthropy: the courage to change.* Medford: Massachusetts: Tufts University Press.

Joel Fleishman (2007) *The Foundation: a great American secret.* New York: Public Affairs Books.

Appendix 5: Further reading

Peter Frumkin (2006) *Strategic Giving: the art and science of philanthropy.* Chicago and London: University of Chicago Press.

Kelin E. Gersick (2006) *Generations of Giving: leadership and continuity in family foundations.* Lanham, Maryland: Lexington Books.

Richard B. Gunderman (2008) *We Make A Life By What We Give.* Bloomington, Indianapolis: Indiana University Press.

Charles Handy (2005) *The New Philanthropists: the new generosity.* London: William Heinemann.

Warren Ilchman and Stanley Katz (1998) *Philanthropy in the World's Traditions.* Bloomington, Indianapolis: Indiana University Press.

Patricia Illingworth, Thomas Pogge and Leif Wenar (eds) (2011) *Giving Well: the ethics of philanthropy.* Oxford: Oxford University Press.

Theresa Lloyd (2004) *Why Rich People Give.* London: Association of Charitable Foundations.

Theresa Lloyd (2006) *Cultural Giving.* London: Directory of Social Change.

John Nickson (2013) *Giving is Good For You.* London: Biteback Publishing.

Teresa Odendahl (1990) *Charity Begins at Home: generosity and self-interest among the philanthropic elite.* New York: Basic Books.

Francie Ostrower (1995) *Why the Wealthy Give: the culture of elite philanthropy.* Princeton, New Jersey: Princeton University Press.

Jerold Panas (1984) *Mega Gifts: who gives them, who gets them?* Chicago: Bonus Books.

Robert Payton & Michael Moody (2008) *Understanding Philanthropy: its meaning and mission.* Bloomington, Indianapolis: Indiana University Press.

Claude Rosenberg (1994) *Wealthy and Wise: how you and America can get the most out of your giving.* New York: Little, Brown and Company

J.B. Schneewind (ed.) (1996) *Giving: Western ideas of philanthropy.* Bloomington, Indianapolis: Indiana University Press.

Dame Stephanie Shirley (2013) *Let it Go: the entrepreneur turned ardent philanthropist.* Luton: Andrews UK.

Catherine Walker and Cathy Pharoah (2002) *A Lot of Give: trends for charitable giving in the 21st century.* London: Hodder/ Charities Aid Foundation.

Oliver Zunz (2011) *Philanthropy in America: a history.* Princeton: Princeton University Press.

Books and reports on how to be an effective philanthropist

Paul Brest and Hal Harvey (2008) *Money Well Spent: a strategic plan for smart philanthropy.* New York: Bloomberg Press.

Charles Bronfman and Jeffrey Solomon (2010) *The Art of Giving: where the soul meets a business plan.* San Francisco: Jossey-Bass.

Leslie Crutchfield, John V Kania and Mark R Kramer (2011) *Do More than Give: the six practices of donors who change the world.* San Francisco: Jossey-Bass.

Nicola Elkins (2009) *Master your philanthropy: how to maximise your strategic giving.* Winnipeg, Canada: Knowledge Bureau.

Caroline Fiennes (2012) *It ain't what you give it's the way that you give it: making charitable donations that get results.* London: Giving Evidence. http://giving-evidence.com

Tracy Gary (2008) *Inspired Philanthropy: your step-by-step guide to creating a giving plan and leaving a legacy.* San Francisco: Jossey-Bass. www.inspiredphilanthropy.org

Randall Ottinger (2008) *Beyond Success: building a personal, financial and philanthropic legacy.* New York: McGraw Hill.

Philanthropy UK (2008) *A Guide to Giving.* Philanthropy UK: London http://tinyurl.com/n2svhzp

Philanthropy Impact (2013) *Talking to Clients about Philanthropy.* London: Philanthropy Impact. http://www.philanthropy-impact.org/ giving-advice/talking-to-clients

Thomas Tierney and Joel Fleishman (2011) *Give Smart: philanthropy that gets results.* New York: Public Affairs Books.

Colin Wilbur and Fred Setterberg (2012) *Giving with Confidence: a guide to savvy philanthropy.* Berkeley, California: Heyday Books.

Reports, articles, lectures and speeches on UK philanthropy

James Andreoni (2006) *Philanthropy*. Madison, WI: University of Wisconsin. http://tinyurl.com/pamwnjd

Barclays Wealth (2009) *Tomorrow's Philanthropist*. http://tinyurl.com/nzero5y

Barclays Wealth (2009) *Philanthropology: the evolution of giving*. http://tinyurl.com/yzbqhmm

Barclays Wealth (2010) *Barriers to Giving*. http://tinyurl.com/ozxzqec

Rene Bekkers and Pamala Wiepking (2007) *Generosity and Philanthropy: a literature review*. http://tinyurl.com/bumotzb

Beth Breeze (2008 onwards) *Coutts Million Pound Donors Reports*, published annually from 2008, available online. http://tinyurl.com/crlzamy

Beth Breeze (2010) *How Donors Choose Charities*. London: Centre for Giving and Philanthropy.

Beth Breeze (2009) *Natural Philanthropists: findings of the family business philanthropy and social responsibility inquiry*. London: Institute for Family Business. http://tinyurl.com/ojjklw9

Centre for Giving and Philanthropy (2012) *Philanthropy and a Better Society*. London: CGAP. http://tinyurl.com/oeaezma

Community Foundation for Ireland (2008) *Trends in Irish Philanthropy: the views of those who advise the rich*. Dublin: Community Foundation for Ireland. http://tinyurl.com/ovvtmmh

Coutts & Co (2012) *Inspiring Local Philanthropy*. London: Coutts & Co. http://tinyurl.com/pzvgjv4

Siobhan Daly (2012) Philanthropy as an essentially contested concept. *Voluntas*, vol 23, no.3.

Lindsay Driscoll & Peter Grant (2009) *Philanthropy in the 21st century*. London: Cass Business School. www.honorarytreasurers.org.uk/docs/PhilanthropyReport.pdf

Laura Edwards (2002) *A Bit Rich? what the wealthy think about giving*. London: Institute for Public Policy Research. http://tinyurl.com/pg5wltg

Stuart Etherington (2012) *Philanthropy, Fairness and Democracy – the 30th Attlee lecture.* London: NCVO.http://tinyurl.com/mpns734

Robert Frank (1996) Motivation, Cognition and Charitable Giving. In J. Schneewind (ed) *Giving: Western ideas of philanthropy.* Bloomington, Indianapolis: Indiana University Press.

HEFCE (2012) Review of Philanthropy in UK Higher Education. Bristol and London: Higher Education Funding Council for England. http://tinyurl.com/p9r5agk

Kym Madden and Wendy Scaife (2008) Corporate Philanthropy: who gives and why? in A. Sargeant and W. Wymer (eds) (2008) *The Routledge Companion to Nonprofit Marketing.* London: Routledge.

NCVO (2010) *Funding the Future: The final report of the Funding Commission.* London: NCVO. http://tinyurl.com/num2qfq

NPC (2013) *Money for Good UK.* London: NPC. www.thinknpc.org/publications/money-for-good-uk

The Philanthropy Review (2011) www.philanthropyreview.co.uk

Jane Allen Piliavin and Hong-Wen Charng (1990) Altruism: a review of recent theory and research. *Annual Review of Sociology,* vol 16 pp.27-65.

Rob Reich (2006) Philanthropy and its uneasy relation to equality. In William Damon & Susan Verducci (eds) *Taking Philanthropy Seriously: beyond noble intentions to responsible giving.* Bloomington & Indianopolis: Indiana University Press.

Adrian Sargeant & Jen Shang (2011) *Growing Philanthropy in the United Kingdom.* London: Institute of Fundraising. http://tinyurl.com/pr5tfrg

Paul Schervish (2008) Why the wealthy give: factors which mobilise philanthropy amongst high net-worth individuals. In A. Sargeant and W. Wymer (eds) (2008) *The Routledge Companion to Nonprofit Marketing.* London: Routledge.

Paul Schervish (1994) The Moral Biographies of the Wealthy and the Cultural Scripture of Wealth. In *Wealth in Western Thought: the case for and against riches.* Westport, Connecticut: Prager.

Paul Schervish (2005) Major Donors, Major Motives: the people and purpose behind major gifts. *New Directions for Philanthropic Fundraising,* vol 47, pp.59-87.

Paul Schervish and John Havens (2001) The Mind of the Millionaire: findings from a national survey on wealth with responsibility. *New Directions for Philanthropic Fundraising,* vol 32, pp.75-107.

Marty Sulek (2009) On the Modern Meaning of Philanthropy. *Nonprofit and Voluntary Sector Quarterly,* vol 39, pp.193-212.

Jayne Taylor, Caroline Webb and Daniel Cameron (2007) *Charitable Giving by Wealthy People.* London: HM Revenue & Customs. www.hmrc.gov.uk/research/report29-giving-by-wealthy.pdf

Karen Wright (2002) *Generosity versus Altruism* (Centre for Civil Society Working Paper 17). London: London School of Economics. http://eprints.lse.ac.uk/29061

Online sources of information including regular news and free bulletins

Alliance magazine – website and magazine by subscription, covering philanthropy and social investment worldwide.
www.alliancemagazine.org

Association of Charitable Foundations – supporting the UK's foundations and grant-making charities, the original publisher of *Why Rich People Give.*
www.acf.org.uk

Centre for Philanthropy, University of Kent – academic centre that makes research reports freely available online and has a blog and e-newsletter.
www.kent.ac.uk/sspssr/cphsj/index.html

Charities Aid Foundation (CAF) – provides financial services and advice to donors, as well as publishes research, notably the annual *UK Giving* report, in collaboration with NCVO – the executive summaries are freely available online.
www.cafonline.org

Charity Commission – website of the Charity Commission for England and Wales, including the Commission's guidance, research, searchable Register of Charities and supporting documents such as annual reports & accounts.
www.charity-commission.gov.uk

Charity Tax Group – campaigns on issues relating to the taxation of charities and donors.
www.ctrg.org.uk

Chronicle of Philanthropy – website of the only (in 2013) weekly newspaper dedicated to philanthropy, the *Chronicle of Philanthropy*. Mainly focused on the US but some global coverage.
www.philanthropy.com

City Philanthropy – promoting more effective philanthropy among city professionals.
www.cityphilanthropy.org.uk

Impetus Trust – merged with the Private Equity Foundation in 2013 – investing in ambitious charities and social enterprises that fight economic disadvantage, offering a free e-newsletter.
www.impetus.org.uk/whats-new/e-newsletter-signup

Institute for Philanthropy – helping donors achieve impact by providing donor education, building donor networks and raising awareness and understanding of philanthropy.
www.instituteforphilanthropy.org

National Council for Voluntary Organisations (NCVO) – the membership body for UK charities and community organisations, undertakes policy and advocacy work for the sector, and publishes research, notably the annual *UK Giving* report, in collaboration with CAF – the executive summaries are freely available online.
www.ncvo-vol.org.uk

New Philanthropy Capital – research and consultancy to make charities and funders more successful in achieving their missions; website includes access to Newsletter and many free reports.
www.thinknpc.org

Pears Foundation Philanthropy programme – including links to annual Family Foundation Giving Trends reports.
www.pearsfoundation.org.uk/#36/philanthropy

Philanthrocapitalism – website linked to Bishop & Green's book which also covers wider contemporary issues.
www.philanthrocapitalism.net

Appendix 5: Further reading

Philanthropy Impact – formed in 2013 by the merger of Philanthropy UK, EAPG and PAF), an online and offline organisation making sense of and inspiring philanthropy.
www.philanthropy-impact.org

Prism the Gift Fund – a fee-based service for donors offering a free e-newsletter.
www.prismthegiftfund.co.uk/newsletter-archive

Society of Trust and Estate Practitioners (STEP) – professional association for practitioners dealing with family inheritance and succession planning, runs occasional publications and events related to philanthropy.
www.step.org

Tactical Philanthropy – A hub of debate about philanthropy issues, written by respected US commentator Sean Stannard-Stockton.
www.tacticalphilanthropy.com

UK Community Foundations – known as Community Foundation Network until 2013, supports community foundations across the UK.
www.ukcommunityfoundations.org

Index

About the authors

Dr Beth Breeze worked as a fundraiser and charity manager for a decade before completing a doctoral thesis on contemporary UK philanthropy. She now directs the Centre for Philanthropy at the University of Kent where she runs a range of research projects and teaches courses on philanthropy, fundraising and volunteering.

Beth researched and wrote the annual *Coutts Million Pound Donors Report* from 2008 - 2012. Her other publications include *How Donors Choose Charities* (2010) and *User Views of Fundraising* (2012). www.kent.ac.uk/sspssr/staff/academic/breeze.html

 **Theresa Lloyd** is a philanthropy expert and leading consultant in strategic planning, fundraising and governance in the non-profit sector. She has also served on several boards and committees in the arts, health, higher education and international development sectors, including the European Association for Philanthropy and Giving (EAPG).

Theresa was the Founder Director of Philanthropy UK (2001-04). She has published three books: *A Guide to Giving* (first edition 2003), *Why Rich People Give* (2004) and *Cultural Giving* (2006). www.theresalloyd.co.uk